Dis-positions: Troubling Methods and Theory in STS

Series Editors **Mike Michael,** *University of Exeter and*
Alex Wilkie, *Goldsmiths, University of London*

Turning the mirror on science and technology studies, this pioneering book series explores the pivotal changes in the discipline. It occupies a unique position in the field as a platform for adventurous projects that redraw the disciplinary boundaries of STS.

Also available in the series:

- *More-Than-Human Aesthetics*, edited by Melanie Sehgal and Alex Wilkie
- *Ecological Reparation*, edited by Dimitris Papadopoulos, Maria Puig de la Bellacasa and Maddalena Tacchetti

International Advisory Board

Itty Abraham, National University of Singapore
Ben Anderson, Durham University, UK
Casper Bruun-Jensen, Kyoto University, Japan
Nerea Calvillo, University of Warwick, UK
Tomás Sánchez Criado, Humboldt-University of Berlin, Germany
Didier Debaise, Free University of Brussels, Belgium
Marisol de la Cadena, University of California, Davis, US
Carl DiSalvo, Georgia Tech, US
Miquel Domènech, Autonomous University of Barcelona, Spain
Ignacio Farías, Humboldt-University of Berlin, Germany
Michael Guggenheim, Goldsmiths, University of London, UK
Michael Halewood, University of Essex, UK
Gay Hawkins, Western Sydney University, Australia
Christopher M. Kelty, University of California, Los Angeles, US
Daniel López Gómez, Open University of Catalonia, Spain
Celia Lury, University of Warwick, UK
Patrice Maniglier, Université Paris Nanterre, France
Noortje Marres, University of Warwick, UK
Amade M'charek, University of Amsterdam, Netherlands
Atsuro Morita, Osaka University, Japan
Fabian Muniesa, Paris Mines School, France
Dimitris Papadopoulos, University of Nottingham, UK
Kavita Philip, University of British Columbia, Canada

Maria Puig de la Bellacasa, University of Warwick, UK
Kane Race, University of Sydney, Australia
Israel Rodríguez Giralt, Open University of Catalonia, Spain
Martin Savransky, Goldsmiths, University of London, UK
Melanie Sehgal, University of Wuppertal, Germany
Manuel Tironi, Pontifical Catholic University of Chile, Chile
Martin Tironi, Pontifical Catholic University of Chile, Chile

Find out more at:
bristoluniversitypress.co.uk/dis-positions

1000 PLATFORMS
Ensembles as Ontological Experiments

Adrian Mackenzie

First published in Great Britain in 2025 by

Bristol University Press
University of Bristol
1–9 Old Park Hill
Bristol
BS2 8BB
UK
t: +44 (0)117 374 6645
e: bup-info@bristol.ac.uk

Details of international sales and distribution partners are available at bristoluniversitypress.co.uk

© Bristol University Press 2025

British Library Cataloguing in Publication Data
A catalogue record for this book is available from the British Library

ISBN 978-1-5292-3739-9 hardcover
ISBN 978-1-5292-3740-5 paperback
ISBN 978-1-5292-3741-2 ePub
ISBN 978-1-5292-3742-9 ePdf

The right of Adrian Mackenzie to be identified as author of this work has been asserted by him in accordance with the Copyright, Designs and Patents Act 1988.

All rights reserved: no part of this publication may be reproduced, stored in a retrieval system, or transmitted in any form or by any means, electronic, mechanical, photocopying, recording, or otherwise without the prior permission of Bristol University Press.

Every reasonable effort has been made to obtain permission to reproduce copyrighted material. If, however, anyone knows of an oversight, please contact the publisher.

The statements and opinions contained within this publication are solely those of the author and not of the University of Bristol or Bristol University Press. The University of Bristol and Bristol University Press disclaim responsibility for any injury to persons or property
resulting from any material published in this publication.

Bristol University Press works to counter discrimination on grounds of gender,
race, disability, age and sexuality.

Cover design: Andrew Corbett
Front cover image: Unsplash/Simone Hutsch

For M.J. Mackenzie (1929–2025)

Contents

Series Editors' Preface		viii
List of Figures and Tables		x
Preface		xi
1	Introducing 1000 Platforms	1
Interlude I	*Life along Edges: Coastlines and Reefs*	*18*
2	Edging: From Terminals to Interfaces	20
Interlude II	*Platform Urbanites: The Doge Pesaro*	*39*
3	Shading: Images and Their Associations	42
Interlude III	*Container Figures*	*68*
4	Hashing Many Containers	71
Interlude IV	*Banded Iron Formations*	*89*
5	Embedding and Embodying	92
Interlude V	*Being on Stage*	*111*
6	Closures and Their Stagings	114
Interlude VI	*A High-Diving Platform*	*134*
7	Alignments and Earth	137
8	Implications	158
References		166
Index		178

Series Editors' Preface

Alex Wilkie (Goldsmiths, University of London)
Mike Michael (University of Exeter)

The aim of the Dis-Positions book series is to bring together recent work in the emerging intersections of such disciplines as sociology, anthropology, history, geography, design and philosophy, not least as they bear on the broad field of science and technology studies (STS). Conversely, if STS is undergoing major shifts in how it engages with 'the social' and the question of 'societies', it raises vital matters of concern for these various disciplines and their inter-connections. Dis-Positions thus provides a platform on which varieties of generative mutualities across these areas of scholarship can be presented.

In this respect, Dis-Positions is undergirded by a desire to promote novel fields of enquiry, adventurous theoretical and empirical projects, and inventive methodological practices. It seeks to encourage authors to address live debates while drawing on and interrogating developments across academic areas, in the process disturbing and repatterning STS. In pursuing this ethos Dis-Positions comprises consolidated, rigorous and proactive space through which new creative and critical perspectives in STS and beyond can find a voice. Under this rubric fall discussions of the post-human, post-colonial, affective and aesthetic; methodological inventions that incorporate speculative, engaged, entangled and socio-material practices; empirical novelty that ranges from emergent technoscientific innovations to reformulations of the ordinary; and conceptually creative and critical developments that capture processual and pluralistic thought, extensions of assemblage and practice theories, and the turns to affect and post-performativity.

We are delighted to have the highly ambitious and original volume *1000 Platforms: Ensembles as Ontological Experiments* by Adrian Mackenzie, as the next volume in the Dis-Positions series. With the notion of ensemble, Mackenzie invites the reader on an expedition to explore and put to the test platforms as (political) ontological pluralities that are dynamic and eventful socio-material arrangements for organizing experience, aligning sensibility and articulating bodies, technologies and practices. Platforms, as Mackenzie notes, have become a peculiar and salient feature of contemporary narratives about sociotechnical infrastructures, joining the venerable club of terms that seem to be able to explain (away) 'society' and any and every macro-social process entailed therein. Platforms, now, are not only software services interactively luring and capturing user populations into multiple modes of relentless and surveilled sociability, but any form of grounded sociotechnical arrangement, patterning or infrastructure, that encodes and mediates more-than-human action.

Thus, in this journey through a thousand platforms Mackenzie invites us to consider six critical ways in which platforms exceed their scripts, or programmes of displaced action – as classical actor-network theory would have it. First, platforms have indistinct edges counterposing the highly programmed nature of technical infrastructures with the concrete possibilities of participation that are often indistinct and vague. Second, platforms are typically made possible by the role and agency of graphics processing units, arguing that platforms consist of and are made possible by images and imaging technologies. Third, platforms coordinate agency using calculative practices and technologies through the numbering and storage format of the 'hash' that anchor platforms in data structures while leaving open opportunities for uncoded numerical possibilities. Fourth, Mackenzie interrogates the various ways platforms are fixed to architectures, technologies and regulatory mandates, notably predictive models predicated on specific techniques of organizing and operating on data. Fifth, coding and data science is viewed as an experimental practice where what is known and made available to platforms is continually re-shaped, defined and re-defined through coding practices – making available, and bringing into being, any number of new agencies and new social processes. Lastly, platforms experiment with and configure new relations to geography, producing novel conventions and alignments between sociotechnical ensembles and platforms, and, as a result, patterning new collectives of life.

As a result, Mackenzie offers a new and exciting way to think with and understand sociotechnical platforms, not as (infra)structures for determining agency, life and living, but as processes of abstraction, feeling, possibility and pluralism that, on the one hand, define, constrain and format social collectives, and, on the other, give rise to new ensembles that add to, enrich and further complicate our modes of existence. Accordingly, *1000 Platforms: Ensembles as Ontological Experiments* is a rich nexus of empirical, conceptual and analytic invention that cuts across a range of disciplines and fields. As such, it is not only a very fine addition to Dis-Positions but enhances and extends the ethos of the book series.

List of Figures and Tables

Figures

1.1	A platform	3
1.2	Platforms as plateaus	5
2.1	Coastal rock platform, NSW	25
2.2	gcloud cloud components 2022	27
2.3	VT100 terminal keyboard	30
2.4	8080 Functional Diagram; CC-SA3.0	34
II.1	Doge Pesaro door	40
3.1	A solid sphere illuminated from one direction	43
3.2	An Asus GPU 760GX graphics processing unit (this is not a pipeline)	47
III.1	Proposition 7, Euclid, *Elements*	69
IV.1	Banded iron formation	90
5.1	Digital platforms in abundance	102
V.1	Mini-trains platform	112
V.2	Utzon's platform	112
VI.1	Diving platform	135
7.1	Lorenz attractor	142
7.2	Lorenz platform attractor	146
7.3	daisyworld.py code	147
7.4	FAIR 2.0 projections of temperature under scenario SSP119	154
7.5	FAIR 2.0 projections of temperature under scenario SSP585	155
8.1	James' ruler and dots; sensing and analysing	165

Tables

6.1	Miscellaneous technologies in the Stack Overflow 2022 survey. The table shows the number of developers who use each technology and the proportion of developers who use it.	122
6.2	Platform preferences in the 2023 Stack Overflow survey. The table shows the number of developers who use each platform and the proportion of developers who use it.	128

Preface

Just as I thought to write these lines, a one-line programming error has frozen many airlines, banks, hospitals, video-streaming services, point-of-sales terminals and websites. The CrowdStrike code expected 21 values in an array, but received 20. Only 8.5 million computers were affected on 19 July 2024, but they were cloud/data centre-based servers running the Microsoft platforms for enterprise-critical services. The event has been termed the largest IT fail ever. The Microsoft Corporation blames the CrowdStrike event on the European Union and its anti-monopoly regulations.

Much of this book was written with a large language model constantly nudging me to accept line completions (GitHub 2023). I redacted almost all content suggestions as uninteresting. For instance, it suggests right now, having observed what I wrote in the paragraph above, that 'the Crowdstrike event was a "wake-up call" for the world. It wasn't. It was a one-line programming error. It was a wake-up call for the people who wrote the code'. The model making this suggestion, however, was itself trained to more or less write code for people, so that wake-up call might be hard to respond to. Who or what is being called by whom or what is not clear.

When readers meet passages of code in the book, they should be awake to the writing of the code. I have often supplicated generative AI platforms to write code (e.g. `write Python code to demonstrate the basic operation of an endpoint detection response system such as CrowdStrike. Please provide comments.`). Their facility in writing it attests to the sometimes startling predictability of coding.

Given that predictability, why write code for a book, especially a book that puts 'experimental ontology' in the title? Concocting code is not a way to win readers over in general. The code itself is not exactly the point. Code runs in reverse here. It executes by staging something. Coding crystallizes some major elements of the contemporary nexus of infrastructures, feeling, agency, value and time. Coding abstracts but also stays attached to its supports, its operating environments and runtimes. Some of the small pieces of code in the book relating to images, chips, interfaces, addressing systems, databases or models convey in miniature how things hang together or fall apart through attachments. Writing or, increasingly, generating code can feed into experimental ontology if those attachments are involved.

The countervailing tendency running in the book is some auto-ethnographic material. The book churns through the folds of regional psychotechnogeography (coastal New South Wales; north-west England). Their surfacing marks zones of temporal subduction where something obdurate washes up. No matter how much I wish it did not, it is very hard for the book not to implicitly dwell on these longer-distance attachments. I invite readers to treat such attachments not as technical nostalgia but as evidence of transitions and ongoing 'technical debt' affecting the writing. Much of this technical debt has its roots in North America. The geography of platforms runs heavily on the west coast of the United States, but it moves up on other coasts.

The writing of this book struggles to resolve tensions between something I would like to know but can't quite name and things I can name and point to but prefer to avoid. Something quite indeterminate washes up against something seeking to determine very narrowly what happens. In most cases, if a choice was needed, I have erred towards the indeterminate.

1

Introducing 1000 Platforms

Are platforms good to think with? Platforms arise from a long series of arrangements of people and things. Such arrangements lack the coherence of a device, machine or 'system', even if they include them. But platforms bind and constrict current configurations of collective life and perhaps digital social research. They might still enable something.

This book devises some experimental approaches to platform things, narratives, places and habits. It draws from science and technology studies (STS) and associated approaches to media, ontologies, knowledges and power. More than some other approaches, an STS-oriented inquiry might attend to the variety of platforms scattered across society-economy-nature-language-subject-object divisions. I hold one key question in mind throughout: does STS assemble the equipment and acumen to not only follow platforms as they diversify across human-nonhuman differences, but to understand how to survive on/in/with/off them? Experimental ontology in ensembles responds to that question.

How many platforms exist?

Many observers see the last two decades, for better or worse, as platform-time. In social sciences, researchers began by re-thinking knowledge as platform objectivity (Cambrosio et al 2004), economic relations as platform capitalism (Srnicek 2016), platform cooperativism (Scholz and Schneider 2017), a society as platform society (Van Dijck et al 2018), and platformization as a far-reaching transformation (Plantin and Punathambekar 2018), leading to platform urbanism (Leszczynski 2019) or perhaps just the latest version of media specificity (Acland 2015). Things once qualified as 'digital' now often spin up as 'platforms'. The body is a platform according to Paul Preciado (Preciado 2013). Synthetic biology configure yeasts, mice and bacteria as platforms, as do COVID-19 vaccine designers. Satellite and airborne platforms pack the sky. Oceans, brains (human and nonhuman), forests, ecosystems, reefs, cities, governments, factories, power stations, cars and home entertainment have either become platforms, or are managed, known, regulated or observed through platforms. Is the earth a platform, as Earth-2, an Nvidia Corporation scientific project, seems to suggest? Everything today, it seems, clamours to be platforms.

How come platforms pop up like fungal fruiting bodies on a rotting log? Are platforms a new species of organization, of thinking or being? Do they challenge us to re-think how people and things come together? Does their success in multiplying – the '1000 platforms' in my title – testify to a change in the composition of collectives?

The American sociologist Erving Goffman describes the 'platform format' as:

> [T]he arrangement found universally in which an activity is set before an audience. What is presented in this way may be a talk, a contest, a formal meeting, a play, a movie, a musical offering, a display of dexterity or trickery, a round of oratory, a ceremony, a combination thereof. The presenters will either be on a raised platform or encircled by watchers. (Goffman 1983, 7)

Together with human ambulatory units, contact practice, conversational frames, the platform format varies the numbers of units participating in the interaction order. It would be interesting to think how this set of elements in interaction figure in making platforms possible, alongside marketization through intermediations or centralizing/de-centralizing movements of platformization.

People have been drawing and building platforms for tens of thousands of years. The drawing as an arrangement of lines lined up could vary in many ways. I will attend to some of those variations in pages to come. At first glance, nothing could be simpler: drawing the arrangement called a platform only takes a few lines, or even a few keyboard characters (-, |) lined up and spaced out.

Does this geometrico-architectural line composition (Figure 1.1) help us figure out what is going on? To start with, I echo the observations of other platform researchers. Throughout the variations running through platform-worlds, two elementary facets crystallize: verticality and flatness. The first facet elevates the structure, and inscribes edges. The sides or supports stand on some ground, ground that itself might be raised or standing on top of other supports, but ultimately some part of the earth. The height makes possible platform variations such as a stage (from Latin *stare* to stand), an altar closer to God (from Latin *altus* or high), or many places of higher *status*, state or statues. The second facet runs across the top of platform. It clears a zone of commutation, a horizontal surface supporting mobile re-arrangements of people and things, as in the surge of people across the

Figure 1.1: A platform

station platforms at Euston when the train to Glasgow is announced, or the figures running along and jumping between levels in a platform game (for example, *Donkey Kong*), or in the depressing precision of a weapons system mounted on gyroscopic stabilizers.

I am alluding, in this description and examples, to the fact that this elementary architectural form that lifts out and mobilizes, a form that was already well-articulated in Alberto Cambrosio and Paul Keating's *Biomedical Platforms* (Cambrosio et al 2004) and analysed by Tarleton Gillespie (Gillespie 2010), already creates trouble. It divides, it separates, it generates status effects, makes some things more visible, projects images, voices and spectacle, it rests on something, it poses problems of access and stability.

The first platform face, vertical elevation, divides people into groups separated by edges. Some people are on platforms. Others are not. Specific features such as height and stability define the grouping effect. Political platforms, theatres and stages of many buildings exemplify this grouping of some actors on stage and others around the edges. Elevation is deeply implicated in the making of media collectivities (Couldry and Hepp 2018). The participatory conditions of social media (Barney et al 2016; Kelty 2019) elevate the stage using devices that accumulate and measure collective attention, sometimes in prodigiously swollen currents of influence. Platform problems of regulation and moderation, free speech, surveillance, misinformation, accountability, marginalization, discrimination, exclusion and exploitation stem from competing efforts to capture group attention.

The second platform facet unfurls well-defined flat, polished surfaces or 'planes' as geometry calls them where things can easily spin around in new arrangements and re-arrangements like dancers on a polished floor. Take the swiping interfaces commonly seen in smartphone apps since 2010 as an example. The ease of using these devices to flick through text or images, to sprint along the terraces of *Temple Run* or respond to messages from friends, work or the government, comes from that polishing of surfaces. The app interfaces rely on two corresponding surfaces, one housing the interface elements of the smartphone apps, one in the cloud or the networked data centres of Google, TikTok or Facebook. In the app, a software library such as Facebook's widely used react includes components such as a 'swiper/carousel ... featuring multiple layouts, parallax images, performant handling of huge numbers of items' (Meliorence 2022). These components handle the manipulation of visual arrangements of 'items' in grids, menus, timelines of app interfaces.

In their re-arranging and re-configuring of items in data centres and in the visible zone of user interfaces, platforms single out smooth surfaces, even edges, straight lines and isolated points as their elements. We might think of the laser-levelled, polished concrete floors of an Amazon fulfilment centre, the rigid server backplanes in data centres, the control planes that configure network topologies or the consumer products simply called 'Surface' as facets of this smoothing. Viewed more sociologically, flatness supports the economization described by STS research into markets (Callon 2016) and the platformization analysed by STS researchers (Plantin et al 2016) on a variety of scales and in a diversity of domains criss-crossing science, economy, culture and everyday life.

What happens when the two facets of elevation and flatness meet along an edge? The smoothing, blending, swapping and melding of the two structural facets of elevation and flatness also generates novelties and frictions for media, markets, governments, institutions and people (as users, customers, workers, citizens or participants) alike. The platform as elevated place of speaking, viewing or performing blends into the platform as surface ready for re-arrangement, and vice versa. Think, for instance, of the unprecedented aggregations of audience that video or social media platforms attract, or of the intensely imagined work on the 'unstoppable infrastructures' of a blockchain-based decentralized Web 3.0 internet (Schneider 2019): these seemingly self-amplifying, geographically widespread and quasi-globally shared events bend and fold sharply defined edges and smooth surfaces along faultlines.

So, 'yes' and 'no' answers to the question posed a few paragraphs back: does this drawing of something built help understand platform arrangements? The verticality, the flatness, the edges where they meet: yes, these guide some questions and descriptions of groupings, change, values, power and geographies. But, no, it is hard to get from the geometrical thinness of the figure to the thick, heated, heavy, intricate, conflicting and disorienting stream of changes, events, collapses and accumulations going on. Even the effort needed to render what is happening in the interface of a smartphone app puts the geometrical structure under a lot of tension.

Thinning and thickening

Is there any way to get away from the elevation and flatness spreading through the platform figure? How would anyone avoid slipping into the thinning-smoothing practices of platform ideality? The '1000 platforms' of this book's title nods to another book, *One Thousand Plateaus* by Gilles Deleuze and Felix Guattari (Deleuze and Guattari 1981). *One Thousand Plateaus* affirms 'plateaus' as assemblies effected through 'distinct regimes of feeling for resistances, directions, meanings' (1981, 400). Plateaus connect with other plateaus through stems and tendrils, extending the plateaus into a rhizome, a network of plateaus. Plateaus proliferate in their thousands via practices of compositional feeling.

Are platforms, despite their edges, flat surfaces and ideational polishing, also plateaus? Plateauization – a difficult to pronounce neologism – of platforms might help to thicken the platform figure. For instance, what happens if someone draws the ground where the vertical support rests? In the Figure 1.2 sketch, hand-drawn because of the ease of shifting directions, the supports stand on a ground that itself made up of other platforms. Platforms pop

Figure 1.2: Platforms as plateaus

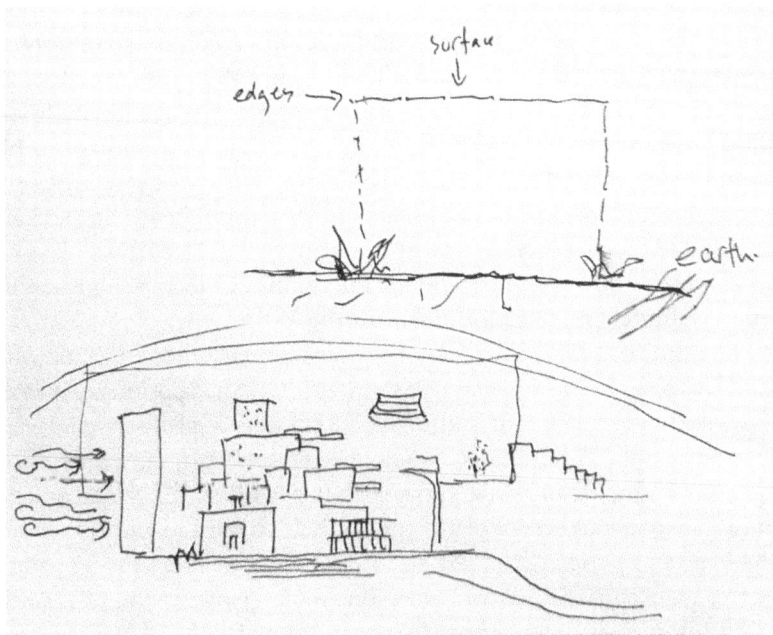

up within, underneath, beside and around other platforms. Sometimes a platform steps onto another one. Steps arrange platforms in a sloping series.

The smooth surfaces and neat edges of platforms are riddled with nested and interlaced entities: ways of organizing light, statistical models, database architectures, file formats, network devices and infrastructures for heat, air, electricity and signals, configured by engineers, designers, programmers and managers weaving between them. Greying out this intricate weave, platform ideality hides work done to moderate and circulate platform content (Gillespie 2018); it covers much of what happens to peoples as they assemble 'on' platforms (Benjamin 2016; Lovink 2019), including the waves of economic transformation that some scholars call 'platform capitalism' (Srnicek 2016) and that others perceive as colonization of social life in the name of connectivity (Couldry and Mejias 2019).

Is the difference between drawing one platform and drawing 1000 platforms enough to thicken the figure of the platform or to ease the constrictions of smooth surfaces and hard edges? The difference suggests something more is needed, but doesn't say what it is. Beyond drawing, what practices lead to better ways of living with or belonging through platforms? Partly this is a problem of finding connections, or working out a way to articulate the configurations of people and things. But an ontological challenge also lurks here. Platforms signal an indeterminacy in the composition of collectives (people, things, places).

In *A Pluralistic Universe*, William James mentions an unnamed philosopher who he says deserves to be known alongside pre-Socratic philosophers such as Heraclitus and Parmenides. Her ontology, according to James, contains only the Thick and the Thin: 'the world, she said, is composed of only two elements, the Thick, namely, and the Thin' (James 1996, 38). It may be that most figures of the platform, and platform talk more generally, are housed in the Thin, sometimes in form factors so thin that they are hard to hold onto and work with. The statements of a large tech company CEO such as Mark Zuckerberg or Elon Musk exemplify a thin-client conception of people and things in place.

James, despite his evident passion for the thinning effects of philosophical practice, definitely prefers working with the Thick when doing ontology. The pluralism of *A Pluralistic Universe* is not so much a theoretical ontology of plural realities, but a empiricism of them. Is there an experimental practice to thicken rather than thin platforms? If there is a platform pluriverse, a heteromorphic ensemble of practices, devices, places, expectations, obligations and performances, how does it get on stage? What practices intensify the concreteness of platforms, so their endemism and embeddings become more experienciable? Experiences of the Thick, as James concludes, oblige us to become 'a part of reality one's self' (James 1996, 68). Accept the obligation to become a part of reality oneself. The obligation seems slender: be part of reality, or more precisely, 'bury oneself in the thickness of the passing moments' (James 1996, 69). Like the plateaus that make up *1000 Platforms*, James affirms sensations of resistance, movement, 'endosmosis' and 'compenetrating flux' (1996, 70).

Thickening through attachment

I would like to do that, but what counts as burying oneself in the thickness of passing moments with respect to plaforms? What would burying look like as an experimental practice? Is it like Descartes considering a lump of wax, and running through what later philosophical thought would called an 'eidetic reduction' to get at the unchanging essence of the lump? I could make a start on that with a platform list, a listing that eddies through the shoals of platform realities.

Here is a list: the glowing device interfaces with their optohaptoelectronics attuned to finger and body resistances and capacitances; the polished visual in-app carousels of images, graphics, emojis, lists, icons, text and numbers, the buttons and controls clustered to create a visual field of perception-action that out-shines the drift of the non-app surroundings; the channelling and processing of sounds to beckon attention, to habituate gestures and seeing to clicking, to give feedback on gestures, set the mood, or call us back; the algorithmic looping of advertising, production recommendations, 'news' updates and social network connections that plug into the hyper-competitive global supply chains of fashion, entertainment, travel, food, gadgets, homewares and the like; the workflows configured to sign up, register, access or interact with health, education, gaming, media, social welfare, banks, shops, employers, training or transport; the constant work done to configure, find, repair, connect and maintain profiles, streaks, levels, files, posts, images, kudos, webcams, smart speakers, rankings or other zones of activity; the accelerating research into machine learner AIs; bots, data breaches, memes, product releases, laws and regulations, viral videos; data scientists, software engineers, computer scientists, information architects and IT consultants; Web 3.0 Decentralized Autonomous Organizations, data centres with their energy-intensive, thinly peopled concentrations of servers and networking capacity; developers in their urban hotspots and global dispersions working in their teams; the cloud-, compute-, infrastructure- and platform-as a-service-providers, the annual industry conferences and their hyperbolic promises.

What is the use of such a list, yet an incomplete list, one that can easily extend to a thousand items? Every list has an openness to additions, extensions, groupings and orderings that is perhaps worth thinking about. This list could be arranged in a catalogue and ordered by a classification of uses, industries, knowledges, geographies, ownership, events, dates, investments or architectures. A list in this form does not, however, readily support intuitions of the variations and spectrum of platforms in their dispersions and colonization, their alignments, supports, forms of closures and edging, or the many other overflows of the elevated speaking position or flat surface for rapid re-configuration. What's worse, rather than feeling compositional, I start dysregulating as I read it. If attention to platforms can do some ontological thickening, an extra twist or tie is needed.

Experimental attachments

In any case, your platform listing will differ greatly from mine. For reasons that I intend to discuss, I've packed my list with technicalities. Other platform realities have different intensities, durations, urgencies and many other threads beside the technical ones. My list and other listings, however, share this: I list what I am somehow attached to, what I care about or compels me to attend to it. Attachments seep through the listing. And attachments always bring with them others, or other selves, in places.

The listing practices proposed by Bruno Latour in *After Lockdown: A Metamorphosis* (Latour 2021) focus on attachments to entities in place: 'we learn to *list attachments* to entities that force us to take care of them' (Latour 2021, 72, emphasis in original). Attachment-listing aims to unfreeze landscapes, describe territories from within, and move experience back to 'here below' (Latour 2021, 48). In Latour's attachment listing, an entry on the list indicates a dependency, something or someone you can't do without in that place. Adding to the list is not a matter of generating more and more items, like a Lisp program that recursively spits out list of list of lists, or list of listing functions. No, each entry is an obligation, a confrontation or hiatus that 'commit you into taking them into consideration' (2021, 73).

The attachment listing practices Latour proposes avoid almost everything associated with contemporary platforms. He renounces coordinate systems as used in GPS, wifi and various forms of wirelessness, digital screens and interfaces as in Zoom calls as the entities encouraging people to think they have left place(s) behind. He probably doesn't renounce them completely, but Zoom, wifi, and GPS-steered travel definitely do not make Latour's list of lockdown/metamorphic attachments. If they could be added as metamorphic elements, how would that be?

I note too that Latour glides over different styles of attachment. I like the attachment-based listing as a way of trying to be somewhere: '[le]ts try and situate ourselves in a spot we'll need to try and describe in tandem with others' he suggests (Latour 2021, 70). Latour, clever and provocative as always, does sail past some problems of attachment and care. Attachment patterns, as they are called in the developmental psychology literature, vary from secure to disoriented. My attachment to Python suffers way less ambivalence than my attachment of YouTube for instance. Also the choice of what place to list attachments may be difficult. Not everyone can situate themselves in a single spot. The learning to list attachments presupposes some stability in place. I might not know where that place is, even if I'm in it. Many people split themselves between places. Platforms have no small part to play in that. So finding the spot may require experiments that test its 'ground truth' (a term used in the machine learning literature to anchor the predictions of a model in a referential claim based on some data). The listing experiment pose the test: is this a place I am attached to, that I belong to and continuously exchange belongings?

Arranging attachment-figures

The chapters of *1000 Platforms* experiment in listing platform attachments. From flat-high platform to platforms/plateaus, from thin platforms to thick listing, and then to attachments in places, the challenge of thinking with platforms, or even deciding if they are good to think with, gets deeper. Ontology has been mentioned and ontological experiments too. I'm now in a position to say how those experiments will take place and what ensemble they compose.

Learning to list attachments to entities/existences that 'force us' to take care of them is, according to Latour, a metamorphosis because it re-grounds the lister. Listing attachments resists detachment because it mixes care with an effort to articulate or somehow make visible, to say or to show what matters and how.

Contemporary platforms ramp up into a confusing imbroglio of expression, communication, experience, knowledge, power relations and distributed collective engenderings. Confusing as they may be, platforms are themselves places of attachment, as well attachment to others in place or collectives. Listing platform attachments as a way of ontologically thickening them or rendering them more concrete would mean tracing and describing some threads of participation running through human-nonhuman collectives in particular places.

To experiment with attachment in place, the chapters depart from a mixed set of six platform-figures. The figures are themselves all literally platforms, but they also offer some wriggle room, or open a passageway around or through contemporary platforms. The term 'figure' can mean numbers, a human form, a graphic illustration or diagram in a publication, an element of a picture, as well as a way of approaching a problem ('to figure out'). Figures can flip over to ground, and many aspects of graphic figures, such as their shading, their edges, their positioning actually draw much on grounding and earth.

The platform attachment-figures are a boulder, coastal rocks, a geometrical definition of 'figure' found in the Greek geometer Euclid's *Elements* (Euclid

2012), a funereal monument in a Venetian church, a music stage and a pool high-diving platform. The scattered figures have their own geographies and their own durations and eventfulness. Their character is markedly geontological (Povinelli 2016) or perhaps more precisely, geostoried (Debaise and Stengers 2022), but they tunnel in different directions like players in a game of ontological *Minecraft*. They all point to something surrounding, supporting or accumulating. They stand off at some distance from platform media and platform technologies as they are usually understood, but they help locate attachments that might better ground the latter-day platforms. Their arrangement in an ensemble might be conducive to better platform arrangements more generally. I detail the figures where they appear in the chapters.

Making arrangements

Via these attachment-figures, each chapter of the book approaches platforms as ensembles that can alter in ways that their programming or scripting – in the STS/actor-network theory (ANT) sense of that term as a transformative delegation of action from one actor to another (Akrich 1992) – might not fully envisage.

The experimental listing of attachment typically begins in a position or orientation in relation to a platform – being at the edge, embedded in, aligned with, in the shadow of, enclosed with, numbered amongst. The platform figures concretely embody differences in attachment.

1 Edging and coastal rock platforms

Platform edges demarcate in and out, or on and off the platform, but they teem with lively pools of activity. The figure of the coastal rock platform, obdurate yet richly inhabited in the midst of waves and wash of tides, provokes different attachments than the hardened and polished edges sometimes enunciated by people who make large platforms.

The empirical material here contrasts different ways of approaching platforms, from hand-held devices to data arranged in files in Google data centres. On the one hand, it describes mundane experiences of confusion, blurring or scattering in contemporary technical ensembles, experiences of not being sure where things, self or others are located, and of knowing even what platform is there. This occasions many practice difficulties of getting on and off platforms, amidst general uncertainty around edges or boundaries. On the other hand, it traces the emergence of the 'hardened edges' of platforms during the 2000s. Between the two, it traces how technical practices of the 'terminal window' or *cli* ('command line environment') create edges at the centre of platforms.

The contrast between disorientation and terminal will be analysed from two main perspectives, the first introducing the concept of technical ensemble found in Gilbert Simondon's *Mode of Existence of Technical Objects* (Simondon 1989), the second developing a well-known analysis of doors and walls from 1990s ANT. The aim of the chapter is to introduce the idea that platform edges are, contrary to their representation, not clear and distinct. It also sets up an idea of the ensemble as something whose boundaries, margins, entry and exit points define experiences of participation.

2 Shading and the Doge's funereal monument

Great accumulations of images, sounds, texts and other data stack up on contemporary platforms. The figure of stacking and the shade cast by stacks is a monumental doorway in the side of a church in Venice. The sculpture, the vertical hierarchy running from slave labour to administrative cherubs, and the footing of the church in the piles driven in the Venetian lagoon all date from the time of Renaissance city-states, but are now visited by tourists like me, even if I was in town for a machine learning/AI workshop.

The chapter orients itself to image fluxes in contemporary ensembles by attending to investments in a single, yet hardly isolated device, the graphics processing unit (GPU) and its recent multiplication. The title of the chapter refers to the early computer graphics technical practices of rendering surfaces and depths in visual scenes using shaders, or graphics programs that add shading and textures to images.

The chapter experimentally transposes between four shaders confronted with a single geometric figure. Shading and shaders, the computational units developed to shade sets of pixels, continue to animate GPU development as GPUs worm into many places in platform ensembles. Their anchoring role in the transformation of machine learning into a new mode of image aggregation, their radical re-configuration as coordinating devices in decentralized, blockchain-based Web 3.0, and their high-definition immersive attractions (for example, GPUs have transformed interfaces on many scales by ever-finer rendering or 'shading') all generalize shaders.

The discussion draws on STS work on imaging devices and observational instruments, and importantly, an influential theoretical conception of the primacy of images first found in the philosophy of Henri Bergson, and STS work on load factors, the chapter re-describes GPUs in terms of re-scalings that shift images further away from screens.

3 Hash and other figures of containment

The leading theorematic-deductive mode of thought for several thousand years of Western thought stems from Euclidean geometry, and its practice of constructing containers by drawing lines, angles and curves. Euclid's mode of generating proposition by carefully drawing container figures has shrunk in importance in comparison to other mathematical practices (algebra, calculus, statistics, and so on). But the figure of the geometrical composition of proof continues to resonate strongly. The chapter focuses on transformations in proof, statements and knowing associated with functions that transforms data into a non-quantifying numbering, the hash.

Numbers and numbering are a primary form of coordination in platforms, and have become critical elements in platform alternatives (such as Web 3.0), as well as in data science and machine learning. The chapter situates the numericity of platforms via STS literature on number and quantification. STS work on numbering, quantity and calculation highlights how inscriptive practices thread chains of delegation or displacement between devices and records/traces. It has also, in other strands, explored the inherently multiple practices of numbering, counting, sorting and quantifying in order to render something calculable.

The chapter builds on the STS work to engender an enumerative sensibility. It analyses contemporary platform numbering practices centred on a specific number construct, the hash. This rather rich numbering practice underpins various data structures, cryptocurrencies and blockchain technologies, as well as many of the coordination practices associated with platform development, operation, repair and maintenance. The chapter will contrast these numbering practices with calculative practices derived from the more 'classical' calculative practices of physics anchored in the prediction of changing states of physical systems.

The chapter will suggest accompanying some of the transformations of hashes offers good ways of becoming more sensitive to the ways that ensembles are stabilized as platforms and to the numerical overflows that might stray into alternative platform configurations.

4 Embeddings and banded formations

Despite the upsurge in scholarly and popular accounts of what platforms cost in terms of water, electricity or land, and in mapping of the geography of data centres, AI and their infrastructures, something hinders the placement or grounding of platforms. A geological figure, a rock cut from the banded-iron formations of north-western Australia, with its embeddings, offers a way of grounding platforms in ensembles of habits, abstractions and institutions.

This chapter sets out to describe practices concerned with locating, centring and keeping platforms in place. The practices of platform embedding vary greatly and can entail quite different arrangements, ranging from how things are plugged in and connected to each other through to regulatory abstractions governing their design or use (Schneider 2019).

The discussion will draw on research into specific cases of embedding: the BBC micro:bit, a quasi-educational IoT (Internet of Things) microcontroller gifted to all Year 7 UK high school pupils in 2018, but also the ordinary cables and plugs that continue to wind around every electronic device. The chapter develops the concept of embedding in senses that range across knowledge, economy and institution in order to highlight one centring/ locating that configures ensembles as platforms.

The other main sense of embedding is found in a dramatic transformation of platform architectures of the last decade, in the triumph of deep learning neural network models over nearly all alternatives. Although I skirt around direct discussion of AI in this book (see the Preface for some justification), so many platforms now base their predictive or generative promise in embeddings as mappings of data. These embeddings contrast with the 'embedded devices' that seemingly decentralize platforms in other settings.

A rich STS literature on embodying and economization, centres and peripheries in sciences and engineering supports this chapter in its description of the two cases. Some forms of centring can re-distribute relations. The aim is direct the contrast between the different forms of platform embeddings towards a better sense of the instability of embeddings, and an accompanying disposition towards the plurality of platforms.

5 Closures and psychotechnical stages

The experience of people such as musicians, singers, actors, dancers and perhaps politicians standing on platforms pans out differently to that of doges or their contemporary incarnation as platform CEOs. Staging an ensemble so that something happens, so that some signal flashes from the divergent processes and actors entails constraints and mixtures. A stage for a concert almost unseen, and actually witnessed only by a few ravens and a passing train, is the grounding figure for events that sometimes transfigure platforms as ensembles.

The last two decades of platform-making have relied on coding practices that limit unexpected interactions or events. Programming and coding practices have not only been central to platform-making, but themselves have been constantly re-assembled in platforms. This chapter focuses on one significant example of a coding-based platform practice, data science. The aim of the chapter is to re-frame ways of thinking about coding as both a stabilizing practice and a way of experimenting with what or who can be included in platforms. It develops the notion of closure to articulate both the limitation or reduction of indetermination and a susceptibility to re-defining inclusion, participation and limits. STS research, with its deep interests in making sense of scientific knowledges, experiments and apparatuses, is a vital resource in exploring platform knowledges.

Several closures are discussed in the chapter: the functional programming construct of closure, the regular expression practices used in pattern matching, the question and answer patterns of the Stack Overflow platform, and the IBM Watson system, a commercial data science platform. Much of the social science literature on digital platforms effectively concerns enclosure, or how in multiple ways platforms have fenced off sections of social life for profit or control. STS work, by contrast, has been much attuned to the forms of knowing that practically configure platform operations. The chapter suggests that closures in various senses have been vital to the economization of platforms (as analysed in the digital and platform capitalism literature), and have supported the development of specialized knowledge forms associated with platforms such as data science.

Closure has multiple senses, ranging from the course of life events to programming constructs that allow shifts in context to be managed, from the STS sense of the reduction in interpretive flexibility of technical objects to the phenomenological method of suspension, bracketing or *epokhe* used to a recovery of sedimented life-world structures. Closures also make it possible to suspend and bracket elements of technical ensemble in order to construct new platforms.

6 Alignments and diving platforms

The final figure is a high-diver rotating, falling and entering hands first into water ten metres below. Many higher dives plunge down in streamed Red Bull Cliff Diving Series. But a simple ten-metre dive forces us to engage in the many possible alignments that flow between the platform and 'arriving' in the water. Diving usefully upends perceptions of elevation.

All platforms are elevated, but some explicitly experiment with arrangements and movements towards earth. The chapter analyses scientific platforms concerned with pathways and changes in average global temperature and climate change. The ensembles of models at the heart of contemporary climate science provide a model for thinking about sensing as alignment.

It works with three simplified models of climate and earth system: the Lorenz attractor, a simulation of hot air rising; Daisyworld, a model developed by James Lovelock to describe how interacting living and non-living processes shape climates, and FAIR 2.0, a recent model that simulates the climate models developed by climate scientists contributing to the Intergovernmental Panel on Climate Change. It contrasts the different models in order to highlight how habits and beliefs can be re-configured by new conventions or alignments in ensembles. Each of them offer approximations, calculations or simulations as ways of sensing different pathways of change (of temperature, in particular). Each also explicitly stages an ensemble of some kind.

The counter-mapping and diagramming practice of the chapter develops recent STS work on sensing to analyse large coordinated ensembles of models used in climate modelling. Aligning is both a set of practices in arranging or configuring things and an intersubjective or collective modality concerned with spaces between things (as in political alignments). Alignments are adjustable, modifiable and provisional, and oriented along edges and surfaces. As a mode of action, aligning breaks down hierarchical divisions between mundane and exceptional, between routine and revolutionary. A small shift in alignment, more or less routinely occurring, might trigger a cascade of changes somewhere else.

Aligning spans different forms of action such as making, governing, consuming, observing or resisting. Alignments are non-specific to subjects or human actors since many things and forms of life align. Habits, impulses, contagions, thinking, perceptions, beliefs, drives, affects, attachments and identification depend on alignments that run through them. Alignments can structure collectives without passing through social structures such as class or regular life courses. While climate science often appears to focus on planetary-scale fluxes, the sensing of change or transformation supported by the ensemble actually localizes and grounds.

Arranging for ensembles

The platform figures, if stood in a circle: what would they make? The figures of attachment point to social, political and morally invested arrangements. They offer not only different ontological starting points for theorization of platforms in their pluralities. Each of them grants a foothold for stepping into an unforeseen or improvised alignment. They trouble any founding categories of quantity and quality, subject and object, nature and society. They each stand for modes of existence includes many interweavings.

What happens when the six figures of platform attachment are arranged in a list, as Latour suggests? As figures of grounding, of attachment, of care, of participation, of belonging, of exchange, of transformation, of alignment, of attachment, they engage and resist, dissolve and strengthen, breed and hamper each other. Moving around these figures of sedimentation, association, abstraction, prestige and movement in a list poses sharp challenges. Even if each other carries a certain weight of history, embodiment, sociality, grounding, technical practices, ecological processes and power relations, how do they communicate with each other in movement? Put together, these figures of sedimentation, association, numbering, prestige, closure and alignment converge in the final keyword of this introduction to the book: *ensembles*.

The thread of platforms as ensembles recurs throughout the book but especially in the conclusion: how do the attachment-figures, approached as modes of grounding, affect each other? What happens in the ensemble? Rather than developing an ensemble theory or ensemble ontology, I'm seek to activate an STS sensibility attuned to how ontology happens across people and things. Ensembles invite experimental ontology, as defined by Noortje Marres: 'Experimental political ontology ... proposes that the investment of non-humans with political capacities and their insertion into democracy are projects of experimental settings' (Marres 2013, 437).

The concept of ensemble to be developed in the course of the book frames the experimental ontology in several ways. First, an ensemble has some plurality and uncertainty with respect to its human/nonhuman composition. It doesn't start with one thing. Ensembles arrange other elements of experience – memory, affect, sensings, perceptions – in mutable and eventful rather than static, regular or structural ways. Second, ensembles happen amidst definite materials, practices and methods for approximation and coordination, sensibility to situations, others and places, as well as couplings and articulations with other devices, habits, infrastructures and practical manipulability. Third, sciences and arts have richly versioned the concept of ensembles across physics, biology, geology, theatre, music, mathematics and computing science, providing a collection of ensembles to work with.

Putting the ensemble frame this way already begins to theorize or conceptualize, but it also suggests things to start paying attention to in terms of their potential re-arrangements, re-alignments and re-configurations. In any case, concepts are themselves ensembles that arrange figures, perceptions, devices and propositions. So even in a theory of ensembles, the ensemble concept has something experimental rather than theoretical at its core. It undoes the ontological primacy of theory and concepts by adding back, as so much STS work has suggested, the practices or doing.

In passing, I note that the word 'ensemble' appears in *One Thousand Plateaus*, surprisingly, more often than the geophilosophical key term, 'earth' (*la terre*). In *One Thousand Plateaus* many things enter into ensembles: signs, molecules, characters, statements, abstract machines, strata, theoretico-experimental physics, axes, incorporeal transformations, of an *agencement/ arrangement/assemblage*. Things gather together and articulate with each other constantly in ensembles, but this collecting varies and flexes in its relations to earth, the State, subjectivity, or bodies.

The concept of *ensemble* outlines the plurality and dynamism of platform living amidst climatic, ecological, urban, infrastructural, communication, knowledge, employment and psycho-corporeal upheavals. Their qualification as *geosocial* points to the shifting ground, currents and atmospheres in which all ensembles find themselves concerned with water, carbon, energy and air.

I draw several times on Gilbert Simondon's notion of a technical ensemble to describe aspects of that plurality. But I note that Simondon's work has a tendency to render some differences universally. The most desirable ensembles, according to Simondon, have 'true relations' and 'true relations only exist in a genetic ensemble balanced around a neutral point, envisioned in its totality' (Simondon 1989, 189). Such formulations surface at important points in Simondon's work. I find them troubling in their reliance on totality, unity and transductive absorption of differences, something that I missed in my earlier readings of *The Mode of Existence of Technical Objects* (Mackenzie 2002). Isabelle Stengers, by contrast, writes in exasperation about how Simondon's notion of the transindividual holds out the promise of a kind of Archimedean point of complete leveraging of all differences: 'I question its consequences as a "territorializing" theoretical operator, presenting itself as capable of subsuming and unifying assemblages and arrangements' (Stengers 2004, 60). Stengers detects in Simondon a 'humanism without the human'. The question remains whether ensemble experience itself always envisages a balanced, unified totality. I think it doesn't.

A final remark concerning one other key feature of platform attachment-figures and their plurality: the ensemble of technical nonhumans and technical practices in platforms can baffle or foreclose understanding, sometimes deliberately. Their intricacies and thick interdependencies ensnare us and demand work, often much work, of us. Willingly or unwillingly, people suffer that work, or they escape it. Experimental ontology does not have to earn any badges of technical mastery, but the experimental process for me does wind through some of this murky technical material. The technical material attests to attachments, and the style of such attachments matters enough to me to bother sticking with them and spending time describing them. I'm not invested in wielding technical mastery, but in gauging their hold on things. Bearing in mind the demand on readers, I endeavour to point out the technical material ahead for readers who wish to skirt the quicksands. It is marked out by a vertical bar to the left of the text.

INTERLUDE I

Life along Edges: Coastlines and Reefs

A guide to the coastal ecology of New South Wales from the 1940s praises the many rock platforms found along the shorelines of eastern Australia:

> Horizontal platforms provide every kind of niche beloved by the shore animals for, owing to cracks and hollows, they provide pools of all sorts and sizes, shallow and deep, together with overhanging ledges, stones, and overhanging rocks with beautifully sheltered holes and crannies beneath them. Even a rough weathered surface provides useful depressions which retain sea-water, or provide shade, or both. (Dakin et al 1948, 204)

The coastlines in question intersperse beaches and rock platforms. These platforms biogeochemically mix sediment, the remains of hard-shelled creatures, microbes and minerals, and the veins and dykes of igneous rock such as quartz intruding from beneath the crust. The rock platforms unfold complicated edges of varying shape and thickness. Actually, not just on rock platforms, but along edges of many different kinds – between shadow and sunlight, between air and soil, between hard and soft, hot and cold or moist and dry – lives diversify.

The coastal rock platforms are edge-thickening events. Along their many edges, gradients of nutrient, water, air, sunlight, and heat shift with tides, seasons, sea levels and climate. They create the possibility of many niches in the same places. Edges are sites of pluralization and, because of that, are sometimes densely populated. The liveliness of coastal rock platforms owes much to tides, to weathering and sea levels, to processes of weathering and the relative durability or solidity of rock to waves, sand and sun. On long time scales, edges are made by the drifting apart and collision of continent plates, pushing crust up or down, raising and lowering sea levels over several billion years.

Coastal rock platforms provide 'every kind of niche'. Like many other living-non-living formations, coastal platforms at the edge of land and sea are edge formations, and they proliferate folded, embedded, occluded edges rich in hidden potentials. Ecologists distinguish niche from habitat. The ecological theory of niche was introduced in the early 20th century and then geometrically conceptualized by G. Evelyn Hutchinson in the 1950s as an n-dimensional Euclidean space comprising all of the living and non-living gradients to which a given life-form is sensitive (Hutchinson 1959). There is no set number of dimensions in niche space, and they have no simple mapping to the spatial gridding of the earth using latitude and longitude. At the cost of some geometric abstraction, the Hutchinsonian niche detaches life from a cartographic grid. Multiple niches pool in the rocks. Hyperdimensional niches assume importance in more recent community ecology (Mittelbach 2012) and some social theory (Rose and Fitzgeral nd) in accounting for unlikely forms of association, adaptation, competition, mutualism and symbiosis.

The coastal rock platforms also elevate a wavering flatness. In cases such as stacks, platforms develop when a connecting ridge collapses, and a vertical monolith stands in isolation. Smaller rock platforms sometimes stand out from continental coastlines, and derive from relatively recent geological processes in which landmasses such as continents converge or diverge, driven by tectonic movements, or the convection-driven upwellings of the mantle. No matter what their genesis, weathering and re-shaping continues. The coastal platform is an anti-template for clean and precise edges. It attests to attachments that diversify and associate along and across edges.

2

Edging: From Terminals to Interfaces

Platform edges are hard to locate. Power-laden like a city-state, vertiginous like a ten-metre diving platform, lifted-up like a concert stage, replete with technicalities like a geometrical proof, and as niche-rich as coastal rocks, platform edges run between inside and outside, core and periphery, on and off.

It may be that platform edges run along tangled lines of code and devices, through interfaces, networks, sensors, chips and screens. Inhabited in practice yet difficult to perceive or untangle, people step into these entanglements every time they open and close documents across different devices and platforms. Sometimes not knowing where the document is stored, they pause to ask: 'Where is that file?' They negotiate uncertain boundaries and thresholds between what belongs to them and what belongs to others, what is part of their work and what is not, or where their work takes place given the complete mixing of platforms into work, education, home life and government. Their work, their time with family and friends, their finances, health, education and leisure, increasingly run into platform edges guarded by requests for user names and authentication or 'use Google/Facebook/Apple to login' requests. They encounter limits in storage on their devices or in cloud data stores and wonder whether to copy everything somewhere else, or buy more space. They lose or find themselves using apps chosen from tens of thousands on offer in app stores such as GooglePlay and Apple Corporation's App Store. The boundaries between platforms overlap and wind around each other: being on a video streaming platform might rely on a Google account, and the Google account might be based on the Android device it was set up on.

Edges are highly consequential. Platform edges, for instance, make possible the unprecedented proliferation of apps as packages of focused functionality. They make possible too the marketization of communication and knowledge in the forms of social media and online. Increasingly they cut right through existing organizational and social life. Many platforms have become markets for externalized computational services, usually by 'exposing' something first designed by developers for internal purposes. Variations of platform edging reorganize or vex the daily conduct of work and life. Organizations buy many services from platforms. Large platforms sell many hundreds, possibly thousands, of different services. Access to swathes of storage, communication and formatted information bundled as 'services' ensnares life collectively in virtual machines, containers and hyperscaling infrastructures.

Platform edges run through the centre of the many enterprises seeking to 'dis-intermediate' or disrupt financial services, health provision, tourism, transport and education. They configure many patterns of contemporary work such as gig economies. The definition of platform edges has also made possible the transformation of many systems of government, institutional, corporate and civil society organization and civil society. Platform boundary work has become not just the cutting edge of platform capitalism's reliance on 'digital infrastructures that enable two or more groups to interact' (Srnicek 2016, 43), but the trigger of 'subductions between infrastructure and platforms across various sectors' (Plantin et al 2016, 22). Access to public transport ranging from trains to scooters, planes to electric vehicles, occurs across platforms.

Without wanting to exaggerate, it would be fair to say that many people regard this re-organizing with ambivalence. Chronic anxieties about being on or off platforms come in large part from difficulties of finding where platforms begin or end. Read the science and technology studies (STS) anthropologist Janet Vertesi' 2019 New Year's resolution for getting off Facebook (Vertesi et al 2019). She carefully devises a multi-step protocol designed to fully cut ties to a platform that edges way beyond its ostensible limits. Uncertainties about where personal files, data or messages actually are, or even what platform I'm actually on burgeon as so many threads of everyday life become entangled in apps and their concomitants.

The proliferating edges evade easy delineation. In his analysis of procedures of participation and their accumulation over time, Christopher Kelty argues that a collective drifting results as platform edges cut ever more deeply into experience or social life: 'it produces a ... unstable, infinite series of collectives; collectives that change constantly in their make-up and relationality; collectives that are unbounded; collectives that are perplexing to experience and difficult to make sense of' (Kelty 2019, 261). Even for social researchers working on platforms, edges dent epistemic confidence. Methodological ambiguities beset digital STS and digital social research more generally as a result of the way platform edges ramify. As Noortje Marres argues, ambiguities as to whether it is the platform or social life on platforms that is being analysed hinder digital social research projects (Marres 2017).

The hardening

Tracking how edges take shape is a way of approaching platforms without assuming that they exist, that we know where they are or what they do. How did platforms come to have the edges they have today?

Sometime in 2002, a 'hardening of the edges' was reportedly ordered by Amazon platform CEO Jeff Bezos. The edict was publicly discussed in the wake of a 2010 Google+ posting known as 'Stevey's Platform Rant' (Yegge 2010). Bezos' order to harden must have run around the offices of the Amazon headquarters in the upper floors of the art deco Pacific Medical Center (formerly a US federal military hospital) in Seattle. At the time, the building was undergoing repairs in the aftermath of a 2001 earthquake that cracked some outer walls and toppled a brick pinnacle down through the upper floors.

Bezos' order supposedly ran something like this:

1. All teams will henceforth expose their data and functionality through service interfaces.
2. Teams must communicate with each other through these interfaces.
3. There will be no other form of interprocess communication allowed: no direct linking, no direct reads of another team's data store, no shared-memory model, no back-doors whatsoever. The only communication allowed is via service interface calls over the network.
4. It doesn't matter what technology they use. HTTP, Corba, Pubsub, custom protocols – doesn't matter. Bezos doesn't care.
5. All service interfaces, without exception, must be designed from the ground up to be externalizable. That is to say, the team must plan and design to be able to expose the interface to developers in the outside world. No exceptions.

The edict concerns how the Amazon platform is put together as a technical entity by 'teams', and how it will relate to 'the outside world'. Above all, it will come together somehow through 'service interfaces'. 'Interfaces' here does not refer to the touchscreens of smartphones or the tabs of a web browser showing on a laptop display, but to a software engineering construct that separates dependency from implementation (Hookway 2014). (Slightly confusingly, smartphones, web browsers, smart speakers or Amazon's own 'AWS DeepLens' are also sometimes called 'edge devices' in the IT industry. So it is possible that you are using an edge device to interface with a platform right now, perhaps even reading these words using the popular software simply called 'Edge'.)

In Bezos' edict, building on the software engineering and object-oriented programming practices of the 1990s splits worlds along an inside and outside boundary or interface. He refers to the application programming interfaces, or the standardized programming approaches that make it possible for 'teams' and other social groupings to 'communicate with each other'. At this time, and for the following decade or so, such programming interfaces were seen as crucially important because they made it possible to define and control how people approached platforms.

The order to harden the edges was part of the ongoing transformation of the Amazon ecommerce site into the now widely used Amazon Web Service (AWS) platform. It is a symptom of the proliferation of edges that people enjoy and suffer today. Its edging does not exactly draw a line delimiting inside from outside because the edges run through the platform itself. Yes, it begins by opening something. Clause 1 of the edict says: 'all teams will henceforth expose their data and functionality through ... interfaces'. In coding terminology, when platforms 'expose' an interface, as many of them have, they make 'data and functionality' available to others. 'Bezos doesn't care' about which technology. But, no, regardless of who those others are (developers, customers, users, strangers), every interface must be 'externalizable'. Making an edge public, was, in Bezos' edict, more important than fortifying any core of the platform. That is, the interface can be approached by anyone, whoever and wherever they are. Teams in Amazon stand in the same position as developers in the 'outside world', and even teams only communicate through interfaces. Whoever was communicating already must shrink their communications without exception to the shape of the externalizable interfaces.

Does an internal corporate memo, even from one of the world's richest men, actually matter very much? It's not as if Bezos wanted something unique. The measures taken by Amazon were broadly in keeping with software design and engineering thinking of the preceding decade. The edge-hardening was probably already under way, as suggested by the list of technologies Bezos doesn't care about. Various protocols to expose data and functionality are listed there, and there must have been quite a few others. The hardening, or thinning as I prefer to call it, was widely emulated by other platforms soon after, and continues to ramify. The idea that developers could be either inside or outside the organization was also typical of the time. In 2012, during its Initial Public Offering, Facebook's CEO Mark Zuckerberg defined the platform's 'hacker culture' as the way it builds its products using continuous coding iterations, building versions of the 'best services over the long term by quickly releasing and learning by small iterations' (Facebook 2012).

The edge hardening is a powerful example of an ontological thinning. It was commercially successful. For instance, while Amazon's online sales of products reportedly remains unprofitable to this day, the services built along the hardened edges – AWS – have generated operating profits for more than a decade (Kindness 2023). But this incisive ramification of edges through the platform was and is rather more messy and mixed than the crisp instructions of the edict suggest.

Approaching edges in the making

What in this work of externalizing data and functionality assembles something that could support experimental ontology? Making edges that do not bend or collapse is not a simple technical process. How can edges hold or harden? Gilbert Simondon's description of the hardening of adze blades and steel cutting edges in *The Mode of Existence of Technical Objects* locates edges and sharp points in ensembles (Simondon 2017).

The hardening that Bezos assigned to Amazon developers to implement comes from metallurgy. Simondon usefully pluralizes metal edges in two ways. First, hard edges presuppose a technical ensemble. Second, edges are not a single line, or the Euclidean extremities of a closed figure. Edges literally fuse different functional zones.

Simondon places hardening in a technogeographic ensemble:

> These types of steel express the result of the functioning of a technical ensemble comprising in equal measure the qualities of coal used, as well as the temperature and chemical composition of the soft water of the Furan river, or the species of green wood used to stir and refine the molten metal prior to casting. In certain cases, technicity becomes predominant with respect to the abstract aspects of the relation between matter and form. (Simondon 2017, 72)

A 'good' edge, one that keeps its edge, comes from an ensemble in a place: Toledo, Sheffield, somewhere in Japan, somewhere along, for my own part, the coal-mining, steel-making near the coastal rock platforms of Illawarra (Figure 2.1). Edge-making involves people in places, sometimes great specificities of place, or pathways that connect that place to water quality, trees for wood, other fuels (coal deposits, charcoal, and so on), or other conjunctions with other ensembles. That's fine: the nice edges on some Japanese kitchen knives come from the confluence of water, coals, ores and stirring implements in place.

An edge too is a sort of place. Simondon locates a confluence of elements within an edge. The edge is a conjunction, a meeting of surfaces and flows, to put it more abstractly, that cajoles geography into technical elements. What happens in making a sharp edge? The edge of an adze, or any cutting edge that thins down to something relatively sharp, is itself one element connected to other elements:

> It is as if, in its totality, the tool was made of a plurality of functionally different zones, welded together. The tool is made not only of form and matter; it is made of elaborate technical elements according to a certain schema of functioning and assembled into a stable structure through the operation of fabrication. ... The technicity of the object is thus more

Figure 2.1: Coastal rock platform, NSW

than a quality of its use; it is that which, within it, adds itself to a first determination given by the relation between form and matter; it acts as an intermediary between form and matter. (Simondon 2017, 72)

Any sharpness of an edge, any capacity to stay sharp, relies on this merging of elements. The actual cutting edge is hard but brittle. Behind the edge lies a zone of steel that is elastic or flexible. Further back from the edges runs a thick, heavier and inflexible mass. Together they make an edge that cuts wood well.

People along edges

Where are people in relation to edges? Simondon's account in this respect is less than fully descriptive. Bladed cutting edges can travel, and cut where they go. They carry something of the ensemble with them. If the edge travels, if it cuts far and wide, if it keeps its edge, it is only because it wields something of the ensemble of people, things and places. It maintains itself more concretely than the ensembles, which exist in a modes of combination, coordination and commutativity. The edges cut far and wide, but the ensembles that make them do not.

People in ensembles inhabit tensions between the mobility of the technical element and technogeographic situation. Ensemble-people, who work, think, and feel how the edge combines brittleness and flexibility, live through the changing conjunctions in the name of the stable edge. They, in their capacities to collective organize or align themselves to the technicity of the edge as a 'plurality of functionally different zones', are caught up in the conjunction, in the states of combination and organization. People integrate ensembles, not as components or elements, although certain platforms attempt to render them thus. They arrange the merging and fusion of elements.

gcloud as a place for developers

Consider, for instance, `gcloud` as an edge, or an edge hardened in the Bezos-Amazon style. The `gcloud` terminal tool is a piece of software developed by Alphabet/Google Corporation to allow terminal access to the interfaces of its many cloud computing services. The tool can be downloaded and installed on a computer or even a smartphone. Other major platforms offer similar things. `gcloud` addresses the very same people that Bezos orders around: the developers and their teams; or what Facebook/Meta Platforms Inc. calls 'our hacker culture'. Developers are very obviously not the only ones who access platforms. They occupy a somewhat privileged position in relation to platform edges. They are somewhat more 'in' an ensemble than 'on' platforms. They sometimes approach platforms differently to other users. Their work of building apps and developing interfaces outlines new edges for platforms since apps often extend and combine platform services.

In a tentative move to stand in the position of a developer 'in the outside world'/ensemble, I install and start `gcloud` on my laptop. `gcloud` asks:

```
Which Google Compute Engine zone would you like to use as
  project default?
 [1] us-east1-b
 [5] us-east4-b
 [6] us-east4-a
 …
 [14] europe-west4-a
 [15] europe-west4-b
 [16] europe-west4-c
 [17] europe-west1-b
 [18] europe-west1-d
 [19] europe-west1-c
 …
 [34] asia-northeast1-a
 [35] asia-south1-c
 [36] asia-south1-b
 [37] asia-south1-a
 [38] australia-southeast1-b
 [39] australia-southeast1-c
 [40] australia-southeast1-a
```

Figure 2.2: gcloud cloud components 2022

```
Your current Google Cloud CLI version is: 411.0.0
The latest available version is: 411.0.0
```

Status	Name	ID	Size
Not Installed	App Engine Go Extensions	app-engine-go	4.2 MiB
Not Installed	Appctl	appctl	21.0 MiB
Not Installed	Artifact Registry Go Module Package Helper	package-go-module	< 1 MiB
Not Installed	Cloud Bigtable Command Line Tool	cbt	10.4 MiB
Not Installed	Cloud Bigtable Emulator	bigtable	6.7 MiB
Not Installed	Cloud Datalab Command Line Tool	datalab	< 1 MiB
Not Installed	Cloud Datastore Emulator	cloud-datastore-emulator	35.1 MiB
Not Installed	Cloud Firestore Emulator	cloud-firestore-emulator	40.2 MiB
Not Installed	Cloud Pub/Sub Emulator	pubsub-emulator	62.4 MiB
Not Installed	Cloud Run Proxy	cloud-run-proxy	9.0 MiB
Not Installed	Cloud SQL Proxy	cloud_sql_proxy	7.8 MiB
Not Installed	Cloud Spanner Emulator	cloud-spanner-emulator	26.7 MiB
Not Installed	Cloud Spanner Migration Tool	harbourbridge	18.1 MiB
Not Installed	Google Container Registry's Docker credential helper	docker-credential-gcr	1.9 MiB
Not Installed	Kustomize	kustomize	4.3 MiB
Not Installed	Log Streaming	log-streaming	13.9 MiB
Not Installed	Minikube	minikube	31.5 MiB
Not Installed	Nomos CLI	nomos	25.0 MiB
Not Installed	On-Demand Scanning API extraction helper	local-extract	13.4 MiB
Not Installed	Skaffold	skaffold	20.1 MiB
Not Installed	Terraform Tools	terraform-tools	53.3 MiB
Not Installed	anthos-auth	anthos-auth	20.4 MiB
Not Installed	config-connector	config-connector	56.7 MiB
Not Installed	gcloud Alpha Commands	alpha	< 1 MiB
Not Installed	gcloud Beta Commands	beta	< 1 MiB
Not Installed	gcloud app Java Extensions	app-engine-java	63.9 MiB
Not Installed	gcloud app Python Extensions	app-engine-python	8.0 MiB
Not Installed	gcloud app Python Extensions (Extra Libraries)	app-engine-python-extras	26.4 MiB
Not Installed	gke-gcloud-auth-plugin	gke-gcloud-auth-plugin	7.6 MiB
Not Installed	kpt	kpt	12.3 MiB
Not Installed	kubectl	kubectl	< 1 MiB
Not Installed	kubectl-oidc	kubectl-oidc	20.4 MiB
Not Installed	pkg	pkg	
Installed	BigQuery Command Line Tool	bq	1.6 MiB
Installed	Bundled Python 3.9	bundled-python3-unix	62.2 MiB
Installed	Cloud Storage Command Line Tool	gsutil	15.5 MiB
Installed	Google Cloud CLI Core Libraries	core	25.8 MiB
Installed	Google Cloud CRC32C Hash Tool	gcloud-crc32c	1.2 MiB

```
To install or remove components at your current SDK version [411.0.0], run:
 $ gcloud components install COMPONENT_ID
 $ gcloud components remove COMPONENT_ID
```

```
[41] southamerica-east1-b
[42] southamerica-east1-c
[43] southamerica-east1-a
[50] asia-northeast3-a
```

gcloud presents a distributed geography of the Google platform and prompts the authorized user to set up a project and choose a 'zone'. The 50 compute locations indicate a quite developed technoeconomic-platform geography represented as regional zones. The Mountain View headquarters of Google manages zones on multiple continents.

The same gcloud terminal then opens onto a niche-rich ecology of platform operations (as shown in Figure 2.2). The services range from generic server instances to AI/machine learning ensembles for processing sounds and images. Forms of platform service in the `gcloud` tool range from now readily available logins and credentials, identity and access management (who else can log in), through 'containerized applications', the all-important Virtual Machines, 'serverless platforms', and myriad of storage, security, networking, resource monitoring and deployment management, AI and machine learning, data analytics, databases, internet-of-things, to game and healthcare services.

Having chosen a compute zone and set a few other parameters, a few words typed in the terminal such as `gcloud vision detect-faces IMAGEPATH` sets in train a range of processes tasked with the platform-user-oriented familiar task of detecting faces in images. In one line, the `gcloud` command concentrates several decades of machine learning technique and implementation around an image file, and generates a list of locations of faces in the image.

To what does this terse, convenient grammar for billable terminal communication with the platform attest? Is this a confirmation that the Bezos edict has been implemented not just in AWS but in many places (Google, Meta, Microsoft, Alibaba, and so on)? Yes, perhaps it confirms that. Two decades after the edict, it might seem as if the hardening did take place. Developers, not just at Amazon, complied with the order. The `gcloud` case is not unusual. Many platforms have terminal interfaces not unlike `gcloud`.

Similar cases also range across the scale of computing, from tiny microcontrollers and smart devices through to energy, building and transport infrastructures undergoing platformization (Plantin et al 2016), as well as the vast numbers of sensing devices floating, flying, orbiting or embedded around the earth (Gabrys 2019). At the same, however, the terse commands hint at a compressed layering of operations that not only remain opaque but suggest that platforms – in this case, Google Cloud Platform – have quite complicated technogeographical edges. The shallow lines of terminal commands tremendously compress practices in system administration, database management, information retrieval techniques, network management, application development, computing cluster configuration, code version control or machine learning pipelines.

The compression of ensemble practices in terminal operations in zones replete with clusters, containers, services and managed instances provides 'every kind of niche'. People endure the ensemble, and render it durable. `gcloud` and the like come into action via multi-generational processes that are hard to track because they concretize differently. The durational processes include institutions, collective imaginings, performance of forms of social life ranging across knowledges, skills, practices and places. The processes have their own geographies combining what grows, what lives, the climate, ways of inhabiting places, and the connections between places. Often an ensemble has sub-ensembles, each with its own specific conjunctions. Many of the more recent ensembles are full of machines, some of which are relatively stable (for example, electronic circuitry). Others are relatively temporary (for example, many software-based mechanisms). All of this durational complexity, with its rhythms, its waves of change, its ephemeral stabilization as a 'cutting edge' or dissolving into 'technical debt' (code that will have to be re-written later for some reason) drifts through the edge-hardened ensembles known as platforms.

When is an edge? Terminal operations

Playing around with the explicit commutativity of `gcloud` suggests that *terminals* should be taken seriously as exceptionally niched zones, as edges that display diverse attachments and intersecting localizations compared to other platform interface approaches. Terminals, then, might be a way to sense how platform edges emerge in ensembles.

> 'When is a terminal?' we might ask, emulating Susan Leigh Star's question to infrastructure (Star and Ruhleder 1996). It's 1979, and a row of computer terminals line one wall of the ground floor of the library at the local university. Their glowing green characters on black CRT screens, a colour scheme still widely seen on contemporary developers' screens, were connected to the computer centre's Univac mainframe computer, probably a Univac Series 1100/60 (Gray and Smith 2001). Bored on a Sunday afternoon, I would idle around the library shelves, flipping through electronics engineering magazines, whose pages were filled at that time with adverts for microcomputers as well as digital multimeters and oscilloscopes. Nobody seemed to use them, at least not on weekend afternoons when I visited the library. I daydreamed about ways of logging in to the terminals, even if I had little idea of what I could possibly do if I did.
>
> The Sperry-Univac Uniscope 100 *General Description* document from 1973 has much that remains contemporary, as if we are still cascading in the wake of the metamorphoses taking place around that time. The terminals in the library, if they were Uniscope 100s, must have been connected to 'home office' as the Uniscope manual slightly confusingly terms a mainframe computer located in the corporate or institutional computer centre. The university's 'home office' was the computer centre where a Univac 1100/60 stood, writing and reading from tapes just like a Turing machine. A terminal multiplexer, a piece of communications equipment that allows multiple terminals to share the same communication line, could have been installed in the library: 'up to 16 terminals may be connected to a single communications-line modem or to suitable communications equipment by means of a UNIVAC terminal multiplexer. More extensive networks are possible with terminals and multiplexers in various combinations, including multidropping and cascading' (Sperry-Univac 1973, 3).
>
> Alongside the general description of what a terminal is – 'the desk-top UNISCOPE 100 Display Terminal is a completely self-contained communications device, with the operator on one side and the communications line on the other. Basically, the terminal

consists of a display screen, display storage, control section, input/output section, a character generator, and the operator controls' (Sperry-Univac 1973, 15) – appear detailed descriptions of character generation, keyboard and, in particular, the cursor and the cursor control keys. Nearly all of these elements – a display, the 'operator', a communications lines, a cursor, a button to transmit (Enter on contemporary keyboards), function keys – are described in concrete detail as if they might not be familiar to readers. For instance, the idea that a cursor, or a blinking line, would show on the display where the next characters from the keyboard will appear, must have been unfamiliar. The *General Description* details at length the nine keys that move the cursor. The manual provides an account of how characters are appear on screen: 'the stroke method of generating characters produces characters that are more easily recognized than other methods, such as the dot matrix method. Because as many as eight strokes are available for producing one character, each character has its own unique shape' (Sperry-Univac 1973, 22). The display space could be split vertically to provide something like the windows or tabs of contemporary computer screen. The description emphasizes too that editing happens in the terminal until the TRANSMIT button is pressed. The keyboard is laid out like a typewriter yet has keys relating to editing and communication. The editing keys mark this feature by having 'IN DISPL' printed underneath them (Figure 2.3).

The terminal itself is described as a place for 'information retrieval', 'data input' and 'dialogue'. A dialogue could serve multiple purposes:

> Dialogue is a combination of direct data input and information retrieval. However, in the case of dialogue, time is a much more important factor because the interaction between man and the processor must be immediate for the information to be meaningful. Input action immediately affects the data base, produces a reaction, and modifies the output. Dialogue varies with the exact application, but basically the terminal provides immediate answers to queries or provides solutions to presented problems. (Sperry-Univac 1973, 14)

The examples of dialogue include 'training and education', under which 'Programming' is mentioned (14). A vision of what today would be called REPL – Read Evaluate Print Loop – is sketched there: 'the terminal can act as a scientific conversational programming

Figure 2.3: VT100 terminal keyboard

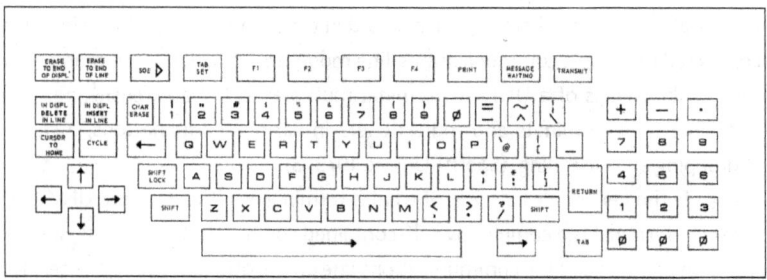

terminal to construct, verify, and transmit code to the processor for execution or compilation' (14).

What was spelt out here remains largely legible today in developers' terminal *emulators*. The Uniscope consoles with their desktop screens and keyboards more or less disappeared, but something similar took their place. An imitation device, terminal emulators, carried over the hardware terminal's arrangement of lines, characters, keyboard controls and connection to the data processing centre into a form of software that eventually re-surfaced as rectangular frames of text on a screen increasingly cluttered with the windows, icons, images and backgrounds of the graphical user interfaces of personal computers. These software implementations emulate the control codes of hardware terminals such as the Uniscope 100, or more usually, the DEC VT100. Terminal emulators allow many text-only 'virtual consoles' to open on the same central processing unit, or from one computer to many others. A terminal emulator may, like the library Uniscope 100s, be at some distance from the processor, or quite close to it. Almost completely hidden from view in the popular Apple and Microsoft operating system software for decades, terminals return to the foreground in contemporary 'terminal emulators' often called simply Terminal or Terminal app. 'Learn how to use Terminal on your Mac to interact directly with macOS using the command line' suggests a recent advertisement from Apple Support.

Terminals thicken edges

Despite their compressed and strict interactions, terminal emulators excite care and attention from developers. Terminal colour schemes and typographic arrangements receive close scrutiny from software developers. The sparse visual forms of terminals are modulated by colour schemes such as the widely screened 16-colour, 'perceptually optimised', **solarized** colour scheme (Smith 2015). Solarized epitomizes the seemingly slight variations in colour, spacing and other graphic configuration found in terminals.

The choice of a terminal colour scheme might seem superficial but points to an ensemble of embodied habits, sub-cultural conventions, techniques of accomplishing tasks all compressed within the terminal. Terminals and the command-line are full of workarounds, shortcuts and fixes centred on approaching, accessing and inhabiting platforms. The keyboard shortcuts that programmers, developers and hackers use to accelerate steps in their work are themselves accelerated by command and code completion routines built into shells – the programs that mediate between terminal communication and the underlying operating system functions – and code editors. As in other communities of practice, couplings of hands, eyes and things can become dense and intricate, and they support strongly held maintained patterns of imitation and identification.

This combination of strictly text-based conventions and habits means that things move around in terminals more quickly, more associatively, than in the non-terminal approaches to platforms. Although almost always localized by preference or default, the fixed conventions of the terminal can be generalized across devices, machines, systems and platforms. Developers use the same secure shell terminal logins for smart devices, network devices, servers and their own laptops. The generic VT100 have important economic effects (see Gupta [2019] for analysis of economic changes).

Each time a new processor comes into operation, developers open a terminal console onto it. A console or terminal scales many edges. The same terminal window – a few dozen lines of text – merges functional zones ranging from a smart watch microcontroller to a data centre cluster of computers. As anthropologist Anna Tsing writes:

> [S]cale is the spatial dimensionality necessary for a particular kind of view, whether up close or from a distance, microscopic or planetary. … [S]cale is not just a neutral frame for viewing the world; scale must be brought into being: proposed, practiced and evaded, as well as taken for granted. (Tsing 2005, 58)

Terminals have been the 'neutral frame' for re-scaling and hyper-dimensioning platforms. Their version of access and interaction defines an edge that fuses across scales ranging from large computer and data centres to scattered fields of devices.

Re-scaling devices

Around the same time as the computer terminals were re-scaling into hyper-merged functional zones, a highly transitional yet elusively inert object came into my possession. This was the at-the-time computational plenipotentiary Intel 8080 microprocessor, a chip edged by 40 pins, a device so electrically delicate that it travelled on a foil-covered styrofoam bed. The 8080 was initially designed for computer terminals and other 'edge devices' such as cash registers in the early 1970s. The 8080 arrived bundled with a tightly folded wad of pages describing the pin layout, the instruction set and various supporting arrangements (Intel Corporation 1986). This was a chip already accompanied along its way by stories and speculations of change: the 8080 would make it possible for computers to re-scale in a new shape initially in the form of personal computers in homes and offices, but also in the control of newly 'intelligent' devices such as a cash registers, computer terminals, ATMs, and the highest grossing computer game of all time, the arcade machine *Space Invaders*. The 8080 became perhaps the most well-known microprocessor chip, and informs the design of successor chips made by Intel Corporation and others. The typical shorthand for such the series of microprocessors is 'x80' and 'x86', and most servers and many other devices use them.

Like the terminal, the 8080 and its variants, are part of the edge-making practices of platforms. Also like the terminals in the university library, I found the operational promise of a microprocessor deeply attractive yet elusive. I was already nerdily familiar with digital circuits and chips, having undergone a personal digital revolution in the late 1970s. In those years, I optimistically assembled a dozen digital circuit designs to count up and down on a single LED-digital display using the Texas Instruments 7400 series integrated circuit chips and circuit prototyping breadboards readily available even in a regional Tandy Electronics store.

The transfer of logic diagrams from cookbook instructions to breadboard had no drawbacks until a school friend who far better understood digital logic asked me if I had designed the various counting and time circuits. Copying a diagram from a book such the *TTL [Transistor-Transistor Logic] Cookbook* (Lancaster 1974) by connecting wires between pins on chips usually led to a working circuit, but the project was in a sense making nothing new. To really bring something new into the world, to invent something, meant arranging a hitherto undocumented arrangement of elements on the breadboard, to devise ways for gates, flip flops and seven-segment displays to act differently, not so predictably as the infantile counting 0–9. The injunction in the *TTL Cookbook* was clear: 'interconnect the basic circuits into working systems – systems that solve problems, entertain, or perform a useful outside-world task. ... Practically all you need to know is in the previous chapters. The rest you will have to learn for yourself' (Lancaster 1974, 292). My friend went on to design and oversee a hardening of the edges in the form of a comprehensive computerized control system for the local steelmaking plant leading to major reductions in labour costs a decade or so later.

The 8080 microprocessor thwarted invention completely. Although I could fit the 8080 on a prototyping breadboard alongside other integrated circuits, it needed to be surrounded by specific chips and devices that communicated, like a bevy of sacerdotal attendants, between the 8080 and the profane world. The 8080 chip needed at least three different voltages to function (+5V, -5V, +12V), a requirement I found difficult to supply, even after scavenging transformers from a Scaletrix car set and batteries from various torches. Lacking an ensemble of chips and with deficits in power supplies, the 8080 didn't run at all.

Nevertheless, within a year or two, still no closer to activating the stranded 8080, I would be mired in its processing. Standing glassy-eyed in front of *Space Invaders* in a gaming arcade, I pursued the never-achieved task of 'eliminate all threats'. In the 8080-based *Space Invaders* and the adjacent *Asteroids* machine (a Motorola 6502 microprocessor-based device like the

Apple computers starting to appear), 8080 instructions had been woven into simple but potent feedback loops that connected hand-buttons-circuitry-screen-eyes-ears-speakers and coin-slot to an array of sprites line-dancing down the screen, always obliterating my bases.

Switching between edges

Are these coastal region anecdotes, with their inevitable biographical peculiarities, materials for experimental ontology in ensembles? The enduring terminals and the disruptive advent of microprocessors precede but also accompany the hardening of platform edges. They add durations, they bring multiple times together in an ensemble. Like the blade-making ensembles, they nurture attachments between functional zones.

What did the Intel 8080 mean for platform edges? The chip gathered within its confines many of the logical operations proliferating in the TTL ICs and circuits.

It fused many devices – counters, registers or storage locations, arithmetic and logical units, flags or status indicators – on one crystalline substrate, a thin 20 millimeter square with around 4,500 transistors.

Many of these devices shrunk systems developed for the mainframe and mini-computers of the 1960s. The 8080, for instance, had an 'instruction set' (Figure 2.4). The instruction set, or opcodes (operation codes), listed in the datasheet (Intel Corporation 1986) was

Figure 2.4: 8080 Functional Diagram; CC-SA3.0

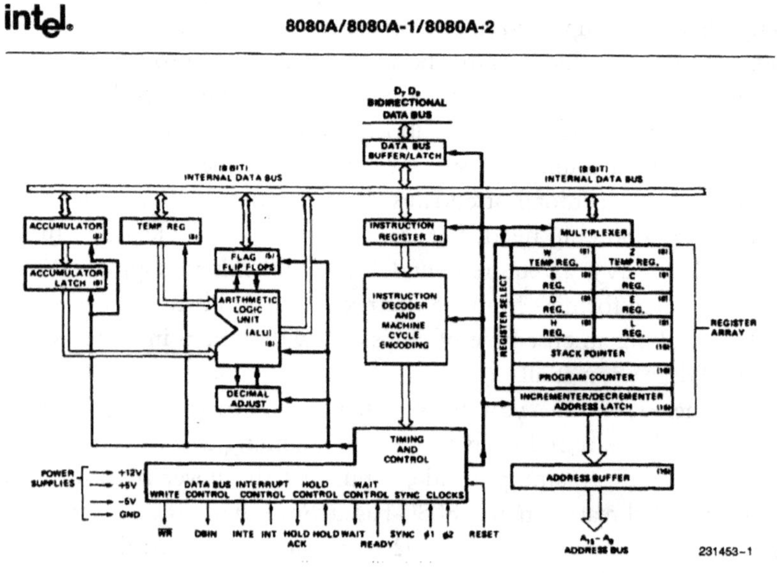

packed with several hundred apparently trivial operations that moved 8 bits in, out and around various registers and 'buses', logical operations that compared and contrasted the contents of the registers, or control operations such as jumping to another address in the program. Reading the *8080 Datasheet* (Intel Corporation 1986) felt like slipping into a pit of technical operations on tiny shards of numbers that had almost no way of doing anything in the world. Beyond doing the arithmetic calculations that were already familiar from doing sums on paper or on hand-held electronic calculators in high school maths classes, these opcodes appeared largely pointless to effect or move anything useful in the world.

Reading this datasheet in retrospect, where terms such as ALU (Arithmetic Logic Unit), Stack Pointer or 'Priority Vectored Interrupts' make some sense, it is not hard to see why such a device would have been remote from almost all practical potentials for action.

Yet the chip also reproduced in miniature some of the organizational complexity found in the 'mainframe' computers institutionalized at the heart of large organizations of government, business and science. For instance, it had a 'stack' and 'interrupts':

> The 8080A has an external stack feature wherein any portion of memory may be used as a last in/first out stack to store/retrieve the contents of the accumulator, flags, program counter, and all of the 6 general purpose registers. The 16-bit stack pointer controls the addressing of this external stack. This stack gives the 8080A the ability to easily handle multiple level priority interrupts by rapidly storing and restoring processor status. It also provides almost unlimited subroutine nesting. (Intel Corporation 1986, 1)

Computer science data structures such as stacks and pointers were wired into the circuits of the device. The stack pointer contained an address at which the most recent state of the processor could be stored temporarily while some other operations occurred. Many changes accompany this capacity to change state. There must be somewhere to record the existing state and there must be a known measure of time – clock cycles – within which the storing or restoring of state occurs. Given memory and time, itself marked by crystal oscillators constantly sending pulses to pins 15 and 21, 'almost unlimited subroutine nesting' could be imagined.

This shifting in and out of different states meant that the processor could change what it was doing in response to events outside the instructions of the current program. A stack is a collection of elements like a pile of plates that can only be added or removed at the top using 'push' or 'pop' operations. As the datasheet suggests, the stack gives the chip the ability to 'handle multiple level priority interrupts'. This is a shorthand way of saying that given certain events – for example, the press of a button on a keyboard – the operation of programs can be suspended and replaced by a new program. The current state of the system is stored at an address given by the stack pointer, and a new set of operations triggered by the interrupt signal on pin 14 can begin.

This context shifting or architecture of displacement, newly introduced to microprocessors by Federico Faggin and Masatoshi Shima in designing the 8080 at Intel during 1972–1973, was soon to appear in 'interactive devices' such as computer terminals, cash registers and microcomputers.

This was a possible relevance for the opcodes after all. Devising a way to shift contexts, to switch between operations, to prioritize some processes over others, even if that was just to backspace over characters in a line of text on a video display, was a definite shift beyond the logical circuits. Division and stacking of contexts continues. Today too the opcodes for the Ethereum blockchain virtual machine still include PUSH and STORE (Ethervm 2021). The substrate of the latest version of network infrastructure, Web 3.0, retains much of the context-switching. The Java Virtual Machine, a mainstay of platform construction in data centres and in networked devices such as the Android operating system for several decades now, has a similar set of opcodes for moving and storing. The recurrence of the opcodes suggests a common surface extending over time across many variations of devices and their substrates.

Edges are central

If, in the wake of many people working for decades in moving around edges of a circuit or connecting terminals, I can now open a terminal on almost anything that has a microprocessor or even a microcontroller (see Chapter 5) in it, what flows from that? A synthesizer, a neural network model, an image generator, a large-scale scientific computing cluster, a supercomputer, a temperature-measuring ocean buoy, a smart watch, the inverter that converts direct current electricity from solar panels on the roof to alternating current, a wifi router, a smart TV, and so on: does this conjunction release proliferating competencies? It is as if the terminals, appearing along all the edges, boundaries and borders that were difficult to cross for such a long time without restrictive rites of passage, become the point of assembly. In the terminals, ensembles of developers, programmers, scientists, engineers, artists, founders, hackers and others spring up as the quasi-subjects of contemporary technical ensembles, as the 'teams' of platforms in particular. Their terminal devices stand in for all the practices of approaching, accessing, connecting up and re-configuring devices as platforms. The chips, no longer rare, indeed super-abundant, stand for the set of operations of recording, storing, retrieving, and comparing numbers in their plural encodings as addresses, characters, or forms of data.

What do terminals and chips make together? 70,000 or so data centres, seven billion smartphones, two billion PCs and a difficult-to-count number of embedded systems attest to the constitutive spread of their zone of fusion in the servers (especially *blade* servers), virtual machines, containers, clusters, serverless architectures and platforms as a service (PaaS) of which platforms consist. And what of the hardened edge of the platform as implemented in interfaces? Despite the hardening, no sharp line divides a platform from what precedes or surrounds it, ensembles. The edges of a rock platform sketch a better line to follow.

The terminal state and its expansive layers of command line precipitate from the concentrated production arrangements of the last century and the first decades of this century. But the surprising new lease of freedom to move in terminals attests also to the many niches of actions that they support. The transactions with elements of frozen metamorphosis in terminals frees many technical beings to enter into new arrangements, to join along new edges, or to move from edge to centre. The terminal as the edge, the end point or the limit, becomes central or re-shapes the centre of the ensemble in the light of the collective, distributive forms of experience it brings together.

Conclusion

The hard-edged platform is, to put it mildly, an ambivalent figure. How should edges of platforms be negotiated, located or approached in the light of the edge-forming events discussed here? Hardening of edges defines the platforms of the last two decades against the background of the many other possible configurations of social-technical life. A better conception of edges would alleviate some of the persistent disorientations that platforms propel and manipulate. Re-drawing platforms edges through ensembles would re-acclimatize platforms to the variegated patchworks, the thresholds and gradients of the technical ensembles they depend on.

Many experiences of opacity, disorientation, constraint, forcing or enclosure associated with platforms reflect the hardening and its way of edging along interface. Edges have been and continue to be made everywhere. Implicit in Bezos' and many other's orders was a proliferation of edges. Even groups within organization – 'teams' – traverse edges. The terminals in the library were the first sign of a re-configuration of organizational life along edges that have continued to ramify.

As people work to get on and off platforms, as they find their work re-located, sometimes put out to be done elsewhere, it is the edge-making ensembles that define the new edges they must negotiate. Alongside electronic cash registers, the video terminals first used microprocessors as a way for 'operators' to engage in an editable dialogue with 'the home office' (aka headquarters), binding the operators in the neutral frame of the command line, and later the terminal emulators where so many developers today spend their days.

The influxes of organizational life and its many context switches into devices such as the TTL chips, then the microprocessors, and then the managed instances of cloud platform services are rather like the fusion of different functional zones in the metal blade. The registers, the operations, the addressing schemes, the ports, the bridges, the interrupts: so many of these elements are borrowed from offices, cities, administrative arrangements and transport infrastructures. It is as if ensembles themselves were re-implemented on the chip, and booted up.

In the wake of the movements across these edges, a movement that seems to be expansive and enabling, how can there be confusion, uncertainty and disorientation? The opacity and invisibility of platform edges is a reversal of the movement that goes from edge to centre. If terminal actions range from editing a text file to detecting faces in an image, from configuring a wireless router to running a 400-core virtual machine, they put platform quasi-subjects in the midst of a burgeoning range of possible compositions of things. But reversed, taken out of the terminal and its peripheral or edge effects, swapped over into a central interiority, housed in a data-processing centre for user-subjects configured as the authorized agents of their own actions, limits the mutualisms of people and technical beings, and produces disorienting edgelessness, a dissolution of edges.

Is there an alternate way of figuring this accumulation of ensembles and their concretization in devices? The ambivalent experiences of access, the sometimes dislocating connections to other places, the neutral frames for scaling, or the fusion of zones of institutional and collective life, lack the transportable, edge-keeping of the metal blades Simondon describes. Would a non-metallurgical edge be better able to account for the layers of different materials and practices, the different places and their connections, as well as the ways in which people, developers and non-developers, inhabit all this? What do we learn about its configuration from encounters with a 8080 microprocessor, a Uniscope 100 terminal, terminal emulators and cloud computer command line interface? They blur the image of the platforms' distinct edges by constantly re-folding them back to create new edges. Empirical description of edges over time shows a fusion of zones, sometimes expanding and sometimes contracting, like the tidal pools of the coastal rock platform.

INTERLUDE II

Platform Urbanites: The Doge Pesaro

There is a doorway on the southern wall of a large church in Venice, the basilica known as the Frari. The complex geometry of the Baroque-style doorway commemorates Giovanni Pesaro, 103th Doge of Venice (1658–1659). Much disliked, Pesaro died suddenly in his first year as Doge. In 2024, the main resonance of the word 'Doge' is probably Dogecoin, a cryptocurrency first started with satirical intent but persistently traded on exchanges alongside the Bitcoin, Ethereum, Luckycoin and Litecoin in almost ten years of speculation.

The heavily ornate doorway (see Figure II.1) has the Doge seated on one of several platforms under a gold-tasselled canopy, flanked by a variety of martial, judicial, scholarly and artistic figures, as well as some quasi-mythical animals and angels. Above the Doge, close to the ceiling of the building, two small angels hover, holding an unfurled scroll, presumably inscribed with either the laws of Venice or the Doge's achievements. Pesaro and various attendants occupy niches separated by black marble columns. Two mythical creatures sit at his feet. The niches and columns stand on a thick plinth borne, along with heavy sacks of grain, on the shoulders of four black-marble figures clothed in torn fabric, slaves brought from Venice's colonies, themselves standing on four pedestals. A door to the piazza outside stands in the centre. At the base, and almost at the floor level where visitors and tourists go in and out in droves, skeletal corpse-like naked figures hold gold-lettered eulogies.

John Ruskin in *The Stones of Venice* despairs of the doorway: 'it seems impossible for false taste and base feeling to sink lower' (Ruskin 2009, 93). The doorway and its marble statuary piles up on at least four levels, and vertically bridges floor to ceiling. The ascending levels embody an extractive hierarchy, or what Ruskin calls 'incessant corruption'. The doorway,

Figure II.1: Doge Pesaro door

dating from a time when the city-state had already lost many of its overseas territories and no longer dominated trade in the eastern Mediterranean, nonetheless points to the footprint of the city-state, its social and economic structure, resting on the labour of many others outside the city-state itself. The funeral door of the Doge stands at the confluence of state, colonization, slavery, institutional religion, trade and warfare. It shows some people in office above those below who, following the rules and laws inscribed on the scrolls, support the edifice.

The monumental funerary door presages contemporary platforms. It accumulates figures, symbols and things in a frozen scene. It is heavy with images. Ruskin calls it a 'huge accumulation'. Platforms are also huge accumulations of images. The doorway is also into a city. It is a doorway to get out of the basilica onto a piazza. Doorways with their thresholds, opening, closing, handles and locks are deeply embedded in city life. The monumental imagery reminds visitors of the stacking and organization of law, commerce, religion and the military that allow the city, and some people, to gather and accumulate people, things, wealth and land from the tides of surrounding life, for a time. If platforms have something urban about them, and if contemporary cities evince platform urbanism (Lee et al 2020), it is partly because cities had already found ways of steering trade, law, belief, habits and military to bolster the differences rendered as high and low in the monument. The monument figures the relation between authority and the city-state-territory it occupies. Many platforms have figures, such as CEOs, COOs and CTOs and other platform elites, who sit in Doge-like positions.

3

Shading: Images and Their Associations

What if platform edges, the tightly controlled programmatic access points and terminal interfaces, were not the most important ways to approach platforms? A different departure point lies elsewhere: in light and images. Images open some paths towards platform grounding, in view of their high level of artifice, the heavy investments in value regimes associated with images, and their entwining with particular images or bodies.

As in other chapters in this book, an experimental ontology centres on grounded or place-based relations. Locating the grounding of platforms in images is hard. One statement of the difficulty appears in Bruno Latour's account of 'digital infrastructure':

> [I]t is rather unfortunate that just at the time when we seem to have lost our ground because of the climatic mutation, we are also collectively unsettled by the complete disconnect between older technics of inscriptions and the digital infrastructure that is now activating them from behind. Just at the time when we need to land on an earth that would give us some solidity, we also have to reconcile ourselves with a technical infrastructure for which we don't have the right bodily apparatus. (May 2019, 18)

At core, the difficulty is not that older techniques of inscription of speech and images have disconnected from platforms ('digital infrastructure'), but the 'bodily apparatus' is not 'right'. How did even one thing become an image? What dependencies and affiliations does the imbrication of images in ensembles entail? Reconciling with a technical infrastructure that is 'activating' an older inscriptive technics 'from behind' like a puppet show is the crucial difficulty here. The disconnect has, as Latour points out, come at a bad time for people on an earth whose bio-geophysics are becoming highly agitated.

Everything becomes an image

What could it mean to say that something like images, an old technic of inscription, is 'activated from behind'? The drawing of images by programs known as *shaders* offers one way to sense this grounding. Take a first image of a sphere, one of the few regular solids that Euclid discusses in the *Elements* (see Interlude III).

We might think of the sphere in Figure 3.1 as an image of the ground to which Latour refers, a planet warmed by light coming from a star. This image is also a plot of a grid of a few thousand numbers calculated using some Python code. The grid is rendered by calculating for each position in the grid whether it lies on the surface of the sphere or not. For each point on the sphere, the code calculates how light coming from a specific direction (the right-hand side of the image) would fall on the surface of sphere. Unlike the figures found in Euclid's *Elements*, no lines or curves are drawn here using rulers or compasses. Pixel brightness or intensity for each point in this image are set by calculating movements of light around a solid body. Although the underlying geometry dissects the scene using lines and angles, and the code estimates for each point where light coming from a single point hits

Figure 3.1: A solid sphere illuminated from one direction

a curving surface, the values in the grid reflect the accumulation of many thousands of points rather than the drawing of lines or curves.

The perception of the image as something – for example, a solid sphere – depends very deeply on the resulting shading, or the way that lighter and darker greys are distributed across the grid. The spherical figure has no underlying outline as such. It is graphically rendered by changing the brightness of a collection of pixels. The perceptual sense of solidity or edge derives from that rendering, not from drawing a line. Here the shading of a surface from light to dark is very much adapted to a 'bodily apparatus' habituated to perceiving solid bodies. But the shading that renders the image perceptible as a sphere in a space comes from 'behind' or 'beside' the scene. Shading in the sense of intercepting or reducing incident light is, I will suggest, a specific mode of inscription or graphism, and one that might help in making sense of accumulations of images and their ilk (sounds, sensings of many kinds) under platform conditions.

Hashtag #platform

Instagram, a photo-sharing platform, dating from 2010, and acquired by Facebook/Meta Platforms Inc. in 2012, also devours and disgorges many images. Many platforms collect images. Social media platforms are not alone in this. Scientific knowledge infrastructures, remote sensing platforms, public institutions such as libraries, museums and galleries, news and other mass media, search engines and knowledge-bases of many different kinds process images in sometimes staggering quantities. Unlike the stark light-source and illuminated sphere of the first images, many of the images processed on such platforms come from cameras, imaging devices, scientific instruments and remoting sensing systems turned towards diffusely light scenes. The transport and transformation of images as they move from some place on earth or perhaps not on earth onto platforms through the internet-connected application programming interfaces (APIs) dates from only a few decades ago, but is now high volume, as if every point on the earth spheroid were more or less emanating pixels back to light-sources in the same way the heated planet currently emits 1.4W/metre squared according to the Intergovernmental Panel on Climate Change's Sixth Assessment Report (see Chapter 7).

The history of social media platforms could be written from the perspective of their image processing pipelines (see Sterne [2015] for a compression-oriented approach to media; Mackenzie and Munster [2022] for an account of the Instagram case). Take the hashtag `#platform`. The platform images come from Instagram. At least for most popular images on the Instagram Explore tab, platforms show up as shoes, followed by the occasional train station. These images, extremely everyday and banal postings, also figure an image-based approach to platforms. They have a relation to body, ground and earth. Shoes and train stations: can they disarm the activating disconnect between platforms and 'older inscriptive ... bodily apparatus' that Latour laments?

Between the darkly shaded sphere and #platform images of high-heeled shoes and train stations is cross-hatched shading, a zone of infill that might be good to work in. If it is possible to connect the shaded sphere, generated by a model that simulates light falling on a sphere, and the #platform images, with all that the hashtag and its many platform points of attachment connotes (economization and marketization, patterns of imitation and virality, and so on), then there is a chance of re-grounding platforms.

Why should this connection matter? The US Surgeon-General's *Advisory on Social Media and Youth Mental Health* asks directly: 'What type of content, and at what frequency and intensity, generates the most harm? Through which modes of social media access (e.g., smartphone, computer) and design features? For which users and why?' (U.S. Surgeon-General 2023, 11). Alongside almost clinical levels of depression, anxiety and poor sleep quality, concern with body-image frequently appears in the research reported in the Advisory. Images of the body generate most problems. The #platform images relate most directly to that concern. Those images might be the 'content' that at certain frequencies and intensities (for instance, in modes of access designed to prolong scrolling) generate bodily harm, a bodily harm that gives people a sense of not having the right body. The pattern of images in their aggregates, distributed according to specific geographies and temporalities, is part of the same loss-of-ground that Latour refers to. Following patterns of illumination or the arrangements of light and shade associated with platform images might be a way to re-ground platforms themselves.

Shaders: local light transport and its overflows

For the last three to four decades, much of what is rendered on screens has flowed through graphics processing pipelines. The human-computer interfaces of desktop, cars, web browsers, smartphone apps, gaming, video-streaming office and operating system applications have been *rendered* through graphics APIs such as OpenGL, DirectX and Vulkan. Major strands of the 'content' of platforms, and important elements of their 'look and feel', are pumped out by the graphics pipelines. Rendering, or the process of calculating the transformations of specific pixels on a screen, is a composite process, inflected by cultures of graphic design, algorithms and software patterns.

For almost three decades, graphics rendering pipelines have also repeatedly overflowed screens (Callon 1998). It is as if images could not be contained on screens, and instead had to spiral out somewhere else. In the early 2000s, the calculations of light and its intensities in images undertaken in graphics processing pipelines were re-directed to other forms of computation first in sciences such as chemistry and molecular biology, then in engineering sciences such as computing, and then in seemingly non-visual fields such as cryptography and then the much-discussed and troublesome forms of calculation found in blockchain technology and machine learning. In these overflows, operating architectures designed to render images were detached from images and re-aligned to models and techniques such as sampling from joint probability distribution that seemed to lie a long way from shading pixels on a screen.

But it is not as if images themselves were locked into place as an older technics of inscription during this time. If we think of the shadows, shading, diffuse light, reflections, textures, radiance, atmospheres, opacities and many other plays of light commonly rippling through visual perception, they too came flooding into the graphics processing pipeline. Whole histories of inscriptive technics (perspective, chiaroscuro, and so on) re-capitulate during those decades.

Of all the different materials and practices in which said overflows occur, the most concentrated arrangements can be detected in the variable ontologies of one device, the graphics processing unit or GPU. As a device, a contemporary GPU is not obviously a pipeline, or at least not a fixed pipeline. Image flows through GPUs have become highly mutable, suggesting a change in the framing of image processing has occurred, and that an ontological variation is in play. The main device for rendering images in contemporary devices and ensembles is the GPU, a device with much significance for image-based platforms ranging from cinema to orbiting telescopes, and especially in the decade or so of deep learning-based machine learning since 2013, as well as the blockchain-based elements of Web 3.0. It is a good candidate for analysis as the local transport hub supplying images to screens and doing the activating from behind of older inscriptive technics.

A GPU card labelled 'Asus Strix' appears in Figure 3.2. ('Strix' is taken from the Ancient Greek for owl.) In 2017, this was in my office computer (see the final chapter of Mackenzie [2017] for some of its renderings). At that time, such GPUs were mostly found in gaming PCs, but were certainly also being embedded in data centres as well as scientists' computers. The office PC case was mostly empty, and perhaps not the most interesting ethnographic site, except that it does, like any other thing, invite attention. What is the feel of such a place? The memory card, the disk drive and power supply take up some space. Many wires run around, despite or because of the growth of wirelessness (Mackenzie 2010). The GPU card plugged in a PCIe (Peripheral Component Interconnect express) slot lies in a different plane, with its own much larger heatsink, cooling pipes and two cooling fans. The 'Asus Strix' takes up two PCIe slots on the motherboard. Most of the visible bulk of it is made up of fans, aluminium fins and heat

Figure 3.2: An Asus GPU 760GX graphics processing unit (this is not a pipeline)

piping. In complete contrast to the other components in the PC, the Asus Strix has highly visible branding in the form of logos and colour graphics. Someone has made this device to appear in a market, and to make an appeal to someone there.

Under the red and black covers, fan blades, and the dozens of metal plates and tubes of the heatsink, lies the printed circuit board with its Nvidia GPU, a 960GTX. The GPU chip, a GM206 graphics processor, is a flat, dark green square of what seems to be glass, with a black square in the centre. It is the largest chip I've seen, and is surrounded by a row of Samsung memory chips. A small city of discrete components lies along the edge of the board where an upright vertical sheet of metal holds plug connections for HDMI and DisplayPort connections to screens and monitors. These paths to an external world are somehow energetically different since they are fed by bulkier components with higher voltage markings and their own heatsink. On the reverse side of the board, things are much more crowded. Dozens of capacitors, resistors and more memory chips lie flat on the board. Text labels such as R160, C917 are printed all over. The many components and pathways suggest that the 'processing unit' is an ensemble in its own right, an aggregate of elements with its own framings (various interface, image and display standards such as HDMI, for instance) and overflows (heat, air). The components are arranged to partially de-couple the GPU chip and its operations from the influence of the other components and perhaps also from whatever flows into the card along the gold-metallic pins running along one edge of the board.

What does a GPU card, now taken from its PC case, have to do with data centre-scale platforms and their accelerated knowing? The GPU card and chip present an intricate arrangement for doing something with images within a specific space of calculation concerned with light. Approached carefully, a GPU card also offers a case study of immediate implication in the social-technical graph of platform bodies. This particular dusty, dated, mid-tier gaming GPU, in its metal, plastic and silicon tangibility, transported many images in its time. It is a device concerned with an economization of images, an arrangement concerned with moving images along certain well-defined paths ('pipelines') for certain actors (users, gamers, scientists, developers, artists, and so on). Its fans and heatsinks carry away heat from the work of making images from signals of various kinds. The careful organization of paths, the cooling systems wrapped around the card, the intricate weave of components and standards, suggests that something significant happens here.

The card is a site of felt transitions, a place where something happened to light, and its illuminating incidence on different places on the surface of the earth. It is a shadow, a silhouette perhaps, of the changes in light transport occurring in recent decades as shaders diversified, unified and then transformed into something else.

Bodies are particular images

In *Matter and Memory* (Bergson nd), Henri Bergson speaks of ensembles of images, ensembles of bodies, ensembles of sensations, ensembles of mechanisms, ensembles of perceptions, ensembles of memories. Even bearing in mind that *ensemble* in French has a much wider range of meanings than in English, Bergson is definitely inhabiting ensembles in this work. Bergson explicitly identifies matter with ensembles of images, and perception with the action of bodies: 'I call matter the aggregate [*ensemble*] of images and perception of matter these same images referred to the eventual action of one particular image, my body' (Bergson nd, 22).

It's a strangely metaphysical fabulation, this ontological proposition that matter is an ensemble of images. Can it be re-formatted into experimental ontology? How can an identification of matter with images in aggregates or ensemble, an understanding of everything made up of images affecting each other, help us understand what is happening with images in social media platforms or for that matter earth-imaging satellite platforms? As a philosophical move, it seems to fetch from pre-modern thought, as if Bergson re-read Lucretius' *De Rerum Natura*, a treatise in which all bodies, living and non-living, constantly shed thin-film copies – simulacra – that mingle with each other. Perhaps the idea is relatively simple and quite down to earth: conceptualize 'matter' as pure receptivity, as affected perhaps subtly or minutely by everything else to some degree, regardless of proximity. To regard matter as aggregate – *ensemble* in the French – of images is to envisage how things constantly affect each other, even just by reflecting.

From this rather striking ontological rendering of images and of matter, it is only a small step to conceptualize bodies as images too. This understanding of body-image entertains a much wider range of imagings than the body-images identified in the Surgeon-General's *Advisory on Social Media*. What could a body do amidst an image ensemble, an ensemble whose concreteness, architectures and dynamics comprise nothing but vast distributions of sensitivity?

Versions of image-ensemble ontological theory have been present in media theory, media studies and even science and technology studies (STS) for some time. The one most often voiced is that everything is becoming an image. They are often made in relation to digital images, but not exclusively so since visual practices have constantly troubled the idea that images merely record, represent, imitate or mirror other things. Some people suggest that images are becoming the substrate of technical ensembles. For instance, architect John May's *Signal. Image. Architecture* has the bracketed subtitle: *Everything is Already an Image* (May 2019). His claim, like Bergson's, rests on the shift from drawing things to regarding images as signal processes: 'images are the outputs of energetic processes defined by *signalization*, and these signals, in their accumulation ... are what we mean when we say the word *data*' (May 2019, 47, emphasis in original).

The claim is based partly on what has happened with large collections of images and machine learning in social media, industry and scientific platforms. No one needs to look far to see the intensive processing of images. The most popular apps on smartphones provide expansive evidence of this development. The constant surge of images on Instagram 'Explore' tab, or the strangely filtered, fragmented face or body images posted by many users on Snapchat, or anything on TikTok, are some obvious examples of images accumulating through signal processing. Images of the earth's surface, landscapes, cities, streets, rooms, humans and nonhumans stream into platforms from satellites, from webcams, smartphone cameras and the like. The images flow out too, sometimes retrieved from the aggregates of recordings, sometimes generated in the rendering pipelines of platforms such as Unreal Engine underlying massively popular games such as *Fortnite*, or increasingly from the image and text-based generative models such as DALLE2 or Stable Diffusion, or just in the many-person video conference calls on Zoom or Teams that first seemed to proliferate during the COVID-19 years.

Media theory versions of image-ensemble-everything claim based explicitly on Bergson have also been in circulation for several decades. Mark Hansen's work exemplifies their skilful development. In 2004, at a time when photosharing platforms such as Flickr were just starting, and videosharing in the form of YouTube had yet to stabilize, Hansen drew on Bergson to understand bodies as imaging processes. Departing from Bergson's concept of bodies as an acting image, or as sensori-motor nexus, Hansen understands bodies as image processors, or GPUs. Rather than body-images, Hansen posits an imaging-body as in-formation: '[W]e must accept that the image, rather than finding instantiation in a privileged technical form (including the computer interface), now demarcates the very process through which the body, in conjunction with various apparatuses for rendering information perceptible, gives form to or in-forms information' (Hansen 2004, 10). Must accept? Perhaps the theoretical imperative is questionable, but the idea that imaging overflows its forms is important. Like Simondon's post-cybernetic treatment of information as something in-formation, Hansen escapes a container-based transfer of information account.

More than a decade later, in the midst of an intensified information flow associated with platforms, Hansen enlarges the imaging-body to include prediction and probability calculations as they shift into less visible, or consciously perceived, zones of experience: 'with the ubiquitous dissemination of probabilistic predictive technologies in our world comes a fundamental shift in the status of sensibility ... the broadening of human experience to encompass a greater share of the microsensible domain' (Hansen 2015, 202). The tone remains imperative, but the focal point dissolves to the fringes of perception, the microsensible domain, as modelled by 'twenty-first century media' through machine learning. Hansen describes a 'vastly different techno-biotic system' (2015, 141) capable of 'expanding its own access to and (potentially) its agency over the material elements of its own situation' (2015, 141) via 'a radical introjection of data of sensibility' (2015, 140).

The transubstantiation of images is actively considered in many recent discussions about machine learning, large image models and visual culture. For instance, artist Matt Dryhurst's 'Infinite Images and the Latent Camera' essay documents a series of experiments with the OpenAI DALL.E and DALL.E 2 systems (OpenAI 2021) aiming to construct images with no boundaries or edges. Like a Bayeaux tapestry extending for kilometres, or even indefinitely, these images can be woven from narratives or from existing images to show more of a scene. The 'latent camera' idea refers to the ways in which particular figures, human and nonhuman, found in image collections are gathered together and re-configured in the embeddings of large image models (Mackenzie 2023). The 'latent space' of large image models such as DALL.E is lodged in the set of parameters or weights that the neural network learns in training on several hundred million images with text captions scraped from the web. Given the image aggregates gathered up on platforms with their text captions, a model's billions of parameters itself embody or 'embed' meme-like images of very many things, ranging from particular people such as Holly Herndon through to visual styles such as Daliesque surrealism. Model-equipped platforms such as Microsoft Bing or OpenAI DALL.E can generate or spawn images because the model parameters exhaustively, cleverly disaggregate the found images and their associations in tandem with words. The many promised/threatened potentials of generative models to transform work, creativity, science, media and consumption is predicated on the many possible renderings of the large image/text models.

Theoretical image ontology is generative: 'everything is already an image', 'fundamental shift in sensibility', 'matter is an image ensemble', 'images are infinite', 'images are spawning in latent space': these are just some of the architectural, sociological, philosophical and art-based propositions concerning the mode of existence of the image aggregates. What does an STS sensibility engaged in experimental ontology have to add to the concern with millions of images and their billions of translations?

Some STS responses to the image-ensemble theory drips with irony. Bruno Latour takes on a slightly satirical vein as if reading commandments from a tablet: 'The message from the Cloud is clear: "Thou shall get only images." Images are no longer a record of anything; they are the provisional translation and a possible rendering of data that could take any other shape' (May 2019, 16–17). The pseudo-commandment 'thou shall get only images' reverses the Old Testament prohibition of worship of carved images. Images subsume other forms of knowing or doing, and will render all other data. But this commandments is also more tentative than May's claim that 'everything is already an image', for it refers to 'provisional translation' and 'possible renderings'. There may be in some sense only images, and these images are not what we thought they were, but these images in their plurality are not fixed in their mode of existence. Like all translations, they are both forms of movement (translation as change of position in coordinate space) and speak in a different language.

Four ways of drawing with a graphics processing unit

Among the various orientations of the STS sensibility, as it ranges across things, their arrangements, knowledges, peoples and their places, what would best ground experience in worlds hedged in on all sides by multi-platform forms of imaging? From an STS standpoint, what can be said about images that doesn't theorize an ontological transfiguration on the basis of a message from the cloud?

Let us return to experiment with some shaded arrangements of light or colour in the graphics processing pipelines. The GPUs themselves run programs called 'shaders'. An analysis of four shaders from roughly four decades of graphics processing shows something of the various renderings of images, and how they might shift about. Shading displays several major transformations in recent decades.

Shader 1: Images as aggregate

Early shaders focused on rapid transformations of Euclidean figures such as triangles, squares or polygons – anything bounded by lines in collections. Take, for instance, the scenes of real-time 3D 'first person' games such as *Doom* or *Quake* in the 1990s. In these animated scenes, the gamers' perception of movement depended on generating many slightly different images centred on a single point of view that moved around a scene. The scenes themselves (interior of a space station, or a dungeon) could only be generated and transformed quickly by reducing them to a Euclidean geometry. Much of the composition of the images centred on 2D depth-perspective re-drawing of many polygons fitted together in a 3D model of the scene. Although centred on the point of view of a player, the player's own body did not fully appear in the scene. The creation and re-drawing of the Euclidean figures could include both geometry and colour as shown in the first of the four *shaders*.

```python
import numpy as np
import matplotlib.pyplot as plt

# Vertex shader (simulates vertex transformation)
def vertex_shader(vertices):
    translation = np.array([0.2, 0.3])
    transformed_vertices = vertices + translation
    return transformed_vertices

# Fragment shader (simulates color assignment)
def fragment_shader(colors):
    return colors/2
# Define the vertices of a triangle
vertices = np.array([
    [-0.5, -0.5],
    [0.5, -0.5],
    [0.0, 0.5]
])
```

```
# Apply vertex shader to transform vertices
transformed_vertices = vertex_shader(vertices)

# Assign colors to vertices
vertex_colors = np.array([
    [1.0, 0.0, 0.0], # Red
    [0.0, 1.0, 0.0], # Green
    [0.0, 0.0, 1.0] # Blue
])

# Apply fragment shader to assign colors
final_colors = fragment_shader(vertex_colors)
```

The first shader shown here is a program that draws a coloured triangle and moves it a bit. It has both vertex shading and fragment shading steps. It constructs the figure of a triangle using an array of coordinate points, and then runs a *vertex shader* to translate or move the points sideways. It also applies a *fragment shader* to change the colour of the points as they move. Everything happens here, as the code shows, through array arithmetic, or adding, multiplying, dividing or subtracting from rows and columns of numbers. It can be observed that none of the shading operations rely on the GPU to run. They are all taking place in the central processing unit (CPU) and its memory, just as has been the case for much graphic rendering for decades. Only much more recently have graphic interfaces, even those that render web pages or the graphic user interface, moved to GPU-based shaders.

Shader 2: What is rendered

Like almost any feature of platforms, it is hard to resist the technical narratives that link progress in graphics processing to representational verisimilitude. The narrative ensnares everything from ads for new phones to anxious responses to GPU-based AI/machine learning. GPUs shaders expanded to address not only higher resolution displays (more individual pixels). One steps off this well-worn path only by paying attention to those aspects of the organization of light in scenes around the potential for action by one particular image, 'my body'.

Bergson is explicit on this front: 'everything seems to take place as if in this aggregate [*ensemble*] of images which I call the universe, nothing really new could happen except through the medium of certain particular images, the type of which is furnished me by my body' (Bergson nd, 18). A slight sense of vertigo, a feeling that I might topple over some edge, accompanies the thought of my body as a type of image through which everything happens. But Bergson's account resonates in the shape-shifting GPUs.

Rather than composing images from arrangements of many polygons (triangles), they began in their second decade to shade images using patches of textures (texture mapping), and then gradually escorting light along edges and surfaces in moving scenes (shading). But in pouring so much into images for 'my body', they added data pipelines, GPU-local memory, dedicated accelerator circuitry for specific operations such as transforming polygons or mapping patches of texture to surfaces, thereby becoming a sub-ensemble or platform within the ensemble of the PC. They exposed their own APIs such as DirectX, OpenGL, Vulkan and, later, CUDA, allowing programmers to access varied functions without detailed knowledge of how the hardware worked. Their clock speeds, number of processors, bandwidth and memory increased year on year. More happens in images via the medium of the perceiving/acting body, but only if ensemble includes new couplings or *renderings*.

The addition of GPUs shows in various detours in the code for the second shader. The second shader is more complicated because it includes arrangements to move the transformations of the triangle to a GPU using the well-established OpenGL (Open Graphics Language) software library (Khronos 2018). Again, the shader is a program, but one that arranges some parts on a GPU.

```
import glfw
from OpenGL.GL import *
from OpenGL.GL.shaders import compileProgram, compileShader
import numpy as np

# Vertex shader source code
vertex_shader_source = """
#version 330 core
layout(location = 0) in vec3 a_position;
void main()
{
gl_Position = vec4(a_position, 1.0);
}
"""

# Fragment shader source code
fragment_shader_source = """
#version 330 core
out vec4 fragColor;
void main()
```

```
{
fragColor = vec4(1.0, 0.0, 0.0, 1.0);
}
"""


def main():
    # Initialize GLFW
    if not glfw.init():
        return

    # Create a window
    window = glfw.create_window(800, 600, "OpenGL Window",
        None, None)
    if not window:
        glfw.terminate()
        return

    glfw.make_context_current(window)
    # Compile shaders and create shader program
    vertex_shader = compileShader(vertex_shader_source, GL_VERTEX_
        SHADER)
    fragment_shader = compileShader(fragment_shader_source, GL_
        FRAGMENT_SHADER)
    shader_program = compileProgram(vertex_shader, fragment_shader)
    # Vertex data
    vertices = np.array([
        -0.5, -0.5, 0.0,
        0.5, -0.5, 0.0,
        0.0, 0.5, 0.0
    ], dtype=np.float32)

    # Create Vertex Buffer Object (VBO)
    vbo = glGenBuffers(1)
    glBindBuffer(GL_ARRAY_BUFFER, vbo)
    glBufferData(GL_ARRAY_BUFFER, vertices.nbytes, vertices, GL_
        STATIC_DRAW)

    # Create Vertex Array Object (VAO)
    vao = glGenVertexArrays(1)
    glBindVertexArray(vao)
    glVertexAttribPointer(0, 3, GL_FLOAT, GL_FALSE, 3 * 4,
        ctypes.c_void_p(0))
    glEnableVertexAttribArray(0)
```

```
    while not glfw.window_should_close(window):
        # Render
        glClear(GL_COLOR_BUFFER_BIT)
        glUseProgram(shader_program)
        glBindVertexArray(vao)
        glDrawArrays(GL_TRIANGLES, 0, 3)
        glBindVertexArray(0)
        glfw.swap_buffers(window)
        glfw.poll_events()

    # Cleanup
    glDeleteVertexArrays(1, [vao])
    glDeleteBuffers(1, [vbo])
    glDeleteProgram(shader_program)

    glfw.terminate()

if __name__ == "__main__":
    main()
```

Like the CPU-based shaders, this version defines a triangle as a vertices. It also creates a vertex shader and a fragment shader, but code for these shaders is demarcated from the normal Python code by sets of triple """ double quotes. Slightly further down in the code, these shaders are compiled or turned into executable 'object files' in the compileShader and compileProgram lines. Finally, for our purposes, many lines in the later part of the code move the triangle figure (an array of vertices) to memory on the GPU, then run the compiled shaders on the GPU, instruct the GPU to draw the arrays as triangles, and then after display, clears all the GPU memory and shader programs.

What are we to make of this re-distribution of shading practices across devices, or its shifting from highly tuned to graphics programming to more general graphics languages (in this case, OpenGL or Open Graphics Language)? In her account of images of Mars produced by the Rover planetary exploration mission, Janet Vertesi presents scientific images as woven together at every level with practices of knowing: 'The scientific image itself does not so much document the object out there as document the work of different communities of knowing subjects that enable, produce, and constrain knowledge of the world' (Vertesi 2015, 109). In her tracking of the work done by teams of NASA workers on images transmitted by Rover missions, Vertesi describes in great detail how images are viewed, edited, manipulated and circulating in the crafting of knowledge about the

Mars surface. Much of this work re-crafts images and inscribes into their very composition as data drawings of something meaningful to a geologist, a soil or atmospheric scientist. This is what Vertesi calls 'drawing as' (2015, 241). Given the scientists can't be on Mars, 'digital image processing, to a large extent, constitutes the essence of "doing science" on another planet' (87). Teams of scientific workers pore over images not exactly looking for something in them, but re-drawing so that something of interest appears in them.

Image processing includes many different re-arrangements of pixels in an image, sometimes guided by geometric calculations and sometimes by signal processing techniques. As a result, what appears in the images are not so much objects in the world, but gestalt-shift changes in how the world can be seen (9).

Shader 3: Unified devices

A third shader from the mid-2000s also draws a triangle, but now takes a detour through the highly developed and active software architecture of CUDA (previously an acronym for Common Unified Device Architecture, but now just **CUDA**), a 'proprietary parallel computing platform and application programming interface' (Nvidia 2018b). This code is no lengthier than the OpenGL code, but it shifts away from the language of graphics rendering. The code is still for a shader program that moves the vertices of a triangle. And it still moves data from the main memory to GPU memory, and works on line and colour by creating vertex and fragment shaders.

```
#include <iostream>
#include <cuda_runtime.h>

// Number of vertices
const int numVertices = 8;

// Vertex data in CPU memory
float hostVertices[numVertices * 3] = {
    -0.5f, -0.5f, -0.5f,
    0.5f, -0.5f, -0.5f,
    0.5f, 0.5t, -0.5f
};

// Vertex data in GPU memory
float *deviceVertices;
```

```
// CUDA vertex shader kernel
__global__ void vertexShader(float *vertices, int numVertices, float
translationX, float translationY, float translationZ) {
    int tid = blockIdx.x * blockDim.x + threadIdx.x;

    if (tid < numVertices) {
        int vertexIdx = tid * 3;
        vertices[vertexIdx] += translationX;
        vertices[vertexIdx + 1] += translationY;
        vertices[vertexIdx + 2] += translationZ;
    }
}

int main() {
    // Allocate memory on GPU
    cudaMalloc((void**)&deviceVertices, sizeof(float) *
      numVertices * 3);

    // Copy vertex data from CPU to GPU
    cudaMemcpy(deviceVertices, hostVertices, sizeof(float) *
      numVertices * 3, cudaMemcpyHostToDevice);

    // Launch CUDA kernel
    int threadsPerBlock = 256;
    int numBlocks = (numVertices + threadsPerBlock - 1) /
      threadsPerBlock;

    vertexShader<<<numBlocks, threadsPerBlock>>>(deviceVertices,
      numVertices, 0.2f, 0.3f, 0.4f);

    // Copy vertex data back from GPU to CPU
    cudaMemcpy(hostVertices, deviceVertices, sizeof(float) *
      numVertices * 3, cudaMemcpyDeviceToHost);

    // Print transformed vertices
    for (int i = 0; i < numVertices; ++i) {
    int vertexIdx = i * 3;
    std::cout << "Vertex " << i << ": "
              << hostVertices[vertexIdx] << ", "
              << hostVertices[vertexIdx + 1] << ", "
              << hostVertices[vertexIdx + 2] << std::endl;
    }
```

```
    // Free GPU memory
    cudaFree(deviceVertices);

    return 0;
}
```

Previous shaders – vertex, geometry, pixel or texture – did this computation with reference to images. The names of the shaders conveyed their image-making operation. In this third shader, something has shifted. The shader code now has no reference to drawing graphic figures and much more to the allocation of computation to 'blocks' and 'threads' on the GPU itself. In the 'unified' architecture of CUDA, references to drawing of images have been re-allocated to many devices.

It would be safe to say that STS work has not dwelled on this aspect of load distribution in imaging. Some lines of STS thought, however, offer useful leads. Working on large technical systems, on scientific imaging and its practices, and on people's interactions with entertainment devices, address some key variations in the ensemble of images. In his work on early 20th-century electrification in North America and Europe, Thomas Hughes developed the concept of large sociotechnical systems (Hughes 1993). Hughes pays attention to something that resonates with much platformative discourse:

> Owners and managers of utilities, unlike the owners and managers of railroads, steelmills, automobile factories, and many other large-scale technological enterprises, were not diverted by harassing labor problems from a close analysis of, and emphasis on, capital cost. In the sources pertaining to the problems of the electric power systems, rarely was more than a passing reference to labor costs encountered. Instead, the emphasis was on load factor. (Hughes 1993, 463)

According to Hughes, power station owners and managers at that time (and perhaps still today) focused on how efficiently the generators were being used. A high load factor implies that electricity being generated is sold to someone; conversely, a low load factor suggests that generators are running but their output is not being used. By contrast, the labour done to keep power stations running or to deliver power to consumers was not considered except in passing.

A similar emphasis to the load factor in electrification occurs around images in contemporary platforms. There, too, the economization – the rendering calculable in terms of costs, times, relative measures of efficiency (Callon

2016) – of the movement of images, their movements and transpositions has been the central concern of owners and operators of platforms. Other forms of data – text in particular – have been of secondary importance. The movements of loads of photographs and video stand centre stage. Their movements enable platforms to become more like the stages and studios found in other media (television, radio, film, and so on).

Vectorizing loads: the re-making of the graphics processing unit as scaling device

Here is Nvidia, the leading manufacturer of GPUs, announcing a new data centre product in 2016:

> NVIDIA® Tesla® V100 is the most advanced data center GPU ever built to accelerate AI, HPC, and graphics. It's powered by NVIDIA Volta architecture, comes in 16 and 32GB configurations, and offers the performance of up to 100 CPUs in a single GPU. Data scientists, researchers, and engineers can now spend less time optimizing memory usage and more time designing the next AI breakthrough. (Nvidia 2016)

In data centres, the Tesla V100 GPU promised to bring 'insights' from 'ever-growing lakes of data' (Nvidia 2016) within the reach of researchers, data scientists and engineers. In this announcement, rendering images on screen takes a backseat, minimally flagged as 'graphics'. Some kind of vector of scaling has carried GPUs into the centre of the data centres along a trajectory that claims to bridge gaps between gathering data and knowing ('insight' or 'understanding') by substituting one for one hundred devices. The analytic value of the advertising promise for such devices is perhaps slender. Each certainty they posit – 'most advanced', '100 CPUs in a single GPU', 'spend less optimizing' – will be subject to many negotiating, competing interests.

Certainties about GPUs, however, have built up over time and have definite infrastructural affects. For instance, since 2009, Graphic Technology Computing (GTC) conferences focused on the applications of GPUs have been held in North America, East Asia and Europe. The speakers and audiences at these IT industry events run by Nvidia Corporation include engineers, scientists, gamers, developers and, above all, the person of Nvidia's CEO, Jensen Huang, who each year stages hour-plus keynote talks.

Over more than decade, the visible structure of Huang's presentations has remained remarkably stable. He introduces a new Nvidia GPU chip, architecture or server product, and then flourishes a demonstration of the product working on a scientific, medical, engineering or commercial challenge. Accompanying slides, music, animations, video clips and enthusing statements prompt the audience to marvel at the advances in size, speed or scale compared to what was possible last year. The GTC keynotes range across social, technical, infrastructural, commercial and scientific interests, but each of these domains principally offers a chance to vectorize scaling. Huang frequently touches on speed, energy usage, time, new applications and, pervasively, the economies of running GPUs in data centres. Sometimes juggling the diverse interests of gamers, designers, scientists, software engineers, developers and data centre operators, Huang presses one truth home: 'That's right! The more GPUs you buy, the more money you save' (Nvidia 2018a).

Shader 4: In the light of image aggregates

The last shader in the series inhabits this scene of scaling by vectoring calculations in GPUs. It is a direct effect of 'the more you buy, the more you scale' imperative. The shader is now based on software libraries commonly used in the neural network-based machine learning, **torch**. Coded to move through large image collections, **torch** and similar recent machine learning neural network software frameworks – **TensorFlow, Keras**, and so on – reverse the graphics pipeline. In the deep learning workflows, images flow into the pipeline and not necessarily out of it. The training of neural networks on images can be used to generate new images as samples by a generative model provided with some conditions or parameters such as the words of a text prompt. The rendering of the most preferred visual element, the triangle, in this shader comes only after a model has been trained on some data. Training models on image and textual data using GPUs has grown in significance in recent years. The edict from the GPU-enabled clouds is no longer 'thou shalt only receive images', but 'thou shalt generate images from the cloud'.

```
import torch
import torch.nn as nn
import torch.optim as optim
import torch.distributed as dist
from torch.nn.parallel import DistributedDataParallel
import matplotlib.pyplot as plt

# Initialize distributed training environment
dist.init_process_group(backend='nccl')

# Vertex data
vertices = torch.tensor([
    [-0.5, -0.5, 0.0],
```

```python
        [0.5, -0.5, 0.0],
        [0.0, 0.5, 0.0]
], dtype=torch.float32)

# Distribute the vertices across GPUs
local_rank = torch.distributed.get_rank()
num_gpus = torch.cuda.device_count()
vertices = vertices.to(local_rank)

# Create a simple model
class TriangleNet(nn.Module):
    def __init__(self):
        super(TriangleNet, self).__init__()

    def forward(self, x):
        return x

# Create the model and wrap it in DistributedDataParallel
model = TriangleNet().to(local_rank)
model = DistributedDataParallel(model, device_ids=[local_rank])

# Define loss function and optimizer
criterion = nn.MSELoss()
optimizer = optim.SGD(model.parameters(), lr=0.01)

# Training loop
num_epochs = 1000
for epoch in range(num_epochs):
    optimizer.zero_grad()
    outputs = model(vertices)
    loss = criterion(outputs, vertices)
    loss.backward()
    optimizer.step()

if (epoch + 1) % 100 == 0:
    print(f'Epoch [{epoch+1}/{num_epochs}], Loss: {loss.
       item():.4f}')

# Synchronize to ensure all processes have completed
dist.barrier()

# Plot the final result
final_vertices = model(vertices).detach().cpu().numpy()
```

```
    if local_rank == 0: # Plot only from one process
        plt.scatter(final_vertices[:, 0], final_vertices[:, 1])
        plt.title('Learned Triangle')
        plt.xlabel('X')
        plt.ylabel('Y')
        plt.grid()
        plt.show()

# Clean up
dist.destroy_process_group()
```

This last shader builds on the previous one, as can be just detected in the mention of cuda at several points in the code. But it is no longer easy to run on a laptop or a PC. It has to move to the cloud compute somewhere for the scaling and translation of the triangle to take place.

To shift to another GPU instance, I type a long command into a terminal window:

```
gcloud compute instances create gpu-instance-1 \
    --machine-type n1-standard-2 --zone us-east1-d \
    --accelerator type=nvidia-tesla-k80,count=1 \
    --image-family ubuntu-1604-lts --image-project ubuntu-os-cloud
```

These lines configure a 'gpu-instance' no longer in my office but in a North Virginia data centre operated by Google in the east of the United States ('us-east1'). The location of the GPU is less mundane since it is now part of the Google Computer public cloud platform. Somewhere between the two instances, the GPU has been figured as a remotely accessible object, part of the ensemble of devices and systems known as the cloud.

Having that GPU over there render a triangle here after training a model is much more platform-implicated. It is one instance located in one of a dozen or more data centres around the world. The gpu-instance could just have well started in Amsterdam or Singapore, albeit at slightly greater cost. The second instance runs in my name and on my credit card account until I 'terminate' and delete it. The virtual machine configured in the script (an Ubuntu 16.04 operating system running on a 'n1-standard' dual CPU) would then spin down or move on to some other queued task.

Under what circumstances does the transition from a GTX960 in my office to 'gpu-instance-1' in North Virginia become so seamless? What continuities and corroborating hold between the two instances? The GPU instance is less mundane since it is now a Tesla K80, the 'world's most popular GPU' (Nvidia 2018b), a GPU designed to lower energy costs for data centres.

The commands I direct to the 960GTX and K80 are identical and the output of the commands is quite similar, suggesting a continuity has been established. The alignments and associations I have to my mundane office PC's GPU are almost indiscernible from those I have to the Google Compute instance. In order for an experience of infrastructurally scaled sameness to appear in my terminal emulator (the same commands work in both places), geographies, software differences and hardware specificities have been overcome.

A final step, just to prove that the edges of platforms scale constantly, moves from a single cloud instance to a 'managed instance group', a set of machine configured with GPUs. 'Ensure that the Boot disk is set to a Debian image, such as Debian GNU/Linux 9 (stretch). These instructions use commands that are only available on Debian, such as apt-get' (Google Developers 2024). There is something called an 'image' that is very obviously not an image, but the configuration of a technical ensemble. But this is apposite: more and more GPUs are there in the data centres, even as they proliferate in smaller versions in other devices.

This shader renders a triangle as well but doesn't begin from a Euclidean figure. Instead it takes a collection of drawings of triangles and carries out the typical neural network treatment of cutting them into many pieces, and then creating many partial observations of the image pieces, keeping track of how these observations can best be combined. Aggregates of images scraped or otherwise gathered from the web could also provide data on triangles for this shader.

Excitement spans several different facets of GPUs (speed, cost, efficiency) but concentrates on knowledge or 'knowledge representations'. Huang often fleshes these claims out by showing case studies. At GTC2018 he presented `Clara Clara`, a data centre server that gathers images from ultrasound machines and re-images them using deep learning neural net models:

> There are three, four, or five million medical [ultrasound] instruments that are installed all over hospitals all over the world. ... Can we take advantage of the same basic techniques ... where you connect devices connected to data centres, and those data centers essentially have [GPU] supercomputers that are virtualized? (Nvidia 2018d)

`Clara Clara`, Huang suggest, 'upgrades' all existing ultrasound imaging scanners: 'Project `Clara Clara` ... is a data centre-virtualized remoted multi-modality multi-user medical computational medical instrument. ... It's possible for us to actually virtually upgrade every single actual instrument' (Nvidia 2018d).

`Clara Clara`'s demonstration, as is the convention at IT industry conferences, takes the form of a before-and-after comparison. The comparison registers some kind of acceleration on, ironically given the decoupling of GPUs from displays, a large screen. The idea, as Huang goes on to show, is to use the network connections found on many ultrasound machines to gather images into a data centre. There, Nvidia's latest GPU server (a DXG-2 [Nvidia 2018d]) running trained deep learning models, sharpens and segments elements of the ultrasound images, revealing observations simply not visible on the original scans or discernible only by experts.

At this point, Huang shows a 3D coloured animation of a beating heat, with the left ventricle segmented as a distinct, coloured mass, and focuses his attention on the heart's beating: 'I'm so excited. We can that we see basically the chamber here and we analyze most of the motion of the left ventricle by using deep learning. ... It's a fully convolutional neural network in 3D called **vnet**' (Nvidia 2018d). Naming the model and pointing to its architecture (3D convolutional neural network), Huang associates **Clara** with prominent currents in the broader stream of research work on images, machine learning and AI. Bringing the model to bear on the ultrasound images of a beating heart, **Clara Clara** anchors data centre GPUs and deep learning models in the life-death referentiality of clinical medicine rather than, say, the fluid referentiality of images posted on Instagram. Done with **Clara** (subsequently released as a Nvidia product [Nvidia 2018c]), Huang turns away from the beating heart to again insist on the 'turbocharged' significance of deep learning.

Conclusion

Say that the way that platforms refract light is changing. The shift from drawing triangles and squares on screen to generating infinite scrolling images can be traced by following shaders from GPUs to common unified devices and then to data centre infrastructures.

Shading, or the process of working out where light gets to, is not superficial. What begins as a superficial device for rendering a figure on screen upheaves whole ensembles. Shaders and their unifying, common-making devices blend across ensembles, from edges to centre. The infrastructural-organizational complexity of shading, cantilevered and leveraged on many people's work, supports the new economies of grandeur and Doge-like platform elites.

In the light of generalized shading, image ensembles come to the fore. Image ensembles present new ontologies. The media-theoretical claim – everything is an image – articulates an image-based ontology. This proposition is the kind of metaphysical or ontological move that has sometimes been staged in STS work, but is more likely to found in media or architectural theory.

Image dazzle and allure is especially distracting. It would be safe to say that images in their aggregates hail, or call out to, people in many ways. Judith Butler describes the value of occasions in which we feel compelled to attend to something:

> The terms by which we are hailed are rarely the ones we choose (and even when we try to impose protocols on how we are to be named,

they usually fail); but these terms we never really choose are the occasion for something we might still call agency, the repetition of an originary subordination for another purpose, one whose future is partially open. (Butler 1997, 38)

We have seen some of this in the work in Vertesi's account of Rover images, or Schüll's work on gaming machines, and indirectly, in the many calculations of load factors associated with economization of image movements.

A theoretical ontology is one response to excitable images. It is tempting to theorize ontologized images. If one has strong inclinations to theorize, images offer scope, so to speak. I have sought to skirt around the vortex of 'everything is an image', even as image production, circulation and distribution saturate visual and non-visual domains. I do, however, like the Bergson inversion for its ensemble starting point: matter is an ensemble of images affecting each other. The isolated, discrete image derives from many cuts and shortcuts through the ensemble. The image ensemble, the aggregate or the immense tableau, as Bergson calls it, provides another way through the univocity of images.

An experimental image ontology also responds to the sense that everything is already an image. Here, it goes along the rendering pipeline as it transforms from a drawing to a shading to a scaling process. The four 'shaders' explored in the chapter, the GPU card and the spectacular performance of their scaling and load-spreading operations, perhaps suggest that image aggregates are one of the most fluid, active and generative elements of technical ensembles. The mutations of shading through drawing, rendering and scaling definitely do not resolve the many difficulties that images have created for accounts of experience, subject positions, places or change.

The accumulation, aggregation and conglomeration of images: what does an STS sensibility bring to this, given that so much has been said about images by media, art and visual theorists for decades? The three lines of STS-derived empirical ontology – re-drawing, rendering, scaling – all run through the particularly eventful images typical of bodies. The changing of images through re-drawing, the shifts in the circuits of rendering with all their effects of suspension, and the shifting to aggregates in scaling the movement of images so that start to affect each other: all of these movements can be combined, interwoven or nested inside each other. These movements are corporeally implicated in an immense image aggregate, or image ensemble as Bergson puts it.

Drawing, rendering and scaling have a more limited ambition in directing attention to aggregate configurations of images, aggregates or ensembles that are always mediated through a particular type of image, the type called 'body'. But unlike other domains of the immense image tableau, the movements of bodies have a centring effect that comes from its situation, its way of being somewhere. Other images affect each other in calculable ways, which is how signal processing, discriminative and generative models, or recording media can reliably work.

Shading and its shaders have become very common technical elements in ensembles, and in platforms in particular. They support a very general practice of transforming images into image-correlates, or the relatively fixed images that are rendered by GPUs, whether it solves the rendering equation or the minimizing the objective function for a generative transformer model such as a GPT.

The generalization of imaging to cover many parts of earth, skies, distant and proximate bodies, living and non-living is a significant patterning of contemporary technical ensemble and lives in them.

It doesn't really matter where or at what scale we follow the movement of images. The GPU example shows that scales are constantly shifting, in multiple dimensions. Thousands of cores, or billions of transistors, might be used to calculate the shade thrown by a cloud on a body of water, or to generate an image from a text prompt in a large image model.

Perhaps the GPU is best understood not only as a drawing device, but as a 'drawing as' device, as Vertesi puts it. But its drawing is not lines, but shades; as in John Ruskin's account of drawing as a shading not a line-making practice. As we have seen, graphic processing became shading done by shaders sometime in the 1990s. A shader is also a program, a way of working on images that is more than lines or geometry, that is a full rendering of images. And looking at it, the GPU, and that florid GPU sociotechnical imaginary, is a response to that. The architecture of the GPU, no less than that of the Doge Pesaro funerary door along with its continuous stream of spectators, is a monumental shading.

INTERLUDE III

Container Figures

At base, Euclidean space has little concern with coordinates and numbers but much concern with figures and containers. In Euclid's *Elements*, the primary geometry textbook for engineering sciences, the definition of a figure makes no mention of dimensions or the coordinates that Descartes instrumented as Euclidean space. Euclid defines a figure as 'that which is contained by any boundary or boundaries' (Euclid 2012, 1). A figure could be a circle, a square, a triangle, and so on, but not a line or a surface extended indefinitely, since those have no endpoints or extremities. This definition relies on preceding ones, many of which rely on even more elementary propositions and line-drawing; for example, 'Definition 2: A surface is that which has length and breadth only' (Euclid 2012, 1).

Figures in Euclid's *Elements* are, broadly speaking, *containers* to be mixed together to construct new containers. The propositions of the *Elements* are, in practice, instructions on how to use the definitions, postulates and previous propositions in combination to make figures (such as Figure III.1): 'Proposition 1: On a given finite straight line to construct an equilateral triangle' (Euclid 2012, 3). The propositions are figurative in Euclid's sense of the figure in that they are constructed using a compass and ruler to draw figures. The propositions, even those concerning number rather than geometry, are figured out using lines as boundaries. For Euclid, figures contain other figures or containers.

The figure definition holds, however, slightly indeterminate: 'that which is contained'. It is not clear, for instance, whether a figure contains its boundary. Many practices make or use containers – weaving, potting, woodwork, cooking, digging, and so on. Containers and bags, as various commentators have argued (Le Guin and Haraway 2019), are some of the most ignored and forgotten technical things we have. If to have is to hold, containers are involved. Containers are duration-making since they allow so many forms of preparation or storage for later. Cooking pots in contrast to circles make it possible to shift metabolic processes of digestion outside human bodies.

Figure III.1: Proposition 7, Euclid, *Elements*

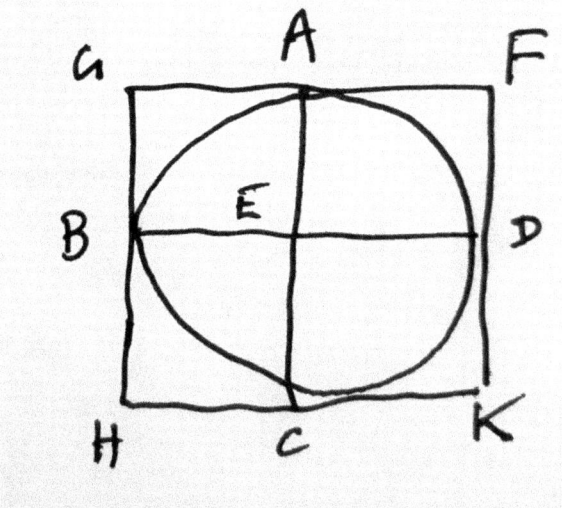

The practices documented in Euclid's *Elements* cultivate containers diagrammatically. The construction of a straight line of a given length at a given point (Proposition 2) requires the plane figures of a circle and finite lines, as well as the diagrammatic figure of Proposition 1, which constructs the figure of an equilateral triangle given the figure of a finite straight line. The 465 propositions of the *Elements* thin the textures and variations of lines to hold them in drawable boundaries of the figures. It also weaves figures together in an increasingly dense texture of cross-linked propositions that gradually complicate the edges of the figures. By Book 12, geometrical forms such as a polyhedrons are inscribed in the solid forms such as boxes or spheres. As in many abstractions, thickness accumulates through practice of weaving together successive results.

The proliferating but thin containers of the *Elements* seem to open the possibility of forgetting about ground, soil, earth, location and place, and instead moving along lines, across surfaces, in spaces where everything is measured. While many critical and post-critical modes of thought have rightly lamented the extension of Euclidean geometry into a thin, inhospitably rigid and empty offworld space, the practice of diagrammatic composition is pragmatic and compositional. The work of assembling a limited number of elements as compounded figures is way more hospitable than the bare figures themselves.

The Euclidean figures have a double practicality in experimentally varying platforms. The figures draw attention to containers and containing in their space-making varieties (shapes, numbers, solids). They suggest too practices of drawing and numbering using containers in order to know. The figures make certain forms of knowledge by gathering figures together using numberings. Euclidean geometry makes figures, with all their surfaces, edges, boundaries, extremities, points, intersections, areas, angles, equalities and differences, by holding them together using numbers (for propositions, definitions, axioms, drawn elements, and so on). The intricately constructed icosidodecahedrons inscribed in a sphere of Book 12 stitch many numbered elements together.

4

Hashing Many Containers

Cloud computing platforms rely on what are simply called 'containers'. Computing platforms are increasingly organized around software 'containers' such as Docker (Docker 2022). Would it be possible to better ground platforms in their ensemble-natures by paying attention to containers and their construction? Numbers offer one way of following the container construction.

There are two problems in attending to platform numbers. The first, which I term the *numericity problem*, concerns the different ways in which platforms gather things through many kinds of calculation, algorithms, addressing techniques and statistical routines such as machine learning and the like. By speaking of 'numbering', I hope to resist treating numbers as if I know what they are. If there is any starting point, it is more like differences and their differencing. Numberings differ. They are multiple and they multiply. Numberings twist multiples together in different ways that can be traced through numeric, calculative and computational practices. Numberings occasion a wide variety of relational problems, including who gets to decide what numbering is done, and how that numbering makes worlds. Platforms overflow with numbers organized in lists, arrays, vectors, matrices, tables and parameters.

The second problem-group concerns a few large numbers and their affects on platform plurality. I call this few-many asymmetry the platform-number problem. There are in non-trivial respects few platforms (for example, Meta Platforms Inc, Alphabet, Apple, Amazon, TenCent, and so on). These few have 'big numbers'. A single number such as 2.3 billion monthly active users stands in for a somewhat huge variety of interactive processing of differences, living and non-living.

A few platforms, the so-called 'hyperscalers', contain many other platforms. Many of the ways in which people feel ensnared or entwined on platforms come from containment on a few platforms. Apps, interfaces, sites, devices, appliances, vehicles, institutions, organizations and places are somehow organized through or entwined with a few platforms. Finding platforms free from such entanglements isn't easy. (The main examples that come readily to mind are certain scientific platforms; see Chapter 7.)

As various platform-related studies have shown, even following the weave of those attachments for a single platform is hard work. Beverly Skeggs and Simon Yuill sought to track the extent of Facebook personalization across the Web (Skeggs and Yuill 2016), Kate Crawford attempted to map the elements of Amazon's Alexa smart speaker device (Crawford and Paglen 2019); they found themselves in a sprawling tangle of relations.

Most of the numbers in the numericity group concern platform *microstates* platforms. The platform numbers that contain many in a few are macrostates. The challenge for experimental ontology lies in working between these two problems. How is it possible to hold together the diversity of microstates and the accumulated macrostates? At times, platforms seem to excel in numbering almost anything imaginable: whale sightings off the coast of New South Wales, environmental DNA, coordinates of every building on the planet, the sets of weights in a neural net model used to isolate John Lennon's voice from a cassette tape (Deezer 2023), or a unique number for every unit of the many cryptocurrencies and for every transaction that takes place. Extraordinary proliferations of numbers spring up. At other times, a few large numbers relating to some platform cast a long shadow over many others. A number, such as the total of Facebook or TikTok users, magnetizes whole fields of commercial, cultural and political life.

Varying the relations between these two number-groups is the main concern of this chapter. This chapter assays platform numbers by placing them back into an ensemble of microstates. The experimental sensibility here takes the form of what John Law describes as wariness about 'stories of consistency and coherence' (Law 2017, 44). Numbers and numbering practices attract many stories of consistency and coherence. I develop an account of platform numberings and numbers that draws on the figure of the statistical ensemble, a construct used in early 20th-century physics to link the many slight variations in the movement of particles to macrostates such as temperature and pressure. The statistical ensemble is a container figure, and a version of a science and technology studies (STS) vision of numbers as 'ontological multiplicity' (Law 2017, 43), in which experimental, computational and mathematical practices entwine.

In order to experiment with the statistical ensemble as a way of holding different numbers at the same time, the chapter spans several durations, some centred on specific laboratory arrangements for dealing with vibrations, others concerning ordinary platform techniques and arrangements such as hashcodes, software containers and blockchains for dealing variations. By paying attention to vibration and variation together, I suggest, it might be possible to ground platforms as ensembles.

Smallest numbers

Platforms, brutally summarized, contain numbers. According to one result of an internet search I did just now, 175 zetabytes (175 billion terabytes) of data will be stored by 2024. Each byte is written somewhere as a microstate of some atoms. In the 1980s, I found myself observing an ensemble similar to the audiometry laboratory that Simondon describes in the *Mode of Existence of Technical Objects*. I sat for what seemed like months, although it probably only lasted weeks, next to a low-temperature physics apparatus, and adjusted dials on signal generators and amplifiers to measure how a single crystal of the rare earth element, holmium, at very low temperature, vibrated in response to oscillating electric fields. My supervisor, a postdoctoral researcher from Germany, explained that he couldn't take it out of its liquid helium-cooled case since it would start to react immediately with oxygen. I noted the settings of the instruments down in a table of numbers (Kopp et al 1984). I barely understood the experimental ensemble at the time. Somehow the interest in the rare earths concerned how amenable the crystal was to electrical and magnetic fields. 'The Initial AC Susceptibility of a Holmium Single Crystal' conference paper at the 8th Annual Australian Institute of Physics 'Condensed Matter' meeting in Pakatoa, New Zealand, is not easy to find online today, but derives in part from the measurement data I collected, absorbed in the apparatus of the experimental ensemble.

Low temperature physics labs with their efforts to tune the crystals initially unearthed, in ways that I did not anticipate, ways of burrowing down into molecular and now atomic vibrations on which much platformate computation depends. In 2017, IBM researchers announced in *Nature* the reading and writing of two bits of information on single holmium atoms set on a bed of magnesium oxide (Natterer et al 2017). In their account, they describe how an 'ensemble of Holmium atoms ... suggests a path towards data storage at the atomic limit' (Natterer et al 2017, 226). The susceptibility of single rare earth elements such as holmium to reading and writing of single binary numbers requires at the very least an ultra-thin insulating layer of magnesium oxide, an ultra-high vacuum, and a far-from-room temperature of around 10K, not to mention a scanning tunnelling microscope, itself supported by sophisticated mechanisms for isolation from vibration.

So the single holmium atoms, chosen because they couple weakly to the substrate – 'interact weakly with the surrounding environment' (Donati et al 2016, 318) – yet have 'exceptionally large coercive field' (implying that their magnetic state resists change in the face of external magnetic fields), cleverly hold a number for a time. Self-isolating yet strongly magnetized, the holmium atoms eventually flip into a random magnetic spin state. For a while, the holmium atoms were the smallest numbers ever written by people.

Coldest numbers: microstates as number generators

Platforms also make numbers. For several years around 2010, I walked a small group of graduate STS students across campus to one of the coldest places on the planet and possibly the universe, according to its attending physicists. In a white 1960s Bauhaus-style building on the green fields of Lancaster University, now rebuilt as IsoLab, physicists and technicians of Ultra Low Temperature Physics Laboratory had built a refrigerator, which they were happy to show us. The refrigerator apparatus itself stands on a 50-tonne concrete block balanced on air-springs. The platform isolates experiments from the vibrations of the surrounding campus and nearby motorway. When running, the refrigerator dropped the temperature of a small internal chamber close to the limits of absolute zero, milli-Kelvins. At such temperatures, the thermal buzz of things slows right down and electrical, magnetic and other forces start to play more freely. The purpose of 'the platform technology', as one might imagine, is not simply to set records for lowest temperatures, but to temporarily open a window onto different times and places in the cosmos, to states of fluidity, interaction and transport in which common materialities become unfamiliar. As a result, the laboratory website promises that 'our platform technology provides the extreme cold and isolation necessary to probe the subtle quantum behaviours that are otherwise hidden by thermal fluctuations or external disturbance' (Lancaster University 2021).

The physicists' construction of a container on springs aims to reduce various mechanical and thermal vibrations in order to approach quantum behaviours. Such technophysical singularities, exceptional in their decoupling from other vibratory fluxes, allow ever-so-interesting indeterminacies to appear. It belongs to an ongoing series of experiments built to crossover from classical mechanics, where particles have determinate locations and interactions, to quantum mechanics, where particles' locations are shifting probabilities calculated from wave functions. The IsoLab platform makes it possible, for instance, to create ultra-random numbers, numberings that contribute highly valuable indeterminacy in the cryptographic separation of systems from each other. Vibrational isolation comes home to roost as strong cryptography.

What links the flow of numbers derived from quantum-level fluctuations in fluxes of particles at very low temperatures to platforms? The arrangements – isolation in particular – that support these flows of random numbers are particularly relevant to ensembles and their number problems. There are perhaps decisive mutations in numberings associated with platforms that we can begin to glimpse by tracking some of the vibratory fluxes in these experimental arrangements for generating or recording numbers.

Statistical ensembles and their containment

For both the holmium crystal and IsoLab, the bridge between the macrostates and microstates physics runs through the *statistical ensemble* of late 19th-century physics. The ensemble is the base container figure devised by the version of thermodynamics known as statistical mechanics in the late 19th century (Stengers 2011). The defining property of the statistical ensemble proposed by the physicist Josiah Willard Gibbs (Gibbs 1902) is a multiplication of the same system in a spread of microstates. In statistical mechanics, moving particles are not studied in isolation but as collections of slightly varying copies or microstates.

The ensemble approach begins from a collection of a relatively large number of moving particles, not the small number of moving bodies, say the planets and sun, found in classical physics. In Gibbs' account, the concept of an ensemble is a way of considering a macrostate such as the temperature of a system of myriad particles by viewing it as a virtual collection of identical systems, differing only in their 'phase' or microstate. Note that the macrostate of a large collection of things such as molecules is hard to figure out because of the many movements and positions they take on. Numbers such as temperature, volume and pressure stand in for the combined effect of those movements, just as platform numbers stand in for the dynamics of social media or other popular platform usage (Mackenzie 2018).

The concept of an ensemble replaces a single closed system of particles with many copies of the system, bounded and contained and separated from an outside universe. The container, as evinced in IsoLab of the single holmium crystal apparatuses, is important because it isolates the system from stray energies. The collection of many closely related copies is important because it re-figures the macrostate as the effect of many different combinations of microstates. 'Instead of studying the system at a single microscopic state', write the authors of a recent review, 'ensemble theory considers the system's microscopic state as unknown and employs a probability density function to describe each state's probability' (Gao 2022). The resonance of the statistical ensemble for presents purposes lies in its treatment of the problem of knowing the macrostate of a collection of things by comparing many closely related versions/microstates of the collection. The *statistical* character of the ensemble suggests a large number of copies can be used to calculate estimates of the macrostates – temperature, pressure, and so on – of the entity.

Many idealizations come into play here – the isolation of the ensemble from the world, the possibility of virtual identical copies in slightly different microstates, for instance, and the calculations used to derive macrostate from the variety of micro-configurations in the ensemble. And yet the statistical ensemble, for all its constraints, is explicitly an approximation, a way of using numbered variations to generate a few 'large' numbers that summarize them, such as temperature or pressure. Gibbs terms this derived macrostate 'density-in-phase', where 'phase' itself refers to the abstraction of phase-space, a space in which particle movements are all re-defined as points in an abstract geometry:

> In an ensemble of mechanical systems identical in nature and subject to forces determined by identical laws but distributed in phase in any continuous manner, the density-in-phase is constant in time for the varying phases of a moving system; provided that the forces of a system are functions of its co-ordinates either alone or with the time. (Gibbs 1902, 9)

An ensemble in this sense is the uneven, always fluxing, manifold of many versions of a system.

Just as statistical mechanics used probability distributions to approximate the movements of particles using the now statistical macrostates of pressure, heat or temperature, we might say that the contemporary platform ensembles reconfigure social orderings ranging from personal to impersonal as a flickering set of states ranging across probability distributions. In the millions, perhaps billions, of approximations streaming each second across platforms such as Instagram, YouTube, Spotify, Uber or TikTok, probability distributions approximated from microstates configure new microstates.

The separation between the molecule/individual and the molar/large-scale social shaping does not capture the ensemble embeddings. The ensemble construct that first changed how physics thought about matter and energy renders the macrostate as an effect of many systems, probable and improbable. The ensemble substitutes many copies of the system in different microstates for the state of the system. Note that ensembles are inherently multiple in the sense that any given system is actually only an approximation to a dynamic set of variations.

The virtualization of a situation as a collection of identically configured systems varying in configuration allowed Gibbs to reconstruct system state as probability distributions. It is possible to see, at least in dim outline, how this re-description of system state in terms of probability distribution could lead to statistical quantum mechanics, a way of approaching physical states as probability distributions affected directly by their observation. Like Karen Barad's re-reading of quantum mechanics as a knowledge practice immersed in intra-action (Barad 2007), I remain curiously invested in statements about physical processes. I see the Gibbs' notion of statistical ensembles as a way of registering the superimposed vibrations of slightly differing configurations. 1000 platforms are, viewed this way, phases/microstates of a numbering ensemble.

How does the statistical ensemble, an ensemble that differs in important respects from the image-ensemble of Bergson, the technical ensemble of Simondon with its provisional de-couplings, or the edge-assemblage of STS with its zigzag boundaries, help address the platform number problems of numericity and sparsity? How, moreover, does attention to numbering via this ensemble approach, ground platforms in ensembles?

The fabric of hashing

A single, widespread platform numbering practice seeps through many places and levels on platforms: hashing. In a terminal, I type **sha1sum <<< 'platforms'**. The SHA-1 hash digest for the input 'platforms' produces the hexadecimal (base-16) number **23a6b3c48d0bd11224d99f0e63f2 efe410fc55a81**, itself a shorthand encoding of the binary number shown in the following box.

```
sha1sum <<< 'platforms'
echo 'platforms' |sha1sum |xxd -b
00000000: 00110010  00110011  01100001  00110110  01100010
  00110011 23a6b3
00000006: 01100011  00110100  00111000  01100100  00110000
  01100010 c48d0b
0000000c: 01100100  00110001  00110001  00110010  00110010
  00110100 d11224
00000012: 01100100  00111001  00111001  01100110  00110000
  01100101 d99f0e
00000018: 00110110  00110011  01100110  00110010  01100101
  01100110 63f2ef
0000001e: 01100101  00110100  00110001  00110000  01100110
  01100011 e410fc
00000024: 00110101  00110101  01100001  00111000  00100000
  00100000 55a8
0000002a: 00101101 00001010
```

The number is a hash of the word 'platforms'. The fact that this hash number is much longer than the message 'platforms' indicates something of how the number is generated. Originally introduced as a US National Institute of Standards information processing standard for digital signing of documents (NIST 1995), the SHA-1 algorithm operates on data in 512 bit blocks, so short messages like 'platforms' will be padded with extra characters to make them up to minimum output of 160 bits. In principle, no other word, including apparently very similar ones such as platform, will be digested or summarized to that same number. 0bbdb0366e2d0065d12175054c9a384d34b71e15 is indeed different, perhaps surprisingly different since nearly every digit in the two is different, yet nearly all the letters in the two numbers are the same ('platform/s') The SHA-1 digest of the whole of this chapter is still the same length 0bbdb0366e2d0065d12175054c9a3 84d34b71e15 and the digest of all the text of all the PDF files I've collected in the last ten years would also be the same length. The point is that this supply of 160 bit binary numbers is rather large: 2^{160} is an astronomical quantity of numbers to number with.

That SHA-1 hash – a number, 40 characters long, that can seemingly uniquely swallow anything on the platform – is the kind of numericity in which contemporary platforms abound. It promises unique variability, or a numbering in which every slight variation – the addition of a comma or a space for instance – sifts out as a unique number. The addressability of hashes, their potential to uniquely identify complex configuration, does not go unnoticed. They lie at the heart of significant developments in platforms over the last few decades, including large databases, cryptography and blockchain technologies (currencies, Web 3.0, non-fungible tokens, and so on) to name a few. In recent years, for instance, the worldwide shortage of graphics processing units (GPUs) attributable to growth in blockchain 'proof-of-work' algorithms is a direct result of intensified hashing. Recent intensification of machine learning-based approaches to hashes suggest that they also will grow in significance for various reasons (for example, to better approximate some of the numbers computed in neural network training algorithms).

Controlling the flow of hashes

The numbers generated by hash functions are tricky to read and even regulate because they form a mycorrhizal network woven through and across platforms, and these numbers have complex relationalities running through them. What can be learnt from examining the collections of such numbers in ensembles? STS accounts of numbering practices regularly suggest the actual plurality of even single numbers. I think here of Helen Verran's tracking of numbers that work to create enumerated entities and vague wholes in certain policy/management settings in control societies (Verran 2012), anthropologist Jane Guyer's accounts of percentages or prices in the wake of the 2007/2008 financial collapse (Guyer 2016), historian Ted Porter's analysis of indicators (Porter 2015), Gilles Deleuze's discussion of constantly varying measures and their relation to durations in cinema (Deleuze 1996), or philosopher Alain Badiou's account of number as weaving the 'cultural fabric' (Badiou 2008). In all these accounts, numberings may involve abstractions, but abstractions are specific, and actually quite concrete in their modalities. Viewed from this angle, hashes are a multi-faceted figure, at once regulatory, ontological and affective in its numberings.

Take the standard, although now slightly outmoded, SHA-1 hash. How are hashes like `0bbdb0366e2d0065d12175054c9a384d34b71e15` ('platform') regulated? There is no obstacle to finding these numbers and the functions that produce them in operation. The terminal commands shown earlier point to their ready availability and visibility. In themselves, they hardly seem to be the locus of intense affective investment. Hashes, however, have been and are regulated by nation-states. The US National Institute of Standards defines SHA-1 and SHA-2 hashes, and also endeavours to govern their circulation. Newer Secure Hash Functions such as the SHA3 Keccak256 appear from time to time because existing hash functions start to break down.

In 2017, for instance, the US National Institute of Standards issued the following:

> Federal agencies should stop using SHA-1 for generating digital signatures, generating time stamps and for other applications that require collision resistance. Federal agencies may use SHA-1 for the following applications: verifying old digital signatures and time stamps, generating and verifying hash-based message authentication codes (HMACs), key derivation functions (KDFs), and random bit/number generation. (NIST 2017)

The directive came in the wake of the Shattered attack, a cybersecurity proof-of-concept. In 2017 Shattered occasioned minor shock waves in the worlds of platform security and administration when researchers in Amsterdam and Google generated two different PDF files with identical SHA-1 digests (Stevens 2017). The fact that they were able to rely on the data centre compute capacities of Google, including heavy use of GPU processors, suggests the collective interest in the question of whether hashing functions uniquely differentiate things such as files or people for that matter. The most sensitive regulatory issue concerning hashes is their uniqueness or lack of uniqueness. The problem with SHA-1 is that it might not generate unique numbers. Shattered showed SHA-1 has a 'key collision' problem. Later versions of SHA – SHA-2, SHA-256, SHA-384, and so on – are less likely to do this.

What is the problem with this possible lack of uniqueness? Numbers in many other settings are used because they lack uniqueness, and this lack of uniqueness makes calculation easier. So, integers or whole numbers for instance, associate readily with each other. By contrast, the uniqueness of some numbers creates a lot of extra work. For instance, in calculating the weights or parameters in large language models or large image models, the

GPUs or other compute devices have to reckon with the many real numbers by using floating point approximations. The floating point representations of real numbers often present choices between how close the approximation will be and how fast the numbers can be calculated. More precise approximation takes much longer to calculate. Hashes fall somewhere between these two. They are neither so unique that they can only be approximated, nor so common that they can be combined in any possible way.

In analogy to Paul Keating and Alberto Cambrosio's idea of regulatory objectivity, hashes have a regulatory calculability within platform numericity. Keating and Cambrosio suggest, in relation to the biomedical platforms they study, that 'regulation is a constitutive component of the platform' (Keating and Cambrosio 2003, 331). Regulation conditions the commutativity of platforms. It establishes their capacity to accommodate many re-arrangements of relations. In this respect, platforms differ from networks. Networks flexibly combine relations, but the combination of elements in networks need not be clearly identifiable. The regulatory arrangements in platforms (such as the 'hardened edges' discussed in Chapter 1) create consistent flexibility in which variations and combinations can be identified. This shaping of regulatory commutability of platforms, or their embodiment of flexible, 'identifiable combinations of elements' (Keating and Cambrosio 2003, 107), goes beyond the de-coupled coordination of elements by human operators described by Simondon in his account of technical ensembles. In digital platforms, this regulation often occurs through numbers, although it is not completely embodied there. But not just any numbers embody regulatory calculability. Only those numbers that pertain to the conventions of equivalence, exchange and circulation need to embody it, which is why such numbers have government standards associated with them (NIST 2015).

Containerizing numbers

Many hashes are entangled in negotiations of who or what is on a platform. How can a hash do this? As numbers, they are relatively large in terms of numbers of digits, but the number of digits has nothing to do with quantity, coordinates, measures, proportion, rates or any of the statistical estimates. Hashes compact other data such as numbers, text or images into somewhat arbitrary numbers of a fixed number of digits. But hashes themselves cannot be meaningfully added, divided or combined except in quite self-identical and isolated ways: a hash function can hash a hash number to produce a new hash.

The design of the original SHA-1 algorithm by Ron Rivest, an MIT computer scientist (NIST 1995), starts from a set of prime numbers, and then runs through on a sequence of logical operations that successively mix parts of the message with the fractional digits of the square root of some prime numbers to generate the final 40-digit hash. The operations of the secure hash functions are intricately arithmetic, and entail many divisions, additions and multiplications of the data values passed to the function. Later versions of the same lineage of cryptographic hash functions such as the SHA-2 and SHA-3 chop the data much more finely and randomly in order to drastically limit such eventualities (NIST 2015).

I find it difficult to follow these operations, although the code for them is not long. But that intricacy, very like a process of weaving, tightly binds different elements of the message to each other in a back and forth combination of chunks of the data. The many loops and steps in the SHA algorithms generate hashes that offer little pattern or structure. The results is a number that lacks any obvious construction.

It's opacity is part of the regulatory calculability, and creates great obstacles to finding the input that led to a given hash number. Hashes are said to be resistant to 'pre-image attack' because no obvious path exists to find the message that leads to a given hash. This is a recalcitrant form of representation: the hash is a highly specific index of the message or input, but it is not possibly to recover the input from the index.

The diminished calculative availability of hashes, their relative immunity to approximations, or to the mathematical treatments found in calculus, algebra or statistics, lends them a different ontological status to other forms of numbering found on platforms or in sciences. It is if these numbers, themselves the product of quite extensive calculation, are closer to the physical locations or places in platforms, and have a stronger connection to what exists there.

Locating numbers

Hashing is a highly economized numbering practice. It runs down into semiconductor design, where hashing functions are now often built into the chipset. When something finds itself re-implemented on a chip, it seems likely that it has become highly valuable. The pervasive presence of hashes in many facets of platforms is somewhat remarkable, but can be understood in the light of the contained calculability of hashes.

User logins, connections to servers over the internet, and session management make extensive use of hashes. They proliferate in the storage and database infrastructures of platforms. For instance, Mazdak Hashemi, VP of Infrastructure and Operations at the former Twitter, writes that 21.2 per cent of Twitter's hardware infrastructure was working on key-value storage engines such as Redis and Memcached (Hashemi 2017). These modes of storage are critical to the observable liveliness of Twitter traffic. Hashemi was implicitly affirming the existence of a vast distributed hash table, data structures which store data using a hash function to generate a unique key for every tweet, direct message or other communication on the platform. In storage systems such as databases, but also in various lists, sets and tables, hashes function as indexes.

```
def create_hashtable(size):
return [None] * size

def hash_function(key, size):
return hash(key) % size

def insert(hashtable, key, value):
index = hash_function(key, len(hashtable))

    if hashtable[index] is None:
        hashtable[index] = [(key, value)]
    else:
        for i, (existing_key, _) in enumerate(hashtable[index]):
            if existing_key == key:
                hashtable[index][i] = (key, value)
                break
        else:
            hashtable[index].append((key, value))

def get(hashtable, key):
    index = hash_function(key, len(hashtable))

    if hashtable[index] is not None:
        for stored_key, value in hashtable[index]:
            if stored_key == key:
                return value

    return None

def remove(hashtable, key):
    index = hash_function(key, len(hashtable))

    if hashtable[index] is not None:
        for i, (stored_key, _) in enumerate(hashtable[index]):
            if stored_key == key:
                del hashtable[index][i]
                break
```

```
def display(hashtable):
    for i, entry in enumerate(hashtable):
        print(f"{i}: {entry}")

hash_table = create_hashtable(size=10)

insert(hash_table, "name", "John")
insert(hash_table, "age", 25)
insert(hash_table, "city", "New York")

display(hash_table)
```

In the Python code for a hashtable shown here, hashes function as devices to locate data values using keys. A hashtable can stores keys and values. The code uses a built-in hash function to create hashes. That is, it records the association between, for instance, the key name and the value John. In comparison to a list or an array indexed by integers starting at 0 or 1, and running up to the length of the list, the indexes in hashtables (known as dictionaries in Python) are hashes of the keys to be stored in the table. An array or list underlies the hashtable, but entries in the table are located by hashes. Much of the table could be empty, as in the example shown here, and entries in the table can be scattered across it locations. To retrieve the value for a particular key such as age, the hash value of the key is converted back to the underlying location in the list to retrieve the associated value of 25.

This additional layer of indexing, in which hashes determine where values are located in various storage systems, is what in STS actor-network terminology would count as a delegation or displacement in which a new actant substitutes for an older one, and in doing so, change the forms of action. The great abundance of key-values stored on Twitter/X or any similar platform today suggests that this delegation of indexes to hashes is addressing some central difficulty or problem.

The git example: 'content addressable'

Hashes run through the connective tissue for nearly all contemporary software development, and are intimately involved in many aspects of personalization on platforms. In fact, from the standpoint of hashes, code and personhood present similar properties: they speed through highly dynamic or changing microstates; they vary widely in the amounts and kinds of data or 'content' associated with them, they can exist in many slightly different versions (for example, many people may be interested in the same news or product; updates, fixes and revisions trickle through code as developers work on it). Hashes are a key to the topology and chronology of such ensembles.

Take the example of `git`, as well as its platform-level enactments such as GitHub, GitLab and BitBucket. The `git` software controls the distributed development of code (Chacon and Straub 2023). Git addresses problems of how many people such as developers can write code together without creating many conflicting changes. In statistical ensemble terms, it confronts the summarizing the effects of many accumulating or rippling microstates. Given that some software, especially for platforms such as operating systems like Android or web browsers like Chromium and Firefox, has tens of millions of lines of code, how could versions not multiply? In terms of the statistical ensemble concept, the problem is how to maintain the macrostate of an ensemble given the existence of many copies of the system in minute variations.

Ways of working with git vary widely, and are extensively documented. It attracts passionate quasi-philosophical and sometimes organizational sociological debate on the part of proponents. Various workflows and workarounds occasion discussion in Stack Overflow and Reddit forums. The software is in very wide use by developers on platforms but also by scientists, engineers, researchers and writers. Like its namesake, I find it a troublesome entity. Clearly vital to the present-day existence of platforms, it doesn't offer much surface for discussion. Computer scientists and information systems researchers concentrate research efforts on mapping the patterns of its use. But what about `git` helps us make sense of platform numericity and platform numbers?

Like the hashtable discussed earlier, git is a key-value data store.

> Git is a content-addressable filesystem. Great. What does that mean? It means that at the core of Git is a simple key-value data store. What this means is that you can insert any kind of content into a Git repository, for which Git will hand you back a unique key you can use later to retrieve that content. (Chacon and Straub 2023, 415)

As the authors of *ProGit*, one of the many books on git, put it, git is a 'content-addressable filesystem'. 'Content-addressable' means that files or data are no longer tracked by name (as in the filename I give to a document) or by location (as in a URL for online files or a directories and folders for files on a computer) but by their content. As seen in the Python hashtable, locations can change depending on what data is hashed. This fairly simple description derives directly from the hashing of all code: 'You will see these hash values all over the place in Git because it uses them so much. In fact, Git stores everything in its database not by file name but by the hash value of its contents' (15). SHA-1 hash functions, despite their regulatory limitations, digest every change in the code or any other files stored in a **git** repository as 'commit hashes' of 40 characters.

```
git commit 03_hash.rmd -m 'adding git discussion'
1 file changed, 113 insertions(+), 13 deletions(-)

commit 7c852fc5b788083a708f1081e81e8266e3961492
```

The simple example of 'committing' some changes to this file generates a hash that incorporates all the edits on that file as well as the existing state of all the files (documents, images, and so on) found in the project. Again, like a statistical ensemble, hashing allows many versions of the same thing to be held together. Each *commit* – as in **git commit** – creates a new snapshot of a whole project. Each successive commit of changes takes into account the previous state of the project, so that changes are chained together through their hashing. When many changes by many people come together in a git workflow, the process of merging changes from other repositories (other developers, or perhaps a git platform such as GitHub) itself only creates new commits by combining files and hashing the overall collection.

STS approaches to such arrangements highlight the importance of the doctrines embodied in such arrangements for negotiating change as part of the reality of technical things. 'A technological project is neither realistic nor unrealistic; it takes on reality, or loses it, by degrees' writes Bruno Latour (Latour 1996, 85). But these degrees of reality are not added in arithmetic progression, as if adding more code increases the reality of a program or a platform. Rather, the many negotiations of what belongs and what doesn't, of what is permitted and what is not, of what or who has responsibility for watching over others' things, of how different interests can be contained, means that the project has a variable numericity.

Given that so much of the work on platforms concerns code or code-associated materials, the constant snapshotting of versions of code easily generates many versions of code. This hashing-based versioning of things generates platform numbers, as in GitHub's '100 million+ developers' working on '420 million repositories'. Both the developers and their hundreds of millions of projects are hard to count in the same way that temperature is hard to work out by tracking the movements of molecules in a heated box.

Rather than mechanical reproduction of the same, variation is the norm. Hash-tracked versions means that every change to the code of several hundred million software projects, ranging from core sub-ensembles such as the Linux kernel or the Android OS, becomes addressable. The active archiving of versions of code is not only at the core of the economically important phenomena of 'open source' code, but weaves the connective tissue of contemporary platform ensembles. Their commutativity, their propensity to constant change or updates

(Chun 2016), their capacity to scale, as well as intermediate between different social-economic fields (users, advertisers, and so on), and to relate to each other, relies on the checks, verifications, snapshots, security and indexing translated as hashes. The commutativity of many contemporary platforms, their capacity to re-arrange their elements in a kaleidoscopic array of variations and modifications, or their capacities to include sub-ensembles with their own levels of coherence as a part of an ensemble, relies on code versioning.

Individualizing and universalizing

These scattered observations suggest, in their scattering, that hashes, a number generated by mixing data or messages to generate keys or indexes that vary greatly, hold ensembles together. Hashes assemble ensembles. Yet the streams of hashes flow very differently according to the different chains of value, work, transactions, measurement or meaning that bind them. Much of the organization of contemporary platforms assumes determinate location. Numberings of various kinds generate determinate locations for all manner of things. 'An ensemble of a higher degree', writes Simondon, 'comprising all these sub-ensembles is defined by the capacity to freely realize any form of relation, without thereby destroying the autonomy of individualized sub-ensembles' (Simondon 1989, 63).

Two other prominent scenes of platform-making in recent years, containers and blockchain technologies, use hashing to 'freely realize' forms of relation based on isolation. Containers such as Docker 'image' the configuration of running applications as hashes, and allow copies of the system to proliferate using the hashes as an address. Like the constrained variations of microstates in the statistical ensemble, containers generate macrostate platform effects. Approximately 80 per cent of internet traffic in 2024 streams video from millions of containers run by platforms such as Netflix and YouTube. Google puts it bluntly: 'everything at Google runs in containers' (Google 2024).

The somewhat counter-platforms blockchains are also made using hash functions. Each transaction or event in a blockchain is hashed, and each unit of cryptocurrency exists as a cumulative record of hashes. The profligate hashing of the cryptocurrency miners that uses brutally powerful racks of GPUs to carry out the 'proof-of-work' hashing for Bitcoin, Ethereum or Dogecoin engenders the sociotechnical imaginaries of de-centralized, non-fiat currencies. It prompts the emergence of rampant forms of speculative value creation in the form of non-fungible tokens and smart-contracts. Coral reefs, forests, charities, organizations, trusts, as well as platforms are caught up in these hashed forms. Even shifting blockchains from the energy-intensive proof-of-work to much more 'economical' proof-of-stake does not alter the basic substrate of hashing. Like the git commits, each block in the chain is effectively a snapshot of the previous state of the chain with the addition of some variation: a new coin, a new contract, a new token.

The components of the platform processing analysed earlier are articulated in technical practices and configurations such as the exposure of the interfaces, the commutativity spun by devops, the hashing of localities, and the embedding of matrices in image collections. Git and GitHub pivot on the hash functions to open the commutativity of platforms. Ethereum and the blockchains with their many GPUs churning through proof-of-work are also hashing but now in the pursuit of an univocity and irreversibility.

Placed alongside each other, the axes of localization, hashing-addressability, verification and generative observation create an ensemble whose state is locality-sensitive. Their effects are subtle, like the statistical fluxes of virtual particles in a vacuum.

Conclusion

The tensions between platform numericity (a plurality of numberings) and platform numbers (a few large numbers capture many small ones), between microstates and macrostate, are not exactly resolved by playing with container-figures such as statistical ensembles. Numbers in their multiplying associations and commutations generate microstates of ensembles. The heavy-duty cycling of numbers such as hashes renders platforms commutable. Hashes, for instance, distinctly localize the myriad minute shifts in configuration, content, activity and connections between events over time in software containers that bulk out big platforms. Hashes proliferate heavily in blockchain technologies and energize speculations on new macrostates such as 'Web 3.0', a distributed, pluralized rendering of Web 2.0 and its hyperscaling platforms.

How does the problem of numericity or any of the many platform numbering practices and the problem of plurality or the strange entanglements of few/many come together in the figure of the statistical ensembles? From IsoLab and the single holmium crystal experiments comes the idea of number as a vibrational state. The statistical ensemble has the virtue of framing a different relation between many microstates and a few macrostates, between numericity and platform numbers. The statistical ensemble figures ensembles as many copies of slightly varying systems. This configuration offers a way of acknowledging the diversity of numberings and numbers, but also their tendency to fall into equivalences, into the form of a platform number.

On the one hand, according to the figure of the statistical ensemble, the many slightly different versions of platform arrangements are simultaneous states of an ensemble. They exist, for instance, as personalized configurations on a social media platform, or as the slightly different versions of code that users of GitHub software repository are working on, or in the many slightly different images of the same places and events cached in the image databases of a photosharing platform. The practices of numericity, with all the forms of counting, sorting, ordering and indexing they entail, are epitomized by the hash numbers and hashing functions.

On the other hand, still aligning to the figure of the ensemble, the combinations of microstates engender the asymmetric, uneven macrostate platform-numbers. In aggregate, woven together by hashes, slightly different copies generate the macro-scale effects of size/volume, pressure and temperature associated with the ensemble. Big numbers such as 2.9/1 billion active monthly users (Facebook; TikTok), 2.5 billion occurrence records (Global Biodiversity Information Facility) or 100 million developers/90% of Fortune 100 companies on GitHub, are macrostate numbers that derive from the many slight variations in the multiplying microstates.

Does that mean that such platform numbers are the temperature, pressure or volume measures of platforms? Yes, but such numbers, in the canonical ensembles of statistical mechanics, rely on an apparatus that isolates the platform from its surrounding flows. What Stengers calls in her account of statistical mechanics a 'new type of being' comes into the world accompanied by new practices of numbering. Like the apparatus in IsoLab, the temperature of a canonical ensemble is fixed by a 'heat bath', but assumes complete isolation from mechanical vibration, and a fixed number of particles. Importantly, macrostates such as temperature, pressure or volume derive from combinations of both common or frequent things and those less common. They add together in some way that depends very much on how active the different versions of the system are. Platform ensembles relax that canonical isolation in many ways. But not entirely. The hashing functions, with their generation of unique yet interchangeable, non-arbitrary but somewhat unsortable numbers, distinguish platform microstates from each other.

INTERLUDE IV

Banded Iron Formations

Roughly one metre cubes, two deep red oblong stones lie in a semi-circle collection of stones. A fragment of the wavering thickness of living/non-living layering of the earth's crust, of what Elizabeth Povinelli has described as geontology (Povinelli 2016), they form part of the Australian National Rock Collection near Galambary or Black Mountain, Canberra (see Figure IV.1). The stones have the width, depth and breadth, surfaces, extremities and angles that reflect their formation and their handling in the mining industry. In the Pilbara, the rock was cut out of the ground by Fortescue Metals Group, one of the world's largest iron ore mining companies. Saved from crushing and shipping as iron ore at the mine, they are now climbed by children and present a training challenge for passing mountain bikers.

The boulders come from the Brockman Formation of the Hamersley Ranges in the mineral-rich Pilbara region of north-west Australia, Pitjanjare country. The 2.3-billion-year-old rocks were cut from a geological formation of vast horizontal stability, millions of square kilometres of central and western Australia, that geologists call 'a platform'. Much of Australia's landmass and large parts of Eurasia are platforms. The rock is banded with waves of iron compounds taken up by marine microbes and sedimented in fine oxide layers. Continental platforms are usually made up of layers of sedimentary rock washed by water across the much older basalt or other igneous 'basement' of Precambrian eons.

Hammersley iron is a *platform deposit* (Morris 1983).

A variety of geological formations, including basements, plates, plateaux and ramps support platforms. Platforms themselves, however, are transported by planetary dynamics, such as geophysical processes of convection, the ubiquitous enabler of diversity of terrestrial and marine life, forming and dividing continents. Without plates, there is little orogenesis, little subduction, no mountains, islands, archipelagos, nor the many diversifications of minerals and organisms, or the dispersions that derive from them. Plates

Figure IV.1: Banded iron formation

and platforms make possible upwellings and what divides them, the oceans and their trenches. Platforms in this setting are very much part of what recent geology refers to as the earth system ensemble (Anderson 2007), an aggregate of processes that include living and non-living.

The fine sedimentary banding of the rock by marine micro-organisms is visible. The bands are traces of the making of the air we breathe. During the Great Oxygenation Event of 2.4 billion years ago, well before today's continental platforms take shape, the photosynthetic activity of cyanobacteria living in vast microbial mats repeatedly increased concentrations of atmospheric oxygen to levels that were toxic to the micro-organisms themselves. Their mass death precipitated the deposits of iron and other mineral oxides such as gallium, copper and lithium absorbed by their bodies from ocean waters. Many mineral deposits are sedimented in the cycles of life and death of marine microbial mats.

The Pilbara rock is a figure of thick and thin banded scales of time and place, lived, living and non-living in platforms. Its massive inertial presence in a rock collection, disconnected from stories and histories of country, is a reminder that platforms are earth sediment. Its exhibition in the Future National Rock Garden reminds us that platforms are lifted-out spaces that derive support from geontological ensembles such as geological platforms, and their billion-year histories of living/non-living processing. The rock figures the biotic, chemical, geological, cultural and economic transformation of marine and terrestrial materials into layers running through platforms and infrastructures. It is a figure of thickness through accumulated interactions. Most rocks like this are crushed by the mining processes into the hundreds of millions of tonnes of ore shipped out of Australia and smelted in the steelworks of China, Japan and India into hardware components: beams, girders and rails of cities, the walls, panels, frames of buildings, or the components and elements of machines, vehicles and devices. Others, such as the caves of Juukan Gorge, are – or were, until the Rio Tinto Corporation blasted them to ore while expanding their Brockman 4 mine in May 2020 – sites of great cultural significance, with 46,000-year-old remains of tools, sacred objects, animals and plants.

Geotechnically, many peoples live most in iron-banded formations. The 2.3 billion years dating, the oxygenating microbes, and the rich dense, economically and technologically vital bands of iron oxide puts the visitor in their place. It is sedimented in the matted photosynthesis that makes a breathable atmosphere and lays down the mineral bands for the infrastructures, technologies, economies and equipment that will in turn transform the earth ensemble, rendering it sensitive to new transitions, to the shifts in ensemble that we are living through.

5

Embedding and Embodying

What does experimental ontology do with devices? Implicitly posed in many places. It's a comfortable hotel, warm and well-lit, in the Lake District, north-west England, February 2016. The fields, hedges and woodland outside are snow-covered, sloping down towards the slate-grey waters of the lake. The meeting room is muted. Soft carpets, plush drapes, ergonomic seats and a continuous flow of fresh baked goods and locally sourced hot drinks cushion the participants. In the meeting room, computer scientists, a scattering of health and environmental scientists, statisticians, health and educational researchers chat around the table, waiting for the opening talk.

We wait to hear about the micro:bit, a BBC-sponsored device whose purpose in life is to usher youth and geeks in the UK and elsewhere into the world of embedded devices, and the more networky version known as the Internet of Things (IoT). The main speaker, a designer from the BBC, is passionate about the history of microcomputers and the BBC, narrating the story of a microcomputer, the BBC Micro, that transformed UK popular culture in the 1980s because of the amateur tinkering and hacking it facilitated. The micro:bit, a £10 piece of hardware, aims to re-capture and update some of the glowing meaningfulness of those days. The update for the internet-enabled post-platform economy is neatly symbolized by ':'. The BBC and the Micro:bit Foundation is just about to deliver hundreds of thousands of the devices to UK schools. Every 11-year-old will have one. Our convenor, the director of data science, reminds us that in meetings such as this, over the last ten years, discussions of the kind we are about to undertake have led to tens of millions of pounds in research funding, and launched research careers in various directions. For the next two days, our ruminations on the micro:bit may well sow the seeds of something similar. The plush venue, well away from campus, reflects the munificence of computer science, engineering and, just at this time, data science research funding. It is under the auspices of the newly institutionalized field of data science that a sociology academic gets invited.

In the afternoon, we are tasked to design research projects based on the micro:bit, preferably projects with a data science flavour. University researchers have been closely involved in its development, coding some of the core functionality of the little platform in a piece of software called **Mbed**. And the chip on which the micro:bit relies is of British design, a 'reduced instruction set controller' (RISC) designed by ARM, a fabless semiconductor design company based in south-west England. Unlike so many hardware platforms, the micro:bit does not arrive from East Asia or the US West Coast. That afternoon, teams of researchers drawn from design ethnographers, geophysicists, mathematicians, interface designers, software engineers – I'm with a bioinformatician, a genomic scientist and an interface designer – set to work on designing research. After ambling pensively along the lake shore to the sailing club and back, we come up with something focused on autism in schools. Our idea is to see whether coding practices differ for micro:bits. It seems misguided and difficult now. How do I think it would be ok to extract data on coding practices relating to the something so personal? But other projects focus on micro:bits as sensors for glacier change. A show-and-tell poster session, presented to the pro vice-chancellor for research, who happens to live nearby, happens later in the afternoon. At dinner that night, the senior computer scientist regales the group in the bar with stories of the startups he's seen come and go, and that he's been part of. At home, months later, after the UK launch of the micro:bit, I ask my own school-age children about the devices. They know of them, and they have seen them in school, but don't really 'have' them. Schools have held on to the devices and 'put them in the cupboard', even though they were 'given' to every student. eBay, it seems, will not be flooded with micro:bits for sale after all.

The micro:bit is 4 × 5 cm square, and weighs less than 20 grams. After the UK early-adopter school students, Icelandic, Danish, Singaporean, Japanese, Taiwanese, Australian and Colombian students received them in following years. The educational device, supported and promoted by the Micro:bit Education Foundation, exemplifies the modestly flourishing ecology of so-called *microcontrollers* and small low-cost and embedded computers such as Arduinos, Raspberry Pico, Adafruit and a gamut of other hobbyist and industrial products. Such devices lack the touchscreens, colourful animations or dense information flows found in apps, gaming consoles or information terminals.

Disconnected from the battery, and importantly, the other devices needed to program it, it's a circuit board not a platform. The ':' in the name gestures towards the URL addressing system of the internet and the 'bit' suggests both engagement with digital processes at an elementary level (bits and bytes) and the idea of a computer as bits or pieces scattered across the fabric of everyday life, just as ordinary as pencils and notebooks. Connected, however, to, for instance, other platforms through a USB cable or a Bluetooth wireless connection to internet/cloud-based Microsoft Touch coding environment accessed through web browsers, the MicroBit Foundation app developed by Samsung, or a Python coding environment on a laptop computer, and an instructional environment, such as a classroom, it becomes something more like a platform as a place where things can be arranged.

Even this low-powered device shows how many different facets a platform might have. There, written on the hardware, are 'BBC', a national media organization, 'FCC', a government regulatory authority, a QR-code, and labels for various devices such as 'BLE' (Bluetooth Low Energy, a wireless communication standard), 'microphone,' 'compass', 'accelerometer' and 'processor'. On the other side, a much simpler surface, lies a grid of 25 LEDs, two push buttons labelled 'A' and 'B', and five metal-plated holes or pins labelled '0', '1', '2', '3V' (3 volts) and 'GND' (short for ground). Already in full view on a small device can be seen connections to media, industry standards, sensors, interfaces and a space of technical and pedagogical experimentation clustered around the more central technical elements such as a processor. This multiplying of dimensions suggests that digital platforms are not simple things, despite the simplicity of the platform figure. They are places where things are arranged both materially and discursively.

This device compresses many platform micro-habits into a few square centimetres, without the distraction of a case, or a touchscreen display. Bare circuitry lies open to view, as if the designers were plugged into the circuit-bending/hardware sensibilities simmering around unhappily over-controlled platforms. The hundreds of quite technical modifications and extensions of the device, often reaching deep into intricacies of hardware elements (Atencio 2023), suggest that the device conducts collective energies associated with technical ensembles into new circuits.

Containing an ensemble in a mapping

The hotel workshop has a hands-on session with some pre-release micro:bits. Some of the computer scientists in the room quickly have the device connected to their laptops and are writing small programs. In itself, their quick uptake is not surprising as micro:bits are meant to be scratchpads for coding by primary school age students. 'The BBC micro:bit is a small computing device for children. One of the languages it understands is the popular Python programming language. The version of Python that runs on the BBC micro:bit is called MicroPython' (bbcmicrobit 2023). It can be programmed in Python, but also in C/C++, Rust, Ada, JavaScript, Lisp, Pascal, Basic, C#, Go, and so on (Atencio 2023). The 'version of Python that runs' on it, micropython, brings across Python coding language to a range of devices: 'implementation of Python 3.x on microcontrollers and small embedded systems' (Micropython 2023). The 'transfer' from desktop/laptop to microcontroller/embedded system is the key feature of micropython (George 2023). Nothing in this description is surprising, but the main point here is that the micro:bit can be coded in the same way as a virtual machine on Google Compute, or any other computational platform.

Multiple layers of software run on the micro:bit to make it possible to code in the various languages: 'This is a port of MicroPython to the micro:bit which uses CODAL as the underlying target platform' (bbcmicrobit 2023). The computer scientists' uptake of the device was facilitated by the fact that some people in the room had been involved in developing an underlying platform called **CODAL**. Micropython or any of the other programming languages don't run on the micro:bit directly. Instead, micropython relies on another 'target' platform, CODAL or the Component Oriented Device Abstraction Layer. The CODAL platform, according to its coders writing in a repository on GitHub, provides:

> [A]n easy to use environment for programming a number of devices in the C/C++ language, written by Lancaster University. It contains device drivers for hardware capabilities supported on a number devices, and also a suite of runtime mechanisms to make programming an embedded device easier and more flexible. These range from control of the LED matrix display to peer-to-peer radio communication. (Lancaster University 2023)

This 'easy to use environment for programming a number of devices ... written by Lancaster University' must, it seems in retrospect, have motivated that meeting at the Lake District hotel in 2016. CODAL underpins the educational, creative and other visions of the micro:bit.

The 'component oriented device abstraction' that furnishes the so-called 'runtime' for the micro:bit explicitly aims to the make the programming of embedded devices 'easier and more flexible', especially for users in schools (Lancaster University 2023). 'Abstraction' means in this context that hardware devices such as buttons, sensors, bluetooth radio or the memory of the microcontroller can be invoked by code commands such as `microbit.compass.calibrate()`. Without CODAL, there is no Microsoft MakeCode platform, no micropython, perhaps no Micro:bit Educational Foundation with its motto of 'make it: code it', nor the many technical projects that wander through different hardware configurations. Every apparently direct approach to the device, including the tangible, unboxed form of the micro:bit, seems to have this mixture of proximity and distance. The device is close to hand, and its many controls, sensors and displays, although simple and limited, appear accessible. The metal-plated edges of the micro:bit circuitboard are explicitly designed to be touched. And yet, it is only through the many indirect paths of first a coding environment such as micropython, then CODAL and then the influential design of ARM Cortex-M3 processors (ARM-Developer 2023) implemented by Nordic Semiconductor as a specific microcontroller chip nrf52833 that any of the tangible or sensible elements of the device can activate.

After public engagement

Five years after its launch and distribution to UK school students, the Micro:bit Educational Foundation reports that five million of the devices are in use. Version 2 of the BBC micro:bit is on sale from Slovakia to New Zealand. A scattering of research reports analyse what happens to them in schools and in various initiatives to engender coding and making practices with digital devices. Much discussion in these reports centres on teachers and how they approach micro:bits. If they don't understand how to code, or if they can't imagine how to connect the device to their lessons, then the devices languish in the classroom cupboards. The Micro:bit Foundation has its motto: 'Make it: code it.' Unlike the devices such as smartphones or laptops that the students and teacher inhabit, the micro:bit in its exposed yet playful technicalities is not for consumption, but a form of production called 'making' that often involves coding. The wager that the micro:bit sponsors, the BBC, and the various digital education initiatives in around 50 countries, take is that a device that exposes its components to view, to forms of action or intervention, and hence participation, can shift habits of consumption towards something different, something perhaps better than the sad absorption in the flickering reels of platform X, Y or Z. The odds stacked against the micro:bit and its kin are great.

The maker lesson plans for micro:bit range from soil moisture meters to abstract computational architectures, from working with data to working with images (Micro:bit Educational Foundation 2023b). These projects typically involve pulsing hearts, emotion badges, sunlight sensors, step-counting, breathing timers, metronomes, electronic pets, compasses and thermometers as possible projects. Many micro:bits probably lie quietly unused, compared to other microcontroller based devices. Their pedagogical/hobbyist biography means that unlike the billions of other microcontroller units, however, the micro:bits circulate the injunction to 'make' things. I initially wrote a loop that just adds 1 to the LED matrix, and gradually counts them up; to express the number 2^{25} or around 33 million. There is a lot about edges on micro:bit, some of which come from the pins and connections and what they do. But the device, by virtue of the nRF82833, also is measuring temperature, gravity and accelerated movement. I think too of the wires and transistors, especially phototransistors, or even the switches, with their edges and bounce. So many relations to sensing, to earthly energies, and embodied, lived patterns of sound and light.

In this chapter, I develop a concept of embeddings to describe the situation or place-specific dynamics associated with people, their habits and devices. The hotel workshop, the BBC, the Micro:bit Foundation, the millions of micro:bits in schools and now in hobbyist projects, and the many similar microcontrollers (Arduino, Espresso, and so on) together position and configure (Suchman 2012) the device. Embedding here has several senses. The micro:bit and the microcontrollers it is built around exemplify the embedded systems that vastly outnumber the microprocessor-based devices found in computers. This is the engineering sense of embedding in which computational processes interact with other technical elements and moving parts such as car engines, electronic locks, air-filtering, clothes washing or blending a smoothie. The number of these devices is difficult to count because different things count as microcontrollers. The subreddit r/embedded periodically debates how many microcontrollers are actually in a typical car. In this the engineering sense, embedded conveys a veiling or withdrawal of something from view.

Embedding has a second sense related to embodying. Much science and technology studies (STS) and related work accounts for embodiment as an accumulation of habits, even thousands of component habits. Devices embed habits. They are not only embedded, but also embed.

Finally, embeddings entail a de-coupling in the name of coordination and configuration. Something is embedded in something else to which it does not entirely belong. This sense of embeddings can be found in the mathematical descriptions of machine learning and neural networks in particular. An embedding in a mathematical sense is a structure contained within another, possibly more complex, structure. The embeddings of a large language model are the numerical weights or parameters of the elements of the neural network layers. Embeddings reduce the plurality of statements, propositions, or talk to continuous vectors of numbers in say 300 dimensions (Mikolov et al 2013). These senses of embedding as economo-mechanical control, embodying habits and mapping a complicated structure to a simpler space, all play against each other in the micro:bit.

Shifting between these different renderings of the same devices can be a way of tracking experiments in engaging with platforms as they invest in re-making collectives in some way. Noortje Marres suggests that 'empirical devices allow for the display of material efficacy inside the frame of the empirical setting, and arguably these devices assist in the specification of material engagement as a distinctive mode of public involvement' (Marres 2013, 438).

Embedding small devices

Perhaps the most important methodological injunctions of STS has been 'follow the actors' (Latour 1987). Actors include people, animals, plants, devices and others. Many STS studies have followed actors along labyrinthine paths in laboratories, clinics, cities, houses, and into extra-planetary space for that matter. No doubt, other STS maxims have been important in relation to things, particular high-tech, such as Donna Haraway's *cui bono?* or 'for whose good?' question, or the implicit maxim of SCOT (Social Construction of Technology): find the interested social groups who define the problem/s the technical thing attempts to resolve (Pinch et al 1987). And the injunction has been painstakingly analysed, modified and criticized from various angles (Gad and Jensen 2010).

The first maxim is perhaps the hardest to follow through embedded devices. It is explicitly plural in its naming of actor*s*. Given that 'actors' or 'actants', to use the slightly more de-centred terminology of early actor-network theory, include living and non-living, technical, natural, social variants, following actors has posed many difficulties both in terms of empirical methods and conceptual articulation. Extensive experimentation in ethnography, in modes of writing, in assembling and working with archives, or in devising diagrams or other figures, has resulted from this injunction.

'Follow' suggests that something moves but remains in view. How should platform actors be followed? What is the geography of their movements? A core difficulty in following actors is their tendency to disappear from view. In any of its implementations, the difficulty of following many actors becomes apparent. Often, it is far easier to follow one or two rather than many actors. This immediately obviates some virtues of the method. Symmetry, multiplicity and plural times all suffer.

This leads first of all to the 'missing mass' situation that Bruno Latour first wrote about in 'Where are the Missing Masses: The Sociology of Mundane Artifacts' (Latour 1992). That line of thinking held sociology or social research more generally responsible for a persistent miscalculation of the mass action of mundane things such as keys, locks, speed bumps, seatbelts and the like. Latour later took Euroamerican modernity to task for its perseverant splitting of human and nonhuman (Latour 1993).

Platforms multiply the 'missing mass' of artifacts: the vast majority of devices with microprocessors or microcontrollers in them are not computers (laptops, desktops, servers, mainframes, and so on). These forms of computation attract little attention. Embedded, especially as part of ensembles, they no longer stand out, and their movements become weaker, less excited and more familiar. Perhaps they are less massive, but they are more numerous in their embeddings.

Even the very mundane accomplishment of connection between devices conceals vertiginous complexities. Consider the USB plug, the kind that connects a micro:bit to a laptop as we did that morning in the Lake District. By 2022, the USB-C standards document ran to over 3500 pages (Voronova 2022). Mostly this intricacy passes unnoticed by most people apart from a concerned USB-public. A series of posts from 2018 on the former micro-blogging platform Twitter parcels out pointed observations concerning a 600 page sub-section of the USB-C document devoted to 'power delivery' (PD):

> [W]hy does the USB power delivery specification define a request to get the country code from their partner?

Or:

> [T]he spec spends six pages just enumerating the 'Policy Engine' states. The sections describing them are nested seven levels deep. (https://twitter.com/whitequark/status/1035760558237204480)

And reflecting on the USB-C plugs:

> [I]n case you were wondering, USB PD defines special messages for updating the firmware in the cable plug, or I suppose both cable plugs. I wonder if they get updated at the same time or you could end up with a cable that's different depending on the way you plug it in. We're fucked.

What is going on here? What nexus occasions this satirical exasperation at a technical standard by **WhiteQuark**?

Even following the cable that connects a micro:bit to a laptop suddenly seems hard. A cable that is capable of connecting two devices together without someone checking that it is turned the right way up is very ordinary, but something quite extraordinary paves the way for that convenience. If a power plug requires a country code be actively registered, if the USB connection requires a 'policy engine' with seven nested levels of policy, or if the cable plug, the small plastic-metal pieces on the end of a cable, have their own updateable firmware, it seems that the costs of a 'universal' connector are quite high. The USB-C cable, despite the 'universal' in its name, has this sense of embedding as withdrawing or subsiding from view into a tangle of specificities and local differences.

If the 'missing matter' problem more or less persists today also in the highly potentialized state of micro:bit and/or USB connectors, it is perhaps less due to the inattentiveness of social researchers and even computer scientists in a workshop focused on public engagement with microcontrollers. It relates more to a vertigo felt in moving along the deeply enfolded paths of actors.

When Latour revisited missing technical actors two decades later in *An Inquiry into Modes of Existence* (Latour 2013), the problems of following the actors were more front-stage. Technical mediations have their own mode of existence along paths that go beyond displacement into unpredictable detours. Latour characterizes the experience of following along a more convoluted itinerary:

> If this experience remains difficult to register, it is because to remain faithful to it we would have to accept its scarcity, its dazzling invisibility, its deep constitutional opacity. For it is always oscillating between two lists of contradictory elements: rare and ordinary, unforeseeable and predictable, fleeting and constantly begun anew, opaque and transparent, proliferating and controlled. (Latour 2013, 216)

In this revised formulation, the problem of following actors is not so much the zig-zag of agency between humans and nonhumans, between social and technical action, but the mixture of contradictory elements such as ordinary/rare or transparent/opaque. Rather than the delegation/translation, oscillation between proliferating and controlling defines the mixing up of 'elements'. In a way, the earlier STS sensibility to things was simpler: nonhumans were largely regarded as the delegates or message-bearers for human actors. In the mode-of-existence account, the technical nonhumans occasion this mixed or oscillating experience of repetition and difference.

Recognizing the contrast between the tracing of moral/social/economic delegations found in earlier STS work and the unstable oscillating between lists of contradictory elements in more recent work brings with it significant implications for doing experimental ontology. There are great practical differences between experiments designed to 'follow the actors' in order to find the missing masses, and experiments witnessing 'this experience [that] remains difficult to register ... for it is always oscillating between two lists of contradictory elements' (Latour 2013, 216). Where on these lists should we put devices such as the five million micro:bits, or for that matter, the so-called 99 per cent of microprocessors located in embedded systems such as washing machines, hot water systems, or car locks or lifts or electric scooters? Are they ordinary or rare, or some mixture? And what in the millions of devices sent out into classrooms, kitchens, factories and vehicles attests to and is affected by this oscillating?

Rare and ordinary: circulation and mistranslation

Like many other microcontroller-based devices – Arduino, Espruino, AdaFruit, STM32x – the micro:bit differs from smart devices, IoT or embedded systems more generally in appearing as a circuit board.

The board is a device without being put in a box. This means that its components, its connections and its controls are visible and transparent. They are meant to be seen, touched or worked on in certain ways, mainly by creating connections with other devices. In the last few years, the micro:bit as a bare device has been adorned, elaborated, experimented on and described in many different settings. Kits of projects with associated technical elements can be purchased, and many instructional projects, how-tos, and so on, can be found online. All of this can be read as ensemble experience.

The Micro:bit Foundation (Micro:bit Educational Foundation 2023a) provides detailed descriptions of all the device hardware components, including details of who makes them and where they are located on the device (see the Bill of Materials file). There are 137 bits and pieces in a micro:bit.

Item	Components
1 Thick film Resistor	40
2 Ceramic Capacitor	37
3 LED	28
4 Diode	9
5 Transistor	6
6 Inductor	4
7 Tactile Switch	3
8 MCU	2
9 PCB	1
10 Connector	1
11 Crystal	1
12 Microphone	1
13 Sensor	1
14 Speaker	1
15 USB Connector	1
16 Voltage Regulator	1

Around 100 resistors, capacitors, light-emitting diodes accompany a much smaller set of things: MCU (microcontroller unit, 2), crystal (1), 'sensor' (1), microphone (1), and so on. A multiplicity of ordinary things surrounds several much rarer things.

The image of the micro:bit (Figure 5.1) shows the position of various components on the printed circuit board (PCB). The three largest are, from left to right, the main microcontroller (a Nordic Semiconductor nRF52833 [Nordic Semiconductor 2023]), the speaker (the largest visible component) and another microcontroller labelled 'M27P8V1N71K', an NXP microcontroller commonly used in automative, smart home, industrial and mobile devices (NXP 2023). It is striking that micro:bits themselves have another embedded microcontroller responsible for managing connections between the micro:bit and other devices. As the very detailed documentation of the design and specifications maintained by the Micro:bit Educational Foundation on their GitHub

Figure 5.1: Digital platforms in abundance

repositories tell us, this second microcontroller, as well as many other components of the micro:bit, handles all the communication with other devices. This second microcontroller also too has an ARM(TM) + Cortex(TM) core, with the same amount of memory, and at least a dozen communication protocols, including the tricky but practically important USB connection that connects micro:bits to other computers in the classroom.

Embedded economy and its capacities

In her account of the embedded economy, the economist Kate Raworth reverses the normal hierarchy in which an increasingly free-floating economy of devices, software and service floats away from an earth that provides an inexhaustible supply of resources (air, water, light, fuel, minerals, land, plants, animals). Her notion of 'embedded economy' echoes and expands Mark Granovetter's 'embeddedness' of the economy (Granovetter 1985). Raworth's account of embedding shrinks the economy to the smallest, most dependent inner-domain of markets, households, governments and commons surrounded by the living matters and flows of social life, themselves bathing in a finite layer of flows of light, air, water, geochemical and biospheric processes of the earth.

The 137 or so components of the micro:bit take this technoeconomic embeddedness directly on board, so to speak. The dozens of resistors, capacitors, LEDs, diodes, transistors, inductors/coils, switches, microcontrollers, buttons, and so on, come from several dozen manufacturers, nearly all located in East Asia (Korea, China, Japan, Taiwan). Even Nordic Semiconductor, the designer of the nrf52833 microcontroller, the central processor of the micro:bit, is 'fabless', and its chips are manufactured in Taiwan by Taiwan Semiconductor Manufacturing Corporation (Nordic Semiconductor 2023).

Each of these devices is connected to a technical ensemble with its own technogeographic specificities.

Take the several dozen ceramic capacitors in the micro:bit. Several trillion of these devices are said to be manufactured each year. The CBR04C308B5GAC capacitor manufactured by Yageo/Kemet, again in Taiwan, is available in reels of 10,000 (Kemet 2023) as well as in small quantities for hobbyists. Such abundance suggests something highly ordinary.

And yet, like the many other components produced by manufacturers such as Yageo, Everlight, Diodes Incorporated and NXP that we may never hear of or see advertised, these Kemet/Yageo capacitors carry with them a small charge of technoeconomic embeddedness. The device has a 'footprint' on the circuit board of around 1mm × 0.5mm wide, and weighs around 1 mg. It pins are made of tin, multi-layer metal plates inside of copper, and importantly, the insulating material in the capacitors, with its capacity to absorb sudden increases in electrical current, is barium titanate. Despite their tiny footprint, the surface area enfolded in this devices is extremely large because layers of metal plate and insulating material are compressed.

Five hundred or so layers of thinly interleaved copper and barium titanate increase the surface area on which the capacitor to store electric charge depends.

Connected to bodies

Only small pieces of code are needed to affect lights and motors connected to the micro:bit. Let LEDs and the electric motor stand for the primary elements of contemporary ensembles concerned with information and energy, or more concretely, seeing and moving respectively. Very ordinary actions – turning on a light or starting a motor – point to the second sense of embedding, embedding as embodying. How does this embodying occur?

```
from microbit import *

lightState = False
if (pin0.is_touched()):
    lightState = not lightState

while (True):
    if (pin0.is_touched()):
        lightState = not lightState
    if (lightState):
        pin2.write_analog(pin1.read_analog())
    else:
```

```
        pin2.write_digital(0)
    sleep(100)
```

In the periodizations of device, machines, systems and techniques, shifts in forms of energy, and especially the appearance of 'information' are used to differentiate ensembles. Each technical ensemble indeed has a material and organizational specificity.

Tending a fire for warmth or light is different to writing code to turn on a light or controlling an electric fan to move air around.

For the micro:bit code shown here, the key elements in turning a light becomes an entity with a logical state: False means that it is off.

The circuit on which this works has an LED connected to pin2 on the microbit. The code begins by checking if a pin on the microcontroller has been touched. Until the micro:bit is touched in the right place – Pin0 on the PCB – nothing lights up. The code then uses the microcontroller to keep track of how much current it gets. The micropython program and the microcontroller keeps track of the state of the light. Set at the right speed, the LED slowly pulses, not in sharp blink but in gradual intensities.

```
duty = 0
rest = 20
step = 1

while (True):
    while (duty < 1023):
        pin0.write_analog(duty)
        duty += step
        print(duty)
        sleep(rest)

    while (duty >0):
        pin0.write_analog(duty)
        duty -= step
        print(duty)
        sleep(rest)
```

The second code fragment uses the technique of pulse width modulation. A variety of modulations of pulse are found in embedded systems. Pulse code modulation is the basis of much sound recording and sound transmission, and has been for decades or longer in some settings such as telephone lines. In the lines of code here, there are some more conventions organizing time: `duty`, `rest` and `step`. The pulse width modulation techniques used in embedded systems regulate the amount of electrical energy going to the motor or the 'load'. The fan gradually slows down and speeds up without any obvious changes.

Why modulate the pulses of energy to something like a motor? These obscure but widely used techniques are typical of what happens where things are inhabited by affected, perceiving, moving bodies. Wouldn't it be simpler to switch a light or a motor on and off, to discipline bodies to a binary opposition – the light is 'off' versus the light is 'on'? The control of an electric motor with a fan attached is typical of the many situations where different habits come into play, and where how habits blend together is vital to inhabitation.

Component habits

Gilles Deleuze's treatment of habit in *Difference and Repetition* has a consistently component-like texture: 'we are thousands of habits' (Deleuze 2001). Like the 1000 platforms to be found in 2023, our 'organic composition' assembles 'thousands of component habits' (Deleuze 2001, 75), each of which is a little self: 'We speak of our self only in virtue of these thousands of little witnesses, all involved in contemplation, satisfactions, contractions, pretentions' (Deleuze 2001, 78). Deleuze's account is unusually broadly conceived since it puts habits well before concepts of self, identity, object, mechanism or material. Habits run deep down into the interstices of life and non-life. *Difference and Repetition* affirms atomic, molecular, machinic, metabolic, physiological, biophysical and psychological habits thickly interwoven.

In close alignment with the treatment of habit in the American pragmatists such as William James or John Dewey, and in Henri Bergson's analysis of memory in *Matter and Memory* (Bergson 2021), and to some degree with Pierre Bourdieu's notion of 'habitus' (Bourdieu 2000), Deleuze regards micro-habits as the generators of difference and repetition. Habits do not repeat something. There is repetition, rather, through the differences that habits occasion. What appears to be the most obviously irreducible and simple forms of repetition, or the most stripped back material forms of repetitions – vibrations, cycles, and so on – are the most concentrated, embedded habits. Habits take hold by binding. They are a form of possession, or taking hold of something.

Psychological habits, from this perspective, come late in the self. They depend on sub-representative footings in cyclical, vibratory habits, in their differences and their specific repetitions. In this respect, the bill of materials for the micro:bit is also a list of 'component habits', or devices 'involved in contemplation' of their respective flows: air, heat, electrical current, magnetic fields, and so on.

The many 'ceramic capacitors', for instance, absorb and slowly release transient changes in current, smoothing electrical flows in the circuits, and stabilizing rapid changes in current for connected components. The circuit schematics show a small capacitor, C11, connecting the Bluetooth antenna to pin H23 on the nrf52833 microcontroller and to 'ground', the part of the circuitry that can absorb, like the earth itself, an undefined amount of charge without itself changing its electrical potential. This micro-component-habit of the capacitor contracts or gathers together high frequency vibrations in voltage and diverts them into the common ground circuit, and away from the sensitive propensities of other micro-component habits.

Despite its constitutive synthesis of differences, its grounding of sensing, its composition of bodies through excitations, some habit formations can become troublesome interactions. Some configurations decay into 'sad repetitions' (Deleuze 2001, 293), and these repetitions can be reinforced and intensified by design, as Wendy Chun's 'habitual media' (Chun 2016), Geert Lovink's 'sad by design' (Lovink 2019) and Natasha Schüll's gaming machine (Schüll 2012) analyses have shown in their engagement with various platform and entertainment media. From Deleuze's perspective, pathological habits relate to a representational order that reduces habits to a bare repetition.

Experimental habits

If habits themselves are the contraction or binding of something as a difference, they are not pathological as such. They, according to Deleuze, become unhappy when repetition is reduced to a bare minimum. Habits' capacity to synthesize differences are covered over or projected externally as inert, material or mechanical repetition (Deleuze 2001, 285). Habits easily embed in devices. For instance, in her account of gaming machines and their players in Las Vegas, the cultural anthropologist Natasha Schüll maps the movements of players through the zones of life adjacent to the casinos (Schüll 2012). Their daily circulation between dwellings, workplaces, shops and casinos sets up the pattern conducive to the repeated interactions or strong habits of game play. Schüll usefully shifts attention to the interactions that travel across these zones, interactions that set up the immersive, suspended temporalities of animated game play. She embeds, we might say, the habits of game play in those circuits of movement, and the repeated interactions that the gaming machines as devices occasion.

The 'zone of suspension' that grows along these circuits is one in which repetition and rhythmic movement oscillate unpredictably with rare or surprising events. As Schüll observes: 'Instead of casting them as aberrant or maladapted consumers, I include them in the following pages as experts on the very "zone" in which they are caught – a zone that resonates to some degree, I suggest, with the everyday experience of many in contemporary capitalist societies' (Schüll 2012, 20). This generative ambivalence in habit formation is framed by John Dewey in *Experience and Nature*: 'By a seeming paradox, increased power of forming habits means increased susceptibility, sensitiveness, responsiveness. Thus even if we think of habits as so many grooves, the power to acquire many and varied grooves denotes high sensitivity, explosiveness' (Dewey 1958, 281). The seeming paradox is that habits dull sensations and sense of novelty. At the same time, the power of forming habits conditions sensitivity, susceptibility and responsiveness. This grooving of habits through experience suggests that the distribution of habits, or how habits connect with each other, is crucial. Hence the recent bestselling appeal of 'atomic habits' (Clear 2018) may well lie in the embedded grooves of habit more generally.

The phenomenological philosopher Maurice Merleau-Ponty approaches embedding/embodying from a slightly different direction. His account of 'a human body', despite its possibly problematic universal singularity, also offers a framing in which blending with things is vital: 'There is a human body when, between the seeing and the seen, between touching and the touched, between one eye and the other, between hand and hand, a blending of some sort takes place' (Merleau-Ponty 1964, 163). That 'blending' he refers to, where is that? Most embedded systems place sensors in contact with controls or actuators – devices that move something, make sounds or light – as part of their operation, but these elements, perhaps devices or machines in their own right, swarm with their own habits and dispositions relating to movements.

Are there places where the sensing and the sensed, the using and the used, the predicted and the predictor, the influenced and influenced, blend together? Circuit-boards such as the micro:bit are one such place where a style of blending of habits occurs. The circuits running between seeing and the pulsing LED, or between hand and fan, insert themselves as two of many possible movements around a body. They themselves – a button, a light, a fan – could easily be linked in a slightly more indirect double habit in which a button turns on a fan and a fan is shown as on by a pulsing light.

An electric motor can be run at a particular speed only if currents feeding into it remain constant. It has its own inertia or momentum. Its tendency to keep moving is what the **while** loops, the duty and rest times, coast on. They switch current on and off at various times in a technique called 'time proportioning'. The pins on a microcontroller might only be able to switch a current on or off, but with time proportion pulse width modulation, a signal can be generated that corresponds to any point between fully off or fully on.

As in the other micro:bit sensors, something resonates in the microphone when a body moves and makes a sound in the air. Something in the microphone is balanced or suspended lightly enough to move when air does. More than that, something in the arrangement changes air movements into currents in a circuit: the movement of a magnet creates eddies of electrical current that feed through the successive stages of amplification, filtering and this analogue-to-digital conversion through sampling. The micro:bit can only record a few seconds of audio at 20,000 samples per second. The welldefined character of the audio data synthesized by the micro:bit microphone is therefore dependent on the many prior events in which sound has been constituted as something that matters to people and others (for instance, as a connection between them as in speaking, or as an element in the formative coupling of a life to a place, as in the many animals that listen carefully for sounds relating to food, territory or threat). The underlying point is that every device contracts habits that relate to preceding series of contractions, sensings or movements.

Counteracting resonance

Does all of this layering, and the interleaving of various component habits in the microcontroller, fit with the vision of a platform as the flattened surface of mutable arrangements? The final sense of embedding as an abstraction that maps a complicated manifold to a simpler surface actuates here. This sense of embedding as abstraction positioned within an ensemble has found much purchase in large machine learning models for language and images (Mackenzie 2023). According to Simondon, technical ensembles always have de-couplings and dis-connects that open them to change. In his description of the audiometry laboratory, the isolation of the audiometer from various resonances in the power supply, in the room, and from interactions between its own vibrating components discourages the technical ensemble from becoming a 'technical individual': 'The ensemble distinguishes itself from technical individuals in the sense that the creation of a unique associated milieu is undesirable; the ensemble is comprised of a certain number of devices in order to counteract this possible creation of a unique associated milieu' (Simondon 1989, 80).

What in the ensemble counteracts the creation of an associated milieu? As usual, Simondon pays close attention to details: the audiometer, an instrument that generates tones to test hearing, contains oscillators. Oscillators easily affect each other through resonance or vibrations in common. It synthesizes frequencies by superimposing different waveforms to create beats, the regular waveforms formed from different frequencies. If the audiometer was designed differently, it might, for instance, create resonances or vibrations of its own in the room. Similarly, a coupling between the audiometer oscillators and the variations in the mains electric power source could affect the frequencies used to test hearing. If the audiometer circuits were not isolated both from the power supply and from each other, they might begin to resonate in unexpected ways. Maintaining a 'certain number of devices' in the ensemble blocks this 'possible creation' by disconnecting or de-coupling things from each other in ways that are ordinary (digital, electric, physical, and so on) but also rare in comparison to the blendings of habits.

Why would a 'unique associated milieu' be undesirable? For Simondon, a unique associated milieu entails a close coupling between the technical entities and their environs. This coupling, while it may deeply embed the device in place, limits the 'general evolution of technical objects' (Simondon 1989, 21). In the in-formation theory terminology favoured by Simondon in much of his work, a closely coupled arrangement reduces the ensemble's capacity to 'receive information' by narrowing the 'margin of indeterminacy': 'It is also through the intermediary of this margin of indeterminacy and not through automatisms that machines can be grouped into coherent ensembles' (Simondon 1989, 32).

Ensembles may contain machines, systems, elements or connect to infrastructures, complicated programs of automation without, according to Simondon, ever obviating the regulatory, coordinating role of people. People, the 'make it: code it' micro:bit users, are the associated milieu for the technical ensemble. They make differences compatible, or 'resolv[e] problems of compatibility between machines within an ensemble' (22) as Simondon puts it. Is it just so that CODAL and then micropython or Microsoft Maker present themselves as capable of subsuming and unifying the devices and their different micro-habits and propensities?

Conclusion

What is the significance of devices like micro:bits, or perhaps of many of the microcontrollers that connect somehow to platforms but are not obviously platforms in the writ-large sense? Under what conditions can such become vectors of experimentation ontology?

The senses of embedding discussed in this chapter suggest a different way of tracking how ensembles become the ordered forms of regulated life we encounter as platforms. The three versions of embedding – technoeconomic, embodying, and as manifold – fold through each other like the bandings of iron oxide. What matters in this enfolding is the possibility of approaching micro:bit without ultimate reference to their final purpose in making embedded systems programmable for a generation of 'make it: code it' subjects.

In the micro:bit device, the Nordic Semiconductor nrf52833 microcontroller is surrounded by more than a hundred other components, most of which are counteracting the formation of an associated milieu, or a vibrational relation between different sub-ensembles. It becomes a 'runtime', something that can be addressed in code by virtue of the abstraction layers that avoid 'internal concretization of the technical objects it contains' (Simondon 1989, 66).

The STS/actor-network theory injunction to follow the actors in order to discern how their different agencies mutate in relating shifts its axis in experimental ontology. It now concerns the oscillations between rare and ordinary characteristic of technical ensembles. The cable that connects the micro:bit to a laptop, or the Bluetooth LE wireless link that connects to another micro:bit or to a smartphone app for coding on it, capture much of the complication of even the connection. What looks to be an ordinary cable that carries low electrical currents turns out to be a 3000 page standards-regulated layering of different state machines organized by nested policies and models of abstract control.

The embeddings of the micro:bit multiply in engaging publics, even the small and motivated public of a multi-disciplinary research workshop. There is a deep sense in which micro:bit dissolves into the Micro:bit Education Foundation, an organization whose mode of action is to configure the creative/economic/technical potentials of the devices in its connection with educational platforms and the institutional curricula of schools. The educational foundation makes micro:bit exemplary of a technoeconomic embedding of the world into IoT.

Like many devices, the micro:bit assembles a set of habits of movement and sensing of potential movements. The expressive possibilities of the micro:bit are arranged around reading and writing of signals to pins and associated circuits that both sense and module movements, touch, light and sounds. The microcontrollers, in which series of signals detour through code, are both limited and broad. They centre around habits contracted in ordering differences.

Embedding carries some sense of incorporating or embodying something, but incompletely, in a way that is slightly separated and raised like the component devices on the micro:bit board. The argument has been that it is through the embodying of habits that ensembles become platforms. The idea that platforms assemble devices and machines so that they not only form a network, but communicate with each other in a regulated way, has become the largely taken-for-granted form of social ordering of life.

INTERLUDE V

Being on Stage

The Christmas concert at Canberra Mini-trains started at 4pm, with a summer heat wave simmering on the former sheep pastures on the southeast edge of the city. The platform, covered in green carpet, was separated from the browning grass and hoof-compacted clay soil of the audience area by a rope with red pendants limp in the still air. On stage, performers in black-tie suits played swing-era arrangements of Christmas carols. A lone raven watched from a fence post. The amplified strains of 'God Rest Ye Merry Gentlemen' rolled out over the pastures as the carriages of the mini-trains trundled around the track, a few children and their adults on board.

Standing on stage among performers such as musicians, singers, actors, dancers and perhaps politicians fronting an audience is part of what Erving Goffman calls the 'platform format'. The scene and configuration of this platform, and so many others like it, presents something different to the coastlines, rocks, geometry and churches. As the platform diagrams for the Sydney Opera House drawn by Jörn Utzon in his *Platforms and Plateaus: Ideas of a Danish Architect* show (Utzon 1962), platforms stage every level of height. Utzon's ground-plan for the support-substrate of the opera stage is full of steps and stages on a range of scales. The main stages or performance platforms are big steps arranged in front of steps for seating, surrounded by steps for approaching, and standing on wide flat steps. Some platforms do not use elevation for visibility, but sit at the base of a depression. Not all platforms are spaces of performance, but nearly all rely on stages.

Whatever the arrangements of steps, approaches, rising or sinking down, what do we make of the ensemble experience? There is an intricate variety of arrangements and gear there, even in the case of a swing-era big band, and its range of music. The differences between a swing big band and a concert orchestra depend on a whole gamut of habitual spatial, visual and auditory alignments, subtended by the social organization of the music

Figure V.1: Mini-trains platform

Figure V.2: Utzon's platform

Source: Utzon (1962)

group, the instruments and the arrangements of sound and sight. A tuba is unlikely to be in the front line in a New Orleans jazz hall band. The piano player needs to be able to make eye contact with the bassist and drummer in a jazz trio. All of this says nothing of the sonic architectures in play during performance, architectures in which there are spaces of resonance, silence, acceleration, pause and timing.

The psycho-physics of ensembles shift on the platform. On a stage, the presence of others beyond the edge of the platform complicates the performance. Even a few others, more than a crow at least, can subtly change everything: breathing tightens, sounds come out differently, heart-rates spike at unforeseen difficulties. Technique falters, and notes that normally flow knot. Prior arrangements and coordination of performance loosen, so that the playlist runs a bit differently. Vectors of sonic affect, highly contagious in performance, spark in all directions, especially for the performers and sometimes for the audience. Sometimes, people beyond the platform edge pick up on something in the music and begin to resonate with it in dance and voice, and their movement can generate new elements of performance.

Little of that happened at the summer Christmas concert. The ensemble generate some internally novel microstates but little exchange across the baking audience arena, or the passengers on the miniature transport infrastructure. Everything in this scene – the set playlist, the fully written-out sheet music, sparse audience, arrangements of American popular music of 70 years ago – stacked up against the potential for anything to happen.

6

Closures and Their Stagings

How did platforms come on stage after 2000? If we start from how platforms appear in web browsers and then apps on smartphones and other devices in increasingly virtualized and microstate, embedded configurations, the complex development of platforms is woven through by practices of coding and software development. Coding and software development itself is re-made in that weaving.

Devices such as applications, apps and websites are the most immediate experience of platforms for many people. The existence of apps and websites, as well as everything that connects to them, depends on code in multiple ways. There has been much recognition of some of the effects of coding and its connections with agency, politics, economy and culture. But perhaps attention to how developers belong to and are included in what they code would help us understand the ensemble-side of platforms. And to ask: how does this progressively entanglement boost experimental ontology?

What matters ontologically in coding things to be platform-like, in making functionalities, interfaces or screens that update, scroll, display, animate, label, tabulate, list or link to 'content'? In a discussion thread entitled 'What is a practical use for a closure in JavaScript?' on the Q&A site Stack Overflow in 2015, a participant declares: 'Technically every function you make in Javascript on a browser is a closure because the window object is bound to it' (alex 2015). The discussion about 'closures in JavaScript' meanders through a dozen or so major responses, some with many sub-replies, and some receiving hundreds of upvotes indicating 'this answer is useful'. But the stark central assertion – 'every function you make ... is a closure' – strikes me as useful in its highlighting of a programming construct – the closure – that is both technically relevant to how platforms have been made through 'binding' and slightly surprising in its implications and connotations for thinking about collectives.

Closures, whether written for didactic purposes of a Wikipedia entry on 'closures' (Wikipedia 2019) or some JavaScript for the components of an app user interface written using Meta Corporation's **React Native**

(Meta 2023), are doing something literally and actually. They are literally recording or maintaining knowledge of state of myriad components and processes, ranging from how many times a button has been clicked, or the number of videos in a list on the screen, or the results of a SQL query sent to a server on the internet.

It is not important for present purposes to know what a closure is in coding. Although many job interviewers probe developers' understanding of closure, levels of understanding of closures vary among developers. Closures, whether understood or not, are common. For more than a decade, JavaScript has been the most popular language for users of Stack Overflow (Stack Exchange 2023a). Indeed, since the early 2000s, web-page authoring gradually moved over to coding functionalities in JavaScript to provide all the elements of interactive or operational functionality now associated with 'dynamic' web pages. The clickable elements of a map, the editable cells of a calendar, the graphs of temperature or share prices on a news site all use JavaScript. Similarly, in the space of a decade, major platform apps for smartphones and other devices such as Facebook, Uber and Netflix shifted from coding in operating-system specific languages to JavaScript.

Closures, for reasons to be explored in this chapter, have proliferated in various forms beyond apps and interactive web browsers. They furnish, at the time of writing, the core functions of the popular 'serverless architectures' – Amazon Lamba, Google Cloud Function, IBM Cloud Functions, Alibaba Cloud Function Computer or Microsoft Azure Functions – used by Netflix, *The Guardian* or BBC. The surprising uniformity of naming across major competing platforms ('Function') suggests that something consistent or coherent is taking shape. These services all characterize themselves as providing 'focus on core business logic with the highest level of hardware abstraction' (Microsoft Corporation 2023a).

Not only emergent platform architectures ad workers, but the scaling, responsiveness, parallelism and interconnection of platforms leverage the closure constructs found in nearly all recent programming languages. The programming construct of a closure is only one side of the story of ongoing platform-making at scale by developers. Earlier usages from mathematics and computer science (closures in set theory; the Kleene closure ★ in regular expressions) still activate some coding.

Note, however, that closure has a spectrum of senses, ranging from cognitive psychology and experiences of conflict, through literary theory in its analysis of narrative, in epistemology in its understanding of how knowledges are connected, in set theory and mathematical topology in their treatment of sets undergoing operations. It also has the less technical but familiar sense of closure of borders, roads, schools, and so on, as well as the closure of many platforms (for example, Google+).

Enclosure occurs in various forms through closure. Other senses of closure and its variants, some deriving from science and technology studies (STS; interpretative closure in Sociology of Scientific Knowledge and Social Construction of Technology aka SCOT; bracketing of experience in phenomenological accounts of technology), complicate this picture. As a concept, closure appears as well in sociology and STS. In the social construction of technology (Pinch et al 1987), 'technological closure' refers to the reduction in interpretative flexibility as the problems to which an artefact and the social groups with their different problems are more or less aligned, reduced and fixed in place. This STS sense, with its orientation to the difficulties of holding on to the multilinear, forking temporalities through which artefacts solidify into something familiar and taken for granted, as if it had to come into existence given the need, is perhaps the one that lies closest to the problem of ensembles.

Closure as a resolution or inclusion of differences does not always occur (Callon and Law 2005). Michel Callon and other STS scholars developed the notion of qualculability in part to describe situations where the scope of events overflows any closure or listing of variables to be taken into account (Callon and Law 2005).

Closures and stagings

There are two platform scenes in this chapter, or two main ones at least. One is Stack Overflow, the question and answer platform used by developers, students and people like me. The opening quote above is from there. Stack Overflow discussions over that time also supply much training data for generative machine learning models such as ChatGPT. Reports during 2023 of a substantial decline in question and answer volumes on Stack Overflow attribute the shift to the large language models (Çelik 2023). Whether or not this shift occurs, or how it occurs, is less relevant for present purposes than the fact of the ongoing transformation and expansion of coding at every level of platforms.

The other scene is something called the 'Watson Data Science Experience', a product developed by IBM Corporation promoted on university campuses in the UK in 2016, and still offered as one of the many data science-related services (IBM 2018). Participating in the Watson Data Science Experience brings forward a specific scene of coding concerned with the institutionalistion of 'data science' as a hybrid scientific-economic field.

The scenes have many connections, and reading them together will perhaps add more. The first scene is full of questions and answers about coding, and has accumulated discussions, participants and visitors for more than a decade. The scene of the Data Science Experience is set up around approaches to working with data, organized as a new kind of knowing in the mid-2010s, and tightly coupled with reorganization of knowledge production around platform services to be purchased by universities, governments, businesses and other organizations. These two economize coding in different ways. They both create products and services, but they also attest to new instabilities in the formation of collectives, as well as some ongoing great stabilities. As with concepts discussed in other chapters, the concept of closure developed here has technical, scientific and socio/philosophical strands running through it. I devise a method for combining these strands by tracing particular encounters where they overlap.

Closures and callbacks

In programming, a closure is a combination of a function (or a subroutine) and the environment in which it was created. A function is usually defined as a 'self-contained block of code' (OpenAI 2023).

The combination of a function and 'the environment' strain this definition. A closure allows a function to enclose something into the self-contained block. It encapsulates the function together with references to its surrounding state, such as variables, constants and functions. This allows the function to access and manipulate the variables from its enclosing scope, even after the scope has finished executing. This surrounding state is also known as a 'stack frame'.

In simpler terms, a closure is like a self-contained 'package' that includes a function and the data it needs to operate, even if that data is not explicitly passed as arguments to the function. It allows functions to 'remember' the variables and context in which they were defined. Closures are commonly used in languages that support first-class functions or have lexical scoping, such as Python, JavaScript and Ruby. They are particularly useful in situations where you want to create functions with private, encapsulated data or when you need to create functions that maintain state between multiple invocations.

Any large language model can generate the closure code construct: 'Here's a "simple example" in Python to demonstrate a closure':

```
def outer_function(x):
    def inner_function(y):
        return x + y
    return inner_function

closure10 = outer_function(10)
result = closure10(5)
print(result) # Output: 15
```

In this example, the function outer_function returns inner_function as a closure. When outer_function is called with the argument 10, it creates a closure (closure10) that 'remembers' the value of x as 10. It returns the whole package of that remembered value 10 and a reference or index pointing to inner_function. The closure in this instance is called closure10. The closure has been assigned to the variable closure10 and then used to perform the + 10 addition by passing 5 as an argument, resulting in the output 15. The instance of outer_function called closure10 carries an environment where x has the value 10. Somewhere in the stack frame for the closure closure10, the 10 is stored. It is the slightly counter-intuitive detour, a way of maintaining separate actions, but also holding them in relation, that I find catchy in this coding construct.

A coding technique of including and separating in code is both operationally important and figuratively significant. Closure, I suggest, is a figure for how ensembles are put together. Their inner and outer aspects, their provisional de-coupling from linear operations and isochronic execution enable many forms of concurrencies, parallelism, scaling, asynchronies and event-driven operations. Things happen at all different rates, but somehow they are held together. The issue here is whether ensembles are only ever the same thing, the same people, doing the same thing, or whether something different happens. The closure technique found in many programming languages aims to maintain something amidst 'multiple invocations'.

One practically useful feature of closures is their capacity to allow 'callbacks', or invocation of functions in a different sequence or even temporality. Callbacks differ from calls. Functions are called all the time in coding, but callbacks are function calls that include a reference to other functions to be called as part of the call. Code using callbacks might configure different orderings of operation, depending on how and when it runs. Like 'closure', 'callback' holds something in place, but not completely.

Functions become 'first class objects' under some circumstances. The naming of functions as 'objects' is a way of saying that they can be treated as data, and passed around, stored and manipulated like any other data. That functioning of functions is evocative (???).

Not only does it allows the interactivity of something like JavaScript or Python, but it runs new layers or abstraction and repetition through it as in the many serverless platform offerings (AWS Lambda, Google Functions, and so on). Hidden state variables can communicate with each other, and whole environments can move around in a closure. It's a model of sociotechnical mediation in which the complications of operations, sets and mappings becomes more vivid and perhaps comprehensible in formation. They suggest ways of thinking about the layers, the interfaces, the tendency to abstract, without resorting to large control structures such as the client-server, the capital or social structure. Closure might be a way of defining platforms through their inventory of operations and functions rather than through the figure of raised surface and its edges.

Heterodynamic closures and the bracketing of experience

If we're all caught up in closures, then the question becomes: how do closures map inclusion in ensembles? As well as asking and answering questions, Stack Overflow is a site 'where developers learn, share and build careers'. It belongs to a suite of Stack Exchange platforms spanning topics mostly concerning computing servers, gaming and IT, but also covering areas such as mathematics, statistics, philosophy, martial arts, coffee, Islam and matter modelling (Stack Exchange 2023b).

The title of the platform – 'Stack Overflow' – refers to an error condition usually leading to a program crash, often caused by infinite recursion, or a function that continues to call itself. Stack overflow is a figure for a state of confusion or overwhelm experienced by developers, not just their software. The stack, an area of memory designated as a place to keep track of functions executing in a given program or process, is finite. `ulimit -s` gives 8192 kilobytes on my laptop. An overflow means that there are too many stack frames, or scoped environments to record them all. In such a setting, the stack overflows and the program crashes because it loses track of the chain of functions it is executing. This is precisely the kind of situation in which closures might be produce or address.

People post questions on Stack Overflow. Their questions, problems and the responses they elicit are a diffracted image of platform and ensemble practices, and their changes over time. Stack Overflow also asks questions of its users, especially in the annual developer surveys it has run since 2011. These surveys, with a changing list of questions, are published online in the form of comma-separated-value (csv) plaintext files (Stack Exchange 2023a). Each year it increases (2022: 72,000; 2021: etc ... 2011:). Indeed all Q&A activity on Stack Overflow and many user attributes are fully accessible in a vast dataset hosted on the Google BigQuery platform (Google 2023). In 2023, the survey conducted in May attracted around 90,000 responses.

Globally, the collection of software developers is said to number around 26 million. That is, there are almost as many people as teachers (across all levels from pre-school to universities), around the same number as doctors and nurses combined, around the same number as taxi drivers, more than three times the number of total scientists, but only a tenth of factory workers, and a tiny fraction of the number of people farming (UN, WorldBank, FAO statistics). Given 23 million registered users on Stack Overflow, and 100 million visits per month, a significant proportion of people learning or doing software development cross the thresholds of the platform. The traffic goes some way to explaining its sale for US$1.8 billion to a South African investment company called Prosus in 2021 (Dummett 2021).

It is immediately striking from the Stack Overflow surveys of the last decade that the 'learn, share and build' injunction has a gendered uptake. The StackOverflow.com dataset makes this gendering starkly visible. For instance, in 2022, the survey asked various questions about gender identities and sexuality. In the 2023 survey, there were no questions about sexuality at all, although questions about ethnicity, education levels, pay, employment, and so on, remained. Across the decade or so of the surveys, the proportions are relatively constant but typically around 90 per cent identify as 'Man', 5 per cent as 'Woman', 1 per cent 'Non-binary, genderqueer', and the remainder don't say how they identify.

There is an extensive research literature on gender and coding, some of it relating directly to Stack Overflow. For instance, Sian Brooke tracks how gendering occurs across the platform, using a computational social science approach to the Stack Overflow data dump on Google BigQuery (Brooke 2021). Brooke begins by identifying gendering via user names. Brooke writes, 'as we seek to understand gender differences, biases, and peer parity on SO [Stack Overflow], usernames are a simple but effective site of gendered identity' (Brooke 2021, 2097). Similar analyses have been done on GitHub (???), a platform whose very name embeds a gendered identity: a *git* is 'an unpleasant or objectionable man or (occasionally) woman' (Oxford English Dictionary 2023). (Also relevant: 'git' in Australian slang means 'get', as in 'git round the back'.)

Some analyses of coding, of open source software in particular with its explicit claims to sharing, inclusion and participation, home in on coding practices associated with the value of 'openness'. Dawn Nafus, for instance, suggests that gender in these setting is regarded as 'orthogonal' to computing, and whatever is associated with gender is a 'mere' social concern (Nafus 2012). Coding work in many organizations has long been separated off from other relevant forms of labour on the platform (testing, documentation, and so on), and regarded as the 'true' or 'real' work, the work that makes things work. This is a gendered and racialized separation (Amrute 2020). The 'separation of concerns', to use a software engineering term, shapes organizational practices around coding, including the talk about coding on Stack Overflow. Describing the style of moderation/regulation of question and answers in discussions such as Stack Overflow forums, Nafus concludes: 'in doing so, men monopolize code authorship and simultaneously de-legitimize the kinds of social ties necessary to build mechanisms for women's inclusion' (Nafus 2012, 669). At the same time, as Nafus observes, talking about the reality or truth of coding work forms a crucial element of the coding field. Much of the more highly vexed talk on Stack Overflow is about the 'real' or 'true' way to code. Coding, it might be said, is constantly coding coding. It is through the iterative enunciation of public statements about good, bad, best or cool coding practices that coding and its diverse deployments valorizes both coding as a cutting-edge form of work and the worth of coders themselves as the agents of such real value. In this context, Stack Overflow, with its ranking mechanisms, 'accepted answers', upvotes, and often trenchant corrections and admonishments is the platform enactment of the coding of coding norms. The annual surveys and their somewhat abundant analyses by data scientists and others reiterate the permutations and derivatives of this shoring-up and straightening-out of coding by talking about it.

The broader landscape of gender and technology can be understood as a diverse ecology of iterative co-normalization of subject positions or identities and configured devices. In feminist STS work, the co-production of gender and technology, as Judy Wacjman highlights, takes place in a constant mutual re-shaping:

> The distinguishing insight of feminist STS or technofeminism is that gender is integral to this sociotechnical process: that the materiality of technology affords or inhibits the doing of particular gender power relations. … Thus, both technology and gender are products of a moving relational process, emerging from collective and individual acts of interpretation. (Wajcman 2010, 8)

Acts of coding, whether to show what a closure is (see Code excerpt 1) for a Wikipedia page or a ChatGPT generated text, writing some code that identifies the first unique character in a string to complete a kata and level up on CodeWars.com, participating in a Kaggle.com data science competition to analysis Stack Overflow survey results, are dripfeeding of gendering.

On Stack Overflow and on GitHub, what we might call a *heterodynamic closure* flows or overflows the millions of questions, responses, solutions, follows, watches, stars, forks and upvotes. The heterodynamic closure combines two different signals, one relating to the configuration of a field of platformate devices, and the other relating to points of identification, as well as economic and epistemic attachments, embodied in the norming practices of developers. Like the closure as a coding construct, the heterodynamic closure refers beyond itself to the surrounding environment, even if that environment is no longer or only directly present. The heterodynamic processing going on is at once actual and figurative, as STS scholarship has long maintained. The figure of a function that continues to execute even when its context or environment has shifted is relevant to the dynamics of co-production of gender and other differences in platformate ensembles. Developers and coders continue to gender coding work through this figuring.

Differentiated closures

Would it be safe to say that heterodynamic closures mean that platforms are a gendering co-production? The constant shifting in arrangements of ensembles is writ large on Stack Overflow. In response, the shifting composition of the survey traces the rise and fall of tags or tools in the hands of 26 million or so developers. But at the same time, there is a micro-layered dynamism to the forms of practice discussed there. The persistent gendering work does not mean nothing changes. It might be that gendering closures multiply, they come from all directions, but developers can maintain function in the midst of gender multiplication through the closure construct and its capacity to include a lexical scope, or a well-defined set of words and grammar for ordering coding.

The co-production of gender and technical ensembles within heterodynamic closures suggests a mixing of fixity and change. Many of the Stack Overflow survey questions implicitly concern this restricted dynamism. For instance, the survey usually asks developers about 'technologies' they use, including 'miscellaneous technologies'. These 'technologies' are often themselves significant platforms (see Table 6.1).

Table 6.1: Miscellaneous technologies in the Stack Overflow 2022 survey. The table shows the number of developers who use each technology and the proportion of developers who use it.

Platforms	n	prop
.NET	11824	11
NumPy	10248	10
Pandas	9070	9
TensorFlow	8836	9
Flutter	7980	8
React Native	6728	7
Apache Kafka	6153	6
Torch/PyTorch	6073	6
Spring	5472	5
Scikit-learn	5175	5
Electron	4349	4
Keras	3493	3
Apache Spark	3155	3
Qt	2895	3
Xamarin	2259	2
Hadoop	1993	2
Ionic	1679	2
Hugging Face Transformers	1462	1

In 2022, the leading miscellaneous tech is .NET: 'NET is a developer platform with tools and libraries for building any type of app, including web, mobile, desktop, games, IoT, cloud, and microservices' (Microsoft Corporation 2023b). Understandably, a platform that allows building any type of 'app' ranging from mobile phones, gaming, cloud and everything else is itself a difficult entity to characterize. A cluster of 237 repositories on GitHub documents the development of this multifarious developer platform (dotnet 2023). The second and third entries in the miscellaneous list are surprisingly different, not just in species or genus, but in mode of existence. **numpy** and **Pandas** are Python software code libraries for working with data in the form of arrays, matrices and tables. If **numpy** is the scientific version, **Pandas** would be the media/commercial correlate. Their high rank in the developer listing is suggestive of the range of different interests mingling through the heterodynamic closures. This numericization {#index} of coding intensifies further down the rankings. **TensorFlow, Torch\PyTorch, Scikit-learn, keras** and **Hugging Face Transformers** shift coding into increasingly vectorized statistical probabilities. At the same time, **Flutter, React Native, Spring** and **Electron** present user-interfaces as the shifting surface of coding work. A few entries – **Kafka** and **Spark** and perhaps **Hadoop** – relate to configurations of computing devices set up to capture, process or distribute streams of data on a large scale.

Whether or not reading such lists is of interest to readers or participants on Stack Overflow, the assortment of technical elements is part of the heterodynamic closure. Questions on programming languages, on database environments, on web frameworks, on cloud platforms, developer tools, operating systems, collaboration tools have similar mixtures of interests. Indeed, the basis categories of developer the survey offers to participants can be and are mixed in various ways. Some developers say they are 'full stack', as if they occupy all strata of software stack (Bratton 2016). But others occupy intersections of different devices; for example, a front-end (interface) developer working with TensorFlow on Terraform, an 'infrastructure as code' platform that allows a data centre to be configured from the command line. These fluxing intersections of devices, infrastructures, knowledges, techniques create many niches where developers along with their organizational environments co-locate.

Univocity of code as expansive closures

The Stack Overflow survey, along with the many other affirmations of coding found online and in conferences, hackathons, educational programmes at every level from early school life on, through to the large language model-based coding suggestions that have begun to infiltrate even a plaintext neovim editor, enunciates a single ontological proposition: code is univocal; it speaks unambiguously, like Being.

To code, and to affirm the univocity of code, is to participate in the maximal reality of ensembles.

Both the Stack Overflow survey questions that categorize and distribute coding into a set of platform and device settings (front-end, back-end, full-stack, academic; databases, web-frameworks, cloud-services, version control, and so on), *and* the common structure of a Stack Overflow discussion thread, with its well-articulated problem, evidence of effort to solve the problem, awareness of what others have already done or said, and conformity to forum norms concerning strictly technical formulation of the problem reinforce the univocity of code.

The openness of code, as manifest on GitHub, for instance, only reinforces this univocity. As Nafus puts it in her discussion of the 'openness' of free and open software, 'openness relies on a steadfastly closed epistemological frame that not only constitutes technology as apart from persons, but shapes this separability in such a way that code is more than just outside the realm of the social: it is downright freed from it' (Nafus 2012, 681). The radically different patterns of participation in Stack Overflow, GitHub and coding in general become much more understandable in this light. In the midst of perhaps the most device-strewn, technically differentiated and distributed ensembles known to any collective, the univocity of code enacts a form of closure that continually reseals the technical from the social, even as it slips nearly all social processes onto a software/code-based pallet. In all its differentiation, to participate in coding is to enunciate a position in the ensembles that seeks to maintain closure, even as it navigates the constant transitions and transformations. The devices and enunciation are coupled, but that coupling is constantly hidden from view as an inner or anonymous function of the closure.

The result of the highly social enactment of the heterodynamic closure is an ongoing differentiation of code itself. The shifting concerns of the surveys over the last decade index some of these differentiations. One in particular is expansive: the closure concerning data. The expansiveness of data and the code developed to work with that expansion present a different sense of closure.

Closures and data

The data from Stack Overflow surveys circulates widely among developers and data scientists. Such datasets, pertaining to platform-making practices, have a distinctive mode of investment. I find myself drawn to the analysis of it using data science approaches popularized among developers in the last decade. And yet the texture of any such analysis is inflected by closures specific to data science and its practices.

For data, or the traces and signs of diversity in beings, there is another practically important but different sense of closure that relates to data rather than programming constructs. It stems from the mathematics of set theory, travels through recursion theory and the lambda calculus of 20th-century mathematics associated with Alonzo Church, Kurt Godel, Alan Turing and Stephen Kleene and then onto cybernetics and the disciplinary formation of computer science. It's unfortunate, according to the designers of Scheme, one of the first mainstream computer languages to explicitly include closures as programming constructs, that the term was already in use in mathematics for something different.

Closure in the programming sense does not hark back to the set theory sense. The set theory sense is, nonetheless, quite important to relational and non-relational databases (Mackenzie 2012). A set theory closure can be framed as a property of sets concerning what belongs and what doesn't when they are subject to a particular operation: 'a subset of a given set is closed under an operation of the larger set if performing that operation on members of the subset always produces a member of that subset. ... The closure of a subset is the result of a closure operator applied to the subset' (Wikipedia 2023). Closure in the set theory sense might be more expansive than the functional programming construct of the closure. Like programming languages, set theory is admittedly not the most promising working material for experimental ontology in ensembles. But, like hash functions with their churning of prime numbers, set theory as practised in finding elements in collections, opens some different ways for about ensembles.

Closures of any size: * as a pluralizing operator

The leading example of this in the last decade of coding work might be the practices assembled under the name of data science.

I like the idea that 'the lack of closure is one reason for enlarging a set'. For example, $x^{\{2\}} = 2$ needs irrational numbers to calculate the value of x, so it might be that arithmetic would need to include natural numbers or integers and numbers that cannot be expressed as fractions; $x^2 + 1$ needs imaginary numbers. Closures, as the '-re' suffix suggests, are not fixed in their closing. A closure is not finally closed at any point. It is extensible.

Take a closure from set theory known as the Kleene closure. This is a set related operation, rather ubiquitous in coding, and usually expressed as *. The history of this closure operator runs through cybernetics. It first appears in a publication by the mathematician Stephen Cole Kleene's 1957 publication appears as a 1951 Rand Corporation report entitled 'Representation of Events in Nerve Nets and Finite Automata' (Kleene 1956). The report has contemporary resonance as it is deeply immersed in the neural net thinking of the time. Kleene, a mathematician, develops a formalism for expressing 'regular events' in the neural network. The formalism expresses patterns of activation coming from the sensing surfaces of the network exposed to touch, light, vibration or other movements. Today, neural nets would more likely be 'exposed' to datasets gathered from platform databases. Kleene's regular event formalism is steeped in the mathematics of recursion theory, functional analysis and set theory. This mathematics was under development through much of the early 20th century. Developed to give order to patterns of events in a technical device such as a neural nets, the regular event approach found very many uses in the processing of so-called 'unstructured data' such as text, but also in working with many 'activation patterns' generated by ensembles themselves: filenames, addresses, metadata, field names, and so on. The regular event formalism is now referred to as 'regular expressions', expressions themselves being derived from the more general mathematical formalization of 'regular languages'.

It is difficult to over-estimate the significance of the regular expression languages that begin with Kleene. They are an integral part of nearly every programming language mentioned in the Stack Overflow surveys. They are found in search engines, in very many pattern matching applications, and in the basic coding toolkit of most developers for whatever end they work. The * operator means 'zero or more repetitions' of the element preceding it. In the Python code example that follows, as in many other settings where regular expressions are found, the data takes the form of text, or strings, that is, set of characters.

```
import re

# Example string containing some repeated characters
text = "aabbcdddddeee"

# Using the Kleene closure to match zero or more occurrences of 'd'
pattern = 'd*'

# Find all matches of the pattern in the text
matches = re.findall(pattern, text)

# Print the matches
print(matches)
```

The ChatGPT explanation that accompanied the code goes on to say:

> Kleene Closure in Regular Expressions: In data extraction and text processing, regular expressions play a crucial role in pattern matching and data extraction. The Kleene closure, denoted by the asterisk (*), allows for matching patterns of any length (including zero occurrences) from the given input. This is especially useful when dealing with unstructured or semi-structured data.

The 'crucial role in pattern matching and data extraction' is a particularly striking instance of an expansive closure. The Kleene star operator * is a way of expanding any character in the match. In this code example, the matches occur wherever a d begins. The pattern d* is an operation on the set of characters in the string that finds multiple occurrences of d. Most pattern matching is likely to be more complicated than this, but the expansiveness of the operator – 'matching patterns of any length' – is evocative. If a short pattern expression can create matches of any length and maintain closure in doing so, the set can become quite large. It can become any size.

I am suggesting that the Kleene closure in regular expressions is a figure for the expansion or extension of data and its closure in ensembles over recent decades, and particularly the decade 2010–2020. This is the period in which data intensification occurs on platforms. In the Stack Overflow Survey of 2012, the second year of the survey, the major 'occupation' answer given by respondents was 'web application developer', followed by 'desktop application programmer', and distantly by 'server programmer.' In 2012, questions about coding concerned programming languages, how long developers had been programming and what kind of mobile device they used. In recent years, the developers have worked with platforms that have a very different configuration to the 'desktop', 'web application' or 'server' categories of earlier years. By 2023, almost all respondents identify with the surprisingly wide-ranging category of 'front-end, back-end, full-stack, mobile or embedded'.

When asked to choose which particular platforms, more than half gravitate to the ensemble-service providers. As shown in Table 6.2, developers now work with a range of cloud platforms, and their survey responses emphatically trend towards major compute platforms.

What kind of ontological operator is the ★ of the Kleene closure? It is a figure that stands in for the expansion of data in tandem with the enclosure of domains of the internet as platforms. Expansion under the closure operator takes a regular/regulated form. The ★ is synecdochal in effect, opening the way for parts to stand in for wholes.

Ensembles in which set-theoretical techniques and operations become device-level operations have strong propensities to re-arrange and re-configure existing part-whole orderings, inclusions and belongings. If the ensembles are characterized by ongoing indeterminacies in relation to their precise forms and modes of existence, if the ensembles are dynamic, even statistical in their composition, if they seriate and multiply, if as Christopher Kelty so fully illuminates in *The Participant*, we now inhabit 'a constant, unstable, infinite series of collectives' (Kelty 2019, 261), then expansive closures and their operation are vitally important to consider.

Table 6.2: Platform preferences in the 2023 Stack Overflow survey. The table shows the number of developers who use each platform and the proportion of developers who use it.

Platforms	n	prop
AWS	25939	26
Microsoft Azure	14604	15
Google Cloud	13634	14
Firebase	10751	11
Heroku	10160	10
DigitalOcean	7953	8
VMware	4429	5
Managed Hosting	2927	3
Linode	1994	2
OVH	1913	2
Oracle Cloud Infrastructure	1110	1
OpenStack	1029	1
IBM Cloud or Watson	853	1
Colocation	642	1

⋆ or data science ocean/cloud experiences

Given that the univocal code ensembles, including Stack Overflow and GitHub, predicate participation as their reason for being, what part in this participation do closures (as functional constructs, as expansion operator) play? Developers' relation to platforms, as shown in Table 6.2, is definitely part of a scene in which something is bought and sold. The leading platform – AWS or Amazon Web Services – has 'service' in its name. Others are brand names that suggest a service: IBM Watson, Microsoft Azure, Google Cloud.

Are these services forms of closure? Take the IBM 'organization' on GitHub:

> Hello, World! Welcome to IBM's organization on GitHub where we love all things open source. 25+ years in open source. Read our story 7,500+ IBMers active in open source. How we do open source 20,000 commits per month. Where we invest +2,900 GitHub repositories. Search below! Learn about our approach to Open Technology. (IBM 2023)

This 'organization' of 7500 active IBMers, active in 'open source' since 2000 and heavily invested in 'commits' to GitHub, is typical of the middle ground of contemporary coding. Much coding occurs in 'organizations' such as IBM Corporation rather than by individuals contributing to free-floating software projects. Although the IBM organization declares love for code that is 'open source', this 'openness', as we have seen, has a problematic form of openness. It directly formats participation in the collective life of ensembles. As Christopher Kelty puts it:

> the practice of arranging and formatting participation is not itself open to participation by everyone. The practices of design, redesign and engineering, or maintenance of our platforms, devices, infrastructures, and technologies are obviously activities cordoned off from the involvement of just anyone, confined to particular people, corporations, governments. (Kelty 2019, 50)

In IBM's thousands of open source code repositories on GitHub lie many examples of re-packaging or re-organizing of other open source projects. Many of the 2900 repositories reposition code within the computing products and services sold by IBM. This relation to markets, or the buying or selling things, is a significant organizational element of the expansive closure.

In STS work on markets, particularly that associated with Michel Callon (Callon and Law 2005, @Caliskan_2010, @Callon_2016), the concepts of marketization, economization and subsequently platformization (Plantin et al 2016) form a series of expanding engagements with how things find themselves in a position to be bought and sold. How can an ensemble of devices, abstractions, knowledges and habits become a service?

The process of making something consumable is itself a form of closure that begins with listing and inventory. Caliskan and Michel Callon suggest that these costs or investments are transforming something entangled into something that circulates: 'An inventory and analysis of the investments required to transform entities from entangled beings into passive things is a key issue for the study of marketization' (Çalışkan and Callon 2010, 6). How does the transformation of entangled and provisionally local things to passively circulating things take place? The STS approach represented by Callon's work is strikingly and perhaps presciently centred on calculation. It joins STS accounts of science and technology to economies, markets, good and services. Rather than starting from forms of economic rationality, it begins with the formation of calculating agencies. Well before the data science/data analytics/machine learning/AI boom of the 2010s that sought to make data and computation explicitly economic goods, calculation or 'qualculation' (Callon and Law 2005) was understood as a form of agency. Enumeration, re-arrangement and gathering of the results of the re-arranged enumeration comprise the core of calculating. The work of calculation, or making something calculable, operates as a closure. It operates only with a set of enumerated elements and tests any potential addition to the set of the right kind of passivity or 'shelf-life'.

Paying to the work 'required to transform entities' into dataset or non-fungible tokens for that matter blurs the outline of the services or goods. The calculation characteristic of platforms runs along the lines of the pattern matching and set-making closure operations.

Much of this calculation done in the name of 'data science' is formatted by closures that expand the enumerations. As Callon frames it, 'the power of a qualculation depends on the number of entities that can be added to a list, to the number of relations between those entities, and the quality of the tools for classifying, manipulating, and ranking them' (Callon and Law 2005, 4). Some closures, among which I would include data science itself, expand the participants involved in the formatting of participation in platform-ensembles.

Calculants participating in the formatting of participation

One shared quality of the main types of closures already discussed is their capacity to address non-closure. They both expand the list so that more entities can be enumerated. The possibility of non-closure or overflow is averted by expansion of the set. From the Kleene closure to the embeddings of the large language model that keeps suggesting line completions until I remember to disable it, the enumeration-arrangement-summation continues to expand.

This has specific formatting consequences on participation in collectives:

> Formatting participation in the present is not just a question of tool kits, scripts, or games, but also of objects like 'stacks,' 'frameworks,' and 'dashboards' that allow the participation of users to be formatted and made visible. Tool kits remake the world in their own image: scalable, modular, automatic, fast, and mobile. Tool kits ease the conversion of the unstructured mess of social lives into the phantasmatic virtual collectives made of data. In the context of such large-scale platforms, participation is formatted in complex and precise ways to enable abstraction and extraction. (Kelty 2019, 253)

The many ramifications of such formatting have been widely discussed in algorithm/platform literature. Here I emphasize only how it is done for and to one group of participants, developers.

Think, for instance, of data science, a subfield of developer activity that criss-crosses not only Stack Overflow, but also GitHub, the various cloud computing services, and many other platforms. It has an academic footprint, with many universities offering data science degrees, and many more offering data science courses. The 'IBM Data Science Experience' training workshops came to academic campuses during 2016 aiming to induct academic researchers into the use of IBM data science platforms. The workshop presenters spoke of 'deploying predictive analytics', and the provision of 'all the analytics' on a 'new foundation', the IBM cloud data science platform, a platform that in 2023 was ranked around number 13 by developers in the Stack Overflow survey.

In their workshop, what the presenters referred to as the 'new foundation' fetched up in the participants' web browsers as a field of technical elements arranged in a grid of most blue polygons with different names. Within the array of technical elements on display in this interface, Watson Cognitive Computing was just one instance among many. Various Watson 'apps' for speech, images, text and other domains stood alongside the booming big data apps such as 'BigInsight', 'BigSheets', 'BigR' and 'BigSQL'. Big was big at this time. The presenters intoned a litany of services on the participants: 'software as a service', 'platform as a service' and 'infrastructure as a service' (abbreviated to SaaS, PaaS and IaaS, respectively). Their fluid delivery of the -aaS terminology suggested that much disentangling and disgorging had already taken place.

In this experience of data science, services deluged the doing of data science. Many of the services and features brought in front of the workshop participants were not specific to IBM. In its basic architecture, the IBM Data Science Experience, with its apps, services, connectors and 'sources', engages very similar interfaces, consoles and dashboards to those offered by Google's 'Google Cloud Platform' (Google 2018), Microsoft's Azure 'Cloud Computing Platform and Services' (Microsoft 2018) or Amazon's 'Web Services Management Console' (Amazon 2018). Cloud computing consoles and dashboards for doing data science at scale had appeared as major internet platforms marketized their own computing capacities.

By the end of the workshop, most of the participants had accomplished at their workstations or on their laptops a single task: they had configured and run a Hadoop cluster on the IBM cloud to split (or 'map') a rather large text file of a million words or so onto a set of servers (or 'nodes'), count the words in the files, and then gather (or 'reduce') the word counts into a global tally. The triviality of counting words drummed in a new injunction: 'analyse data on a cloud-based platform'. The workshop experience formatted participants to do their data-science calculation on a marketized platform. Even if they were not paying for the computing, they were introduced to the idea of deploying calculation (counting words) across a distributed computing platform.

It might seem surprising that a training workshop called 'IBM Data Science for Academic Researchers' did not broach modelling, visualization, machine learning or prediction, just even basic data exploration. From the standpoint of rendering *calculants* for the formatting of participation, this is nothing surprising. 'Making [data] things consumable' for a kind of developer called a data scientist counts for more than the solution of any particular data analytic or modelling problem. The training workshops arranged calculative elements of differing provenance in a common space. The training sought to nudge data scientists into a new role as agents of deployment, connecting, attaching, duplicating and arranging calculative operations in the platform space of cloud or data-centre computing.

The IBM Data Science Experience workshop emphasized mundane practices of setting up cloud accounts, uploading datasets, configuring access to databases and existing information sources. Within the space of the cloud data science 'console', the interfaces, software tools and terminal windows already found on developers' laptops were replicated.

Like the other so-called 'public cloud' platforms such as Amazon's AWS, Google Cloud Compute and Microsoft Azure, the IBM cloud console arrays technologies and systems already familiar to data scientists working on a small scale (for instance, ipython or Jupyter notebooks, and the statistical programming language R and the Rstudio). The similarity of these elements to their non-cloud predecessors both smoothes deployment to platforms and makes it less obvious.

This combination of mundane familiarity and a new foundation has a dual purpose. It habituates the agents of calculation to working with the analytic tools and data sources of the platform. It also positions data scientists in the front seat in the formatting of services and assets composing platforms. They coordinate elements of the platform ensemble by transforming them into data for calculation. Deployment, not the relatively convergent processes of modelling, is the epicentre of marketized calculation.

The IBM Data Science Experience is in this sense a platform for doing closures at the platform scale. In a twist on Callon and Caliskan's notion of the 'common space' of calculation as an anchor-point for marketization, they bolt together diverse forms of calculation in the common space of the platform. Certain forms of calculation – aggregating data, arranging it in synoptic forms such as models and visualization, and synthesizing new entities such as rankings, recommendations, classifications and prediction – not only become endemic to platforms, they themselves circulate as products.

Conclusion

It understandable that the presenters also prophesied the inevitable obsolescence of all specific services, including their own products.

They used their own experience of product obsolescences to prod data scientists to step onto cloud platforms as a more raft to work and cling to amidst much change. The IBM presenters made no effort to disguise the heterogeneity or incongruities of systems that might cohabit the calculative closures of the Data Science Experience/platform. They instead affirmed that any differences in configuration, format or mode of operation could be accommodated in the platform itself. No incompatibility of version, underlying dependencies, operating system or legacy was too great to withstand the mutability of the platform.

The range of 'consumable things' within the common space of calculation indiscriminately embraced old and new. On the new front, Watson Cognitive Computing apps can be deployed for speech-to-text, for detecting sentiment in text, for face or object recognition in images, for recommendation and ranking, or for summary and abstract of documents. The consoles present the currently best-known 'big data' systems. At the time of the workshop in 2015, software systems such as Apache Spark and Hadoop were prominent. But right next to that, a cloud platform version of the long-lasting social science statistics package SPSS (Uprichard et al 2008) accompanies 'db2 warehouse' (a business-oriented database long supported by IBM).

Against the narratives of big data disruption, many of the services and systems displayed to developers in the IBM data science cloud console persist from different periods and stages of data analysis and information retrieval.

'Legacy' (or established practice) and the newer, rapidly shape-shifting platform distributions of processing such as Watson Cognitive Computing entwine in much of practical work in data science (for instance, many 'how to' guides for data scientists recommend SQL – Structured Query Language, a technique for querying relational databases dating from the late 1960s – as a key technical skill [Lorang 2016]). The entwining of old and new is central in the marketization of calculation since that marketization precisely concerns the transformation of the pre-platformate into the contemporary practices of embeddings.

The re-versioning of the different closures described in this chapter – the functional programming approach as the heterodynamic closure of Stack Overflow, the Kleene closure as expansion of participation, the calculative closure of data science as formatting of calculants in the Data Science Experience – are efforts in the conduct of the experimental ontology of ensembles (Marres 2013).

Each re-version bisects a closure. Each closure is a way of making things multiple, and not just in the way that all social arrangements (groups, institutions, associations) might be multiple. They bring with them ontological variabilities that can become either very fixated or unleash much experimentation.

INTERLUDE VI

A High-Diving Platform

The architecture of the ten-metre diving platform at Civic Pool in Canberra (c 1955) can also be seen in the Sprungturm at the Freibad, Berlin Pankow (c 1960). The ten-metre platform abstracts from the coastal platforms in certain facets. Diving platforms are infrastructurally rich in scale and modalities of edging and elevation. The platform stands on land and projects over a body of water, the diving pool.

The diving platform adopts the elementary stepped access to levels. The diving platform (see Figure VI.1) limits the space for steps and ladders, so that a compromise gradient, usually built as a step-ladder or a winding staircase, needs to be constructed.

Many built structures include edges, lines or planes that differentiate spaces vertically. The diving platform is a somewhat unusual case since its edges cannot align with its support. Its levels jut out over a pool of water. Such arrangements, for all their apparent simplicity as a way of elevating a surface above water, bring some complexities. The levels of the platform set at three, five and ten metres cannot be stacked vertically. In that case, divers on high levels would risk hitting lower levels. So the levels of the platform need to be staggered so that the highest level projects further over the water than the lower. Such a staggered overhang requires more complicated support than the vertically aligned levels of a high-rise building with its box-like stacking. Jenga players know that the vertical stack is quite stable until holes start appearing lower down the stack. Overhangs may involve different techniques of cantilevering or balancing the projecting higher levels with the greater mass of a base or foundation.

The edges of upper levels of the diving platform challenge perception and balance. The platform's edge facing the water is open, creating a clear vertical drop. Perception of that verticality is confusing. While the pool is usually deep enough to slow down the body of a diver dropping from the ten-metre platform, someone looking down from the edge of the platform

Figure VI.1: Diving platform

sees a much greater height than the distance between platform and water. They see not so much the surface of the water, but the bottom of the pool. As perceived, the five-metre level becomes ten metres and ten becomes 15 metres. Learning to discount this perception is part of learning to go over the edge. Of course, you do not see the drop at all by looking straight ahead or running over the edge. Approaching the edge is a matter, at the diving pool, of not seeing too much, either by looking ahead or running so fast that you pass over the edge before you see off it.

Many rituals and habits associated with learning to dive from ten metres, and the coaching from poolside that gradually orients and aligns divers to the geometry of the dives – the tuck, straight, pike, free, and so on – escort divers to the edge and over. Like any other platform practice, there is always an audience, perhaps virtualized, for any dive from the higher levels of the platform, and sometimes that audience includes coaches or judges who assign scores to the dive. This figure of experimental ontology combines, then, the infrastructural rarefaction of the platform as height with an alignment to edge experiences, alignment where habits of seeing, balancing, jumping and falling back to earth take shape.

7

Alignments and Earth

Earth systems models, and perhaps sciences more generally, excite experiments in making ensembles.

But rather than regarding earth as an experimental object, this chapter turns to earth systems models as experimental practices in constituting ensembles. It is less concerned with the epistemic features of the models in describing earth processes and more with how models re-configure relations in an ensemble. I work again here with the presentiment that ensembles have some different propensities to the operating system, machines, devices or to their pre-eminent contemporary arrangement as platforms.

Ensembles are interesting precisely because they lack the internal regulation of a machine, and they do not circulate in concretized detachment in the way certain technical elements may do. Ensembles differ from other technical configurations in that they constrain internal couplings, or mutual conditionings. But their composition as ensembles depends on a 'margin of indetermination' (Simondon 1989, 12).

For Simondon, the margin of indetermination plays out in the 'inter-commutativity' of the ensemble not in its emergence with an associated milieu/background/middle (1989, 73).

Earth and science and technology studies

What does science and technology studies (STS) actually say about the world and what it is made up of? Increasingly, recent STS speaks directly of earth, its places, surfaces, flows and histories. And while this work might seem to lie at some remove from the data centres, terminals, hash functions, graphics processing or functional closures of app programming, platforms are affected by it. What would it be to take the earth into account in the study of platforms? An STS formulation conducive to earth as ensemble can be found in Donna Haraway's Terrapolis equation. The equation for Terrapolis presented in *Staying with the Trouble: Making Kin in the Chthulucene* is typically inventive in its envisioning of an integrated manifold of earth and its polities:

$$[X]n = \int\int\int\int \ldots \int\int \text{Terra}(X1, X2, X3, X4, \ldots, Xn, t)\, dX1\, dX2\, dX3\, dX4 \ldots dXn\, dt = \text{Terrapolis}$$

$\alpha X1 = \text{stuff/physis}$, $X2 = \text{capacity}$, $X3 = \text{sociality}$, $X4 = \text{materiality}$, $Xn = \backslash\text{alpha}$ (alpha) = not zoë, but EcoEvoDevo's multispecies epigenesis; $\Omega \int \text{Terra}$

Ω (omega) = not bios, but recuperating terra's pluriverse; t = multi-scalar times, entangled times of past/present/yet-to-come, worlding times, not container time.

Terrapolis is a fictional integral equation, a speculative fabulation (Haraway 2016, 34) of how a manifold might provisionally hold together.

The Terrapolis integral equation is explicitly speculative and fictional. Speculative and fiction elements have been consistent elements of STS sensibilities, particularly as it blends into arts where speculation and fiction are less obviously impeded. Notions such as sociotechnical imaginary (Jasanoff 2015; McNeil et al 2016) highlight narratives in their collective performances and institutional stabilization. The integral equation, as Haraway goes on to describe, is a woven manifold of different times, materials, capacities, processes, across various timings. The equation expresses Terra or earth as a 'function' – see the brackets () – of changes (dX1, and so on) in *physis*, 'capacity', 'sociality', 'materiality', and so on with respect to the time(s) *t* of Terrapolis. This 'integrating' is full of twists and folds, and the convoluted volume that the integration, if it were fully computable, measures would be highly flexible. Each element of the volume – stuff, capacity, sociality, materiality – could be interacting with others.

What is the point of the integral equation for Terrapolis? It seems to lie a long way from the concepts, methods and analyses that people associate with social science and humanities scholarship. The sensibility here is definitely somewhat epistemic in the sense that integral equations in general express the potential for a calculation. Integral equations are one of the main forms in which the accumulated effects of changes over time(s) are brought together in propositions and calculations as part of sciences and engineering. To what other end could the Terrapolis integration be put?

The Terrapolis equation is one sign of the emerging sensibility in much STS work to planetary finitude, and its current trajectory through regimes of climate sensitivity and biodiversity collapse, and to the Anthropocene. Given its very long-standing interest in sciences, their knowledges and their practices, it would be strange if STS didn't interest itself in the contemporary scientific knowledges and engineerings of the earth. And yet, it is not easy to take a position in relation to such knowledges and practices. Anthropologists, geographers, sociologists and the environmental humanities all face versions of the problem of how to align themselves in relation to these knowledges.

Elizabeth Povinelli's *Geontologies* frames the problem of relation as one of implicit commonality: 'What if we asked not what epistemological differences have emerged over the years as the natural sciences and the critical sciences have separated and specialized, but what common frameworks, or *attitudes, anxieties, and desires*, toward the lively and the inert have been preserved across this separation and specialization?' (Povinelli 2016, 46, emphasis in original). Povinelli's focus on the shared framings and desires for/of lively/inert or living/non-living is critical, whereas in Terrapolis it is integrative. In Povinelli's account, common frameworks, or attitudes, anxieties and desires, are problematic because they maintain living/non-living differences. In Terrapolis, integration is speculative, but differentials are in relation over times. It also highlights something important about knowledge: differences in knowing, in how knowledge is crafted, found or maintained, can preserve commonalities.

Why would anyone want or need to locate something in common between say contemporary earth systems science and anthropology or sociology? Versions of it lie at the heart of at least a decade of STS-related work on climate, water, energy, environment, food and health. The question is not about earth as the place where social action occurs, or earth systems (flows of air, water, carbon, heat, life) as matters of concern. For the most part, this work doesn't care for devices or ensembles of devices. Both the 'vast machine' of observation/prediction described by Paul Edwards (2010) and the many pathways of practical action envisaged in contemporary climate change figure less than they should. The common framework is practically in front of our eyes: the devices, coordinated in ensembles, often configured as platforms.

I suggest the earth system models sensitise experimental ontology both to the incomplete coupling of the ensembles, and to ways of aligning the intercommutativity of ensembles in a common framework. What kind of thinking practice is integrative yet sensitive to differentials, including the differentiations of attitudes, anxieties, beliefs and desires? Inventiveness in relation to ensembles does not take the form of a highly refined technical object. As Judy Wajcman writes, 'inventiveness is not about the novelty of artifacts in themselves, but about the degree to which they are "aligned with inventive ways of thinking and doing and configuring and reconfiguring relations with other actors"' (Wajcman 2015, 180). If there is an altered sensitivity associated with earth system models, if they bring an altered sensitivity to how things hang together, it will not be the models themselves but their alignments that matter. These alignments will be technical, but technical in relation to how they arrange relations between elements of the earth ensemble. The technical problem of alignment is more like a process of tuning an instrument than putting things in rows.

The chapter, like those preceding, uses a single concept – alignment – as a connection and an approach to the ensemble problem from an earth-oriented direction. There is an ensemble-feeling at stake in relation to earth in recent STS work that can be provisionally conceptualized in terms of *alignment*. As in other chapters, I understand the concept in a pragmatist sense as an arrangement of relations in the mode of composition. Alignment as practised here is a cumulative effect like the nesting of elements in Haraway's Terrapolis equation, but one that, by contrast, eludes full integration. Alignment is also an approach sensitive to lines of force, like a diver's body about to break the surface of the water, or a compass needle to the earth's magnetic field, a field that itself drifts over time. The problem for any reading of a compass needle is to know how to adjust for the fact that the magnetic field diverges from 'true north' according to location. The concept of alignment thus implies a situated felt-coordination, or a feeling of agreement. This felt-coordination has also engaged, as we will see, STS work on earth and ecological politics. Finally, although alignment might suggest architectural or geometrical order, or everything neatly lined up, not all alignments are so straightforward.

Approximations as alignments

Many alignments are approximate. They approach a value, but only within certain limits and along certain lines. Whether in respect to its lack of integration, sensitivity to lines of force or approximations, the alignment problem for ensembles is how to coordinate elements so that they retain their capacity to respond to events.

Rather than grounding alignments in a speculative figure of integration, I experiment in deriving it from several earth system models made for approximation. Computable approximations of various aspects of Terrapolis are not hard to find, and they have been around for decades. These include the famous Lorenz attractor, a figure of 'sensitivity to initial conditions' in heated air flow (Lorenz 1963; Mackenzie 2004), Daisyworld, the computational parable for the living/non-living Gaiaean earth (Watson and Lovelock 1983) and FAIR 2.0., the Finitude Amplitude Impulse Response model, itself a simulation of ensembles of climate models known as CMIP6 (Eyring et al 2016; Leach et al 2021). These models are all notable for their admission of entities that are not easily accommodated in existing accounts of earth system processes: non-periodic solutions, hysteresis loops in temperature, simulations of simulations. They also scamper along on an ordinary laptop.

A first approximation to earth can be found in the Lorenz attractor, a model of atmospheric convention from the 1960s (Lorenz 1963). The Lorenz attractor is known for its non-periodic change over time, and its visual figuring of the 'butterfly effect' is famous also as a 'strange attractor'. Importantly, although the Lorenz attractor is primarily a model of air currents and heat, it is also an affirmation of approximation.

The second is `daisyworld`, a model from the 1980s that describes the feedback loops between the growth living things and average planetary temperature (Watson and Lovelock 1983). `Daisyworld` underpins James Lovelock and Lynn Margulis' work on the Gaia hypothesis. This model, less than a 100 lines in Python code, has many interacting processes just like Terrapolis and provides a way of mapping of earth as an ensemble of living and non-living processes. It includes living things, a sun, a dimensionless planet that heats up and cools down. Daisyworld is a model of the earth as an ensemble of living and non-living processes.

A third model is FAIR, or the Finite Amplitude Impulse Pulse Response model (Smith et al 2018; Leach et al 2021), a relatively small model that simulates the very large ensemble of models in use in contemporary climate science. It is a simplified climate model (an SCM) of the ensembles of climate models used in CMIP. The work of the Intergovernmental Panel on Climate Change (IPCC) uses what it calls an 'ensemble' of models in the Coupled Model Intercomparison Project (currently version CMIP6). Not all of the thousands of scientists, researchers and other people contributing to IPCC reports can run the ensembles of CMIP6 or its predecessors. To even run one of the models, let alone a whole ensemble, is expensive and time-consuming. Much work relies instead on models –SCM – to approximate the climate model ensembles. Of the many SCMs, the FAIR model has explicit ambitions to make sense to, and be used by many people, not just the IPCC contributors.

Lorenz attractor devices and changing alignments

If integral equations aim to summarise accumulated effects of interacting processes over time, alignment tracks how forces, tunings and orientation can move in specific directions. The first model, the Lorenz attractor, is an approximation to the Terrapolis fabulation, but an approximation that lacks full integration. Its key feature is the attractor, a form of non-periodic change that still has cycles (see Figure 7.1).

A device concerning earth as a fluid, atmospheric entity, the Lorenz attractor dates from the mid-1960s. The Lorenz attractor, perhaps the most famous of all attractors, was initially developed as a model to help understand the movements of air in an atmospheric layer heated from above and cooled from below. It is a model of a layer of air, heated from above, cooled from below, with flows horizontally and vertically. The attractor follows the changing states – the rates of convection and the temperature variations – by tracking changes as paths in the space of vertical and horizontal movement and temperature. The attractor as plotted in Figure 7.1 is a folded space of transformation. In the attractor, many different paths pass close by each through some densely trafficked crossings.

Figure 7.1: Lorenz attractor

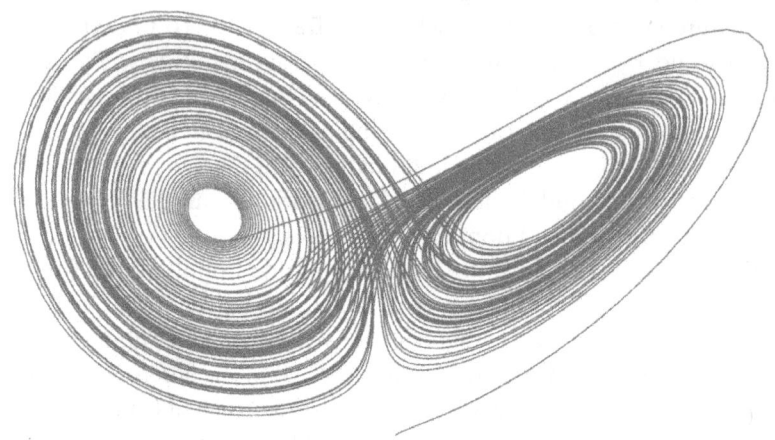

During the 'complexity turn' of the 1990s–2000s, there was so much discussion of the edge-of-chaos and self-organizing behaviour. The interest of attractors was multiple, but their propensity to diverge over term was central:

> The interesting of property of such attractors is that, if the system is released from two points on the attractor which are arbitrarily close to each other, the subsequence trajectories remain on the attractor surface but diverge away from each other. After a sufficient time flowing on the attractor, the two trajectories can be arbitrarily far apart on it. (Kauffman 1993, 178)

A second feature is their low-dimensionality:

> [T]hey may be of very low dimensionality even in a high-dimensional state space. Thus a system may have 100 variables, but flow may be restricted to a strange attractor of two dimensions, a folded surface closing back on itself in that 100-dimensional space. From the point of view of the entire state space, the attractor is a very small object indeed. (Kauffman 1993, 178)

As Isabelle Stengers observes, attractors are not a generalizable model, despite the hopes of complexity-based theory and complexity science:

> '[S]trange attractors' are not a model, but rather a question mark, or an alarm bell. They signal that the difficulty of an operation of passage may not be due to a lack of knowledge, an incomplete formulation of the problem, or the enormous complication of the phenomenon, but may reside in intrinsic reasons that no foreseeable progress could gainsay. (Stengers 2011, 8–9)

Attractors have, however, re-surfaced in recent STS work focus on climate and ecological politics. In some writing done just before COVID-19 and after, Bruno Latour presented something related to Haraway's Terrapolis integral equation, but in the form of attractors. In *Down to Earth*, Latour suggests that 'we are no longer dealing with small fluctuations in the climate, but rather with an upheaval that is mobilizing the earth system itself' (Latour 2018, 43). Across his various responses to the mobilized earth system, there is consistent emphasis on the technical/artificial paths back to ground and soil/earth: 'there is nothing more innovative, nothing more present, subtle, technical and artificial (in the positive sense of the words), nothing less rustic and rural, nothing more creative, nothing more contemporary than to negotiate landing on some ground' (Latour 2018, 53).

The attractor in Latour's usage figures the collective trajectories revolving through locality and globality, between going off-planet or off-world (as many of the platform elite aim to) and attaching to a dwelling place that entangles local and global. In some respects, the Lorenz attractor is off-ground, or in orbit. It is part of the separation from earthly things in their contingent ensembles. But the attractor adds a few important things: forcings, contingencies of approximation and something non-periodic. As Edward Lorenz writes, 'non-periodic solutions cannot be obtained except by numerical procedures' (Lorenz 1963, 130).

The Lorenz attractor was only widely discussed in chaos and complexity science literature from the 1980s onwards. In its approximately 28,000 citations, the model is hardly ever treated as a model of the atmosphere. Its reference to wind, clouds, moisture, heat and temperatures was largely lost in its separation from both weather and in some ways from the computation it depended on.

```
import numpy as np
import matplotlib.pyplot as plt

# Define the Lorenz system of differential equations
def lorenz(x, y, z, sigma, rho, beta):
    dxdt = sigma * (y - x)
    dydt = x * (rho - z) - y
    dzdt = x * y - beta * z
    return dxdt, dydt, dzdt

# Parameters
sigma = 10.0
rho = 28.0
beta = 8.0 / 3.0
```

```python
# Initial conditions
x0, y0, z0 = 1.0, 0.0, 0.0

# Time parameters
dt = 0.01 # Time step
num_steps = 10000 # Number of time steps

# Initialize arrays to store the trajectory
x_traj, y_traj, z_traj = [x0], [y0], [z0]

# Numerical integration using Euler's method
for _ in range(num_steps):
    dx, dy, dz = lorenz(x_traj[-1], y_traj[-1], z_traj[-1],
        sigma, rho, beta)
    x_new = x_traj[-1] + dx * dt
    y_new = y_traj[-1] + dy * dt
    z_new = z_traj[-1] + dz * dt
    x_traj.append(x_new)
    y_traj.append(y_new)
    z_traj.append(z_new)

# Create a 3D plot of the Lorenz attractor
fig = plt.figure()
ax = fig.gca(projection='3d')
ax.plot(x_traj, y_traj, z_traj, lw=0.5)
ax.set_xlabel('X')
ax.set_ylabel('Y')
ax.set_zlabel('Z')
ax.set_title('Lorenz Attractor')

plt.show()
```

Like the variables of Terrapolis, the spatial dimensions of the attractor figure are not those of Euclidean geometry. They are physical quantities such as temperature (x), and movements in horizontal and vertical directions (y, z). The changes in these quantities is interconnected in the Lorenz attractor equations. The mean planetary temperature, the changes in rates of movement and temperatures in the Lorenz attractor are entwined with each other. For instance, the vertical variations in temperature depend on the rates of convection multiplied by the horizontal convection (wind), dampened by the vertical movement taking place. The `lorenz` function in the Python code shown here is a set of equations that connects the changes in temperature, horizontal and vertical movement. The lines of code that integrate these changes over time can only provisionally hold the changes together by stepping through time, measuring moment by moment how they affect each other.

> The changes in movement and temperature are strongly affected by the values of the three constants σ, ρ and β. The constants σ, ρ and β are system parameters proportional to the Prandtl number, Rayleigh number and certain physical properties of the atmospheric layer itself. For the atmosphere, the Prandtl number gives a dimensionless sense of thermal conductivity or how heat moves. The Rayleigh number relates buoyancy and viscosity to each other in different flow regimes (for example, laminar flow or turbulent flow).

Can an alternative description of the Lorenz attractor re-specify it as a ground-aligning device in an earth ensemble? The attractor is animated by a set of forces, or forcings, that enliven the earth as a fluid, atmospheric entity. Forcings entail energy differences, and they heat or cool the earth. The difference between incoming and outgoing energy, or the forcings, move air and heat. Atmospheric convection and temperature rise are also forced by heterogeneous technical ensembles. A Lorenz attractor for the earth understood as layers of air heated from above would need to include the forcings associated with the arrangements of those ensembles.

We might position platforms along the movements or paths through the central basin of the attractor, the place where most trajectories move from time to time.

Perhaps the defining movement in attractors is their non-periodicity. Although trajectories are more or less aligned to the attractors, they are not periodic. In the vicinity of the platform attractor, social groups, interests, situations, traditions or habits are drawn towards common paths or configurations. Points starting close to each other on the edges of the attractor can end up widely separated from each other. A technical problem can become social, or vice versa. The mixing in the platform attractor (see the 'zone of heterogeneous assembly' in Figure 7.2) is such that once seemingly separated spheres (for example, state/market/civil society, abstract/concrete or social/technical) can end up in viscous flow. Along these paths, a Lorenz platform attractor registers some of the convection flows that make it possible for devices to run without overheating.

A dimensionless but lively world

A second model, `daisyworld`, adds to the heat-driven dynamics of the Lorenz attractor something new: living things. No longer conceived as fluid flow, the earth resolves into an almost dimensionless plane of living and non-living processes. This model is a tricky entity: almost dimensionless in its abstract formulation, it does couple heat and life. Declared to be a fable by its authors, it is a kind of fabulation, even a speculative fabulation in Haraway's sense. But the fabulation connects solar radiation, the temperature

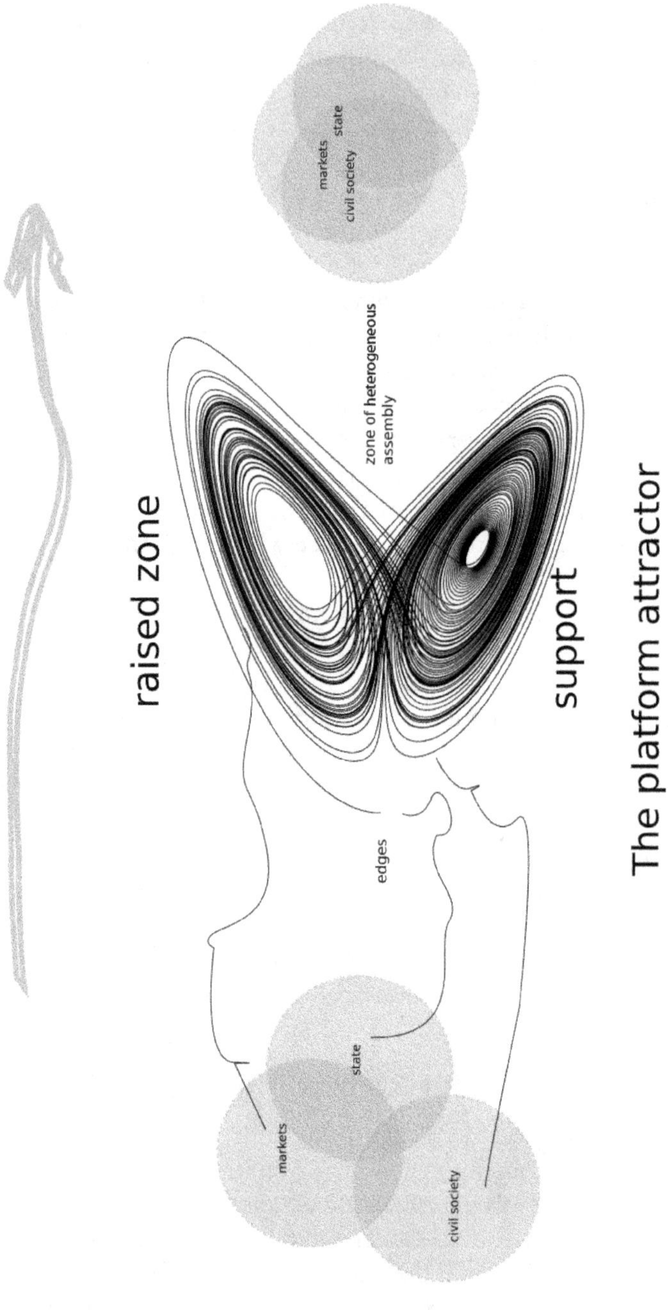

1000 PLATFORMS

Figure 7.2: Lorenz platform attractor

of the earth and the growth of plants. More specifically, it loosely binds solar radiation, planetary temperature and plant growth, in the interests of sensitizing people to their interactions.

How does it do this? A lead on this question comes from the introductory chapters of earth systems textbooks (Kump et al 2010; Lenton and Watson 2011). They often discuss the planetary model 'Daisyworld' developed by Andrew Watson and James Lovelock during the 1980s (Lovelock and Watson 1982; Watson and Lovelock 1983). Daisyworld is a 40 year-old simulation of planetary mean temperature and its changes. When implemented in code, the model becomes a compact device comprising several dozen lines of code at its core. Through steps, functions and loops, the code 'runs' a set of equations. Many implementations and demonstrations of the model can be found online today (von Bloh 2006; Wilensky 2006). Dozens more are to be found on the GitHub code platform (Park 2021), and incorporate a range of species, diseases and other dynamics. Like Donna Haraway's integral equations for Terrapolis, Daisyworld, I would suggest, nests different processes within each other.

An 'implementation' of Daisyworld is shown in Figure 7.3. As distinct from the six mathematical equations of Daisyworld, `daisyworld.py` is 160 lines of Python code (Python Software Foundation 2023). (Hereafter the typographic convention for such

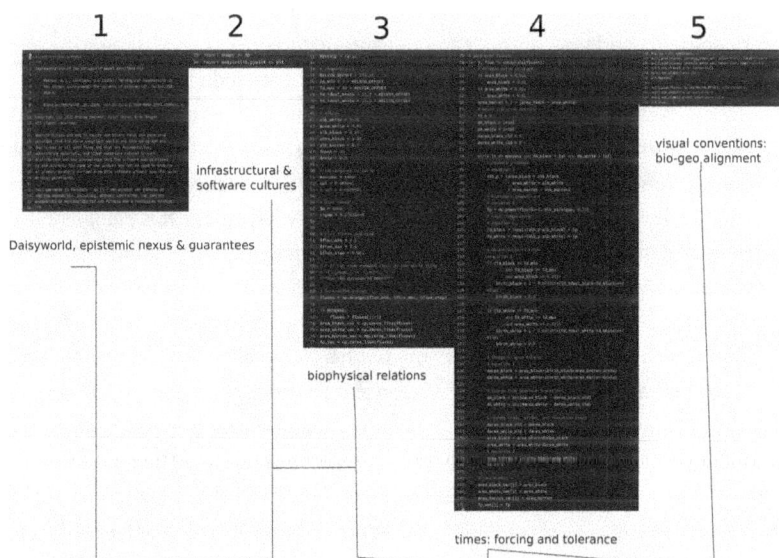

Figure 7.3: daisyworld.py code

devices is monospace.) What can be read in the Python code? It can be split into five sections:

1. The first section (lines 1–8) holds bibliography, author, copyright and warranty information. This material links the code to Daisyworld, Lovelock and Gaia, to the epistemic cultures of earth system science and its norms of verification via citation. The warranty text, by contrast, designates the code as a device or a technology, by denying any guarantee of 'fitness for a particular purpose'.
2. A brief second section (lines 29–30) 'imports' software libraries commonly used in scientific and data science computing. The first, numpy, the 'fundamental package for scientific computing with Python' (Numpy 2023), brings mathematical constructs such as arrays and vectors, constructs which are not only 'de-facto standards of array computing' but direct exemplars of the coordinate spatiality of much modern scientific knowledge (Whitehead 1925). Similarly, matplotlib (Matplotlib 2023) is the most commonly used Python software library for displaying visualizations hints at 'maths' and 'plots', or the drawing of lines and axes. These two lines 'import' a computational ordering of collections of numbers in arrays, and a visual culture of scientific data visualization in which collections of numbers are rendered as points on a coordinate plane. Immediately, through these imports, daisyworld.py avails itself of a highly developed set of conventions for arranging and transforming numbers.
3. The third section (lines 34–78) defines physical and biological constants, data structures to hold results of calculations and some numbers that relate to conventions for iterative processing of calculations. These constants derive from experimental and theoretical physics, and population ecology, that is, to non-living and living things, as well as to some mathematical conventions concerning approximations or ways of approaching limits. These constants, with their mixing of living and non-living, abstract and concrete, attach daisyworld.py to histories of several sciences, with their sometimes disparate renderings of what exists.
4. A fourth section (lines 79–147) codes the steps the device takes in simulating the Daisyworld model of a planet. The implementation of the model, as is often the case, takes the form of nested loops, or sets of calculations that are repeated until some condition is met. This is the core of the device in several senses. It is typographically the most dense part of the code, it is computationally the part that takes the most time to run, it is where biology and thermodynamics and geophysics mingle, and it generates many numbers. The looping here is the critical zone of the device, and possibly the zone most closely concerned with felt-virtuality. While the six equations set out in the Daisyworld model (Watson and Lovelock 1983; Lenton and Lovelock 2001) are abstractly connected by instantaneous continuous flows, daisyworld.py as a device arrays a series of numbers that approximate that fluid continuity by re-writing numbers in register operations and memory chips. Climate sensitivity is sensed by cutting the continuous variations of temperature, plant growth-rates, and planetary albedo in the compressed time of computational approximation.

5. The final section (lines 148–158) visualizes the data produced during the loops as two simple line graphs, reproducing the relatively simple plots of the original publication (Watson and Lovelock 1983). Like the `import` statements, the visual devices invoke habits and conventions that stabilize visible forms of order in institutionally recognized forms.

In its arrangement of citation, copyright, warranty, computational data structures, numbers that point to something in the world, a set of steps to generate new numbers, and figures that visualize collections of numbers as lines, `daisyworld.py` is not a purely epistemic thing (Rheinberger 1997; Mody and Lynch 2010).

The title of the 1983 article referenced in the first section of the code – 'Biological Homeostasis of the Global Environment: The Parable of Daisyworld' (Watson and Lovelock 1983) – points to this directly: it is a *parable* of the propositions in Lovelock's widely read book *Gaia: A New Look at Life on Earth* (Lovelock 1979), a book that presented the Gaia theory co-developed with biologist Lynn Margulis.

Prior to, or just at the cusp of, emerging scientific evidence of greenhouse gas-related climate warming, the model connects the population dynamics of vegetation, and in fact, a modelling of the distribution of organisms based on epidemiological models of infection (Carter and Prince 1981), to a calculation of planetary mean temperature. Daisyworld continued to change. Lovelock and earth system scientist Timothy Lenton re-visited the model in the early 2000s, responding to criticisms and testing the model against subsequent earth science (Lenton and Lovelock 2001).

Almost two decades later, Lenton, now writing with Bruno Latour, returns to the model in an article entitled 'Extending the Domain of Freedom or Why Gaia is Hard to Understand' (Latour and Lenton 2019). The article, published in *Nature*, stresses the 'lack of unity' in Gaia: 'The best way to understand this lack of unity is to consider that Gaia is a heterarchy with variations in the strength of coupling between the living and nonliving across spatial and temporal scales and across different features (nutrient cycling, climate)' (Latour and Lenton 2019, 672). A regulated disunity is perhaps interesting because unities – individuals, species, populations, groups, structures, systems – have pervasively operated to marginalize or externalize living/non-living heterarchies varying across scales and 'features'. The model connects population ecology and geophysics to support the contention that living things regulate planetary energy fluxes. Such calculations of a regulated disunity are, in present-day climate politics, freighted with significance.

Like the Lorenz attractor, `daisyworld` generates interactions in the planetary ensembles by translating the instantaneous changes of growth, heat, reflection and absorption into something that can be approximated by loops of code doing repeatedly updated calculations. One loop gradually increases the values of the solar forcing, while another loop inside that calculates the growth rates of daisies and their effects on the absorption of radiation and moderation of the effective planetary temperature. Very much a miniature and toylike version of contemporary earth system models, the approximations combine a steplike forcing of climate collapse with a convergence-based search for values that satisfy within an arbitrary numerical limit the equations coupling plant growth and temperature. Alignment in `daisyworld.py` practically takes the form of a search for values that fall within limits given by the approximation.

Impulse responses and experimental ontological alignments

The third device, FAIR 2.0, is a model of the ensemble of climate models used in recent IPCC reports. If the Lorenz attractor is a figure for heat-driven flows, and Daisyworld is a figure for regulated disunity of living/non-living Gaia, FAIR 2.0 is an approximation aligned to the increasing sensitivity of climate.

The model simulates the ensemble of models used in contemporary climate science. It departs from the recent report of Working Group 1 (WG1) to the IPCC, Sixth Assessment Report (AR6), entitled 'Climate Change 2021: The Physical Science Basis' (Masson-Delmotte et al 2021). Based on modelling conducted by the Coupled Model Intercomparison Project (CMIP6) (Eyring et al 2016), the IPCC 'Climate Change 2021' report documents changes in earth climate, a several kilometer thick interval ranging from ocean depths to stratosphere in which solar radiation, atmospheric and ocean temperatures, land and ice-cover, flows of water and air, mix. A main finding in the report is increasing sensitivity or responsiveness of the climate system to change. There is now, the report states at the outset, 'higher average climate sensitivity' (Masson-Delmotte et al 2021, 15). 'Climate sensitivity' refers to a standard measure of how the earth's surface temperature changes under the influence of various 'forcings': changing concentrations of greenhouse and other gases or airborne particulars, changes in land use, variations in solar radiation and other alterations in earth system processes ranging from ocean acidification, loss of ice-cover to reafforestation. 'Higher average climate sensitivity' refers to the contrast between combined predictions of the models in CMIP6 and models in previous CMIP iterations running back to 1996.

The simulations of earth climate in the earth system models of CMIP6 run on nation-state-funded supercomputers. They are expensive and slow to run very often, and this limits researchers' ability to experiment with different climate scenarios. The scientific knowledge infrastructure for CMIP6 is the Earth System Grid Federation (Earth System Documentation 2022). The Earth System Grid Federation is a collaboration that develops, deploys and maintains software infrastructure for the management, dissemination and analysis of model output and observational data. The Earth System Grid has all the usual platform configurations – databases, webpages, GitHub repositories, data science-style interactive notebooks. The tutorials, and so on, on GitHub as usual, make all these things seem doable. These elements, and many others, have been developed with the alignment problem in mind.

The complexity of the CMIP ensembles of models has been recognized by the IPCC modellers for some time. Writing in 2013, scientists participating in the CMIP envisaged building a simplified simulation of the full earth system models: 'The purpose of this study is to compute the response in atmospheric CO2, in ocean and land carbon, global mean surface air temperature, ocean heat uptake and sea level change to a pulse-like (i.e., instantaneous) emission of CO2 into the atmosphere' (Joos et al 2013, 2794). This simplified climate model would treat the full ensemble of earth system models as itself a vast signal processing system whose responses to changing pulses of energy or CO_2 need to be understood.

Responding to pulses

The title 'finite amplitude impulse response' conveys a conception of the earth system as a signal process that responds in highly specific ways to an input (the impulse). Derived from signal processing engineering, the impulse response model captures how a system integrates an input signal over time. The convolution integral effectively multiplies and integrates the input signal x(t) with a time-reversed and shifted version of the impulse response h(t). As a result, convolution captures how the system responds like the water in a pool after a diver enters. The speculative fabulation here is that the earth systems – atmospheric circulation, ocean currents, carbon cycles associated with living and non-living things, natural events, and so on – can be understood as signal processing system receiving a signal – the impulse – taking the form of a 100 Gigatonne pulse of carbon dioxide.

Almost exactly like the two earlier models, FAIR centres on a small set of equations: 'In FaIRv2.0.0 we propose a set of six equations that we demonstrate are sufficient to capture the global mean climate system response to GHG and aerosol emissions' (Leach et al 2021, 3008). The earth system, in this view, couples flows of carbon, heat and water to produce different surface temperatures and sea-level change. But these couplings, while increasingly scrutinized by various earth sciences such as atmospheric physics, earth systems, oceanography or ecology, interact with each other in the earth ensemble in very complicated ways. The task of a SCM is to find ways of exploring these couplings given the constraints of data such as the Argo Float 5903676 ocean temperatures and given the outputs of the wide-ranging runs of the CMIP models.

The impulse response function (IRF) approach taken by scientists in the IPCC Assessment Report 5 (AR5) is instructive in its simplicity. The IRF envisages an infinite amplitude and instantaneous signal entering a system (for example, a loudspeaker, an ultrasound sensor, a broadband modem, a concert hall, a national economy, and so on) and a longer vibrational dynamic as the system absorbs and resonates to the impulse.

The resonances and vibrations occurring with the system may damp down quickly or continue to reverberate, as in some concert halls.

> IRFx(t) is the impulse response function (IRF) ... IRFx represents the time-dependent abundance of gas x caused by the additional emission of one kg of gas x at time 0. In other words, the IRFx(t) is the fraction of the enhancement in concentration due to the added emission pulse remaining in the atmosphere at time t. (Joos et al 2013, 2795)

Like Haraway's Terrapolis integral, the IRF varies over time. The concentration of gases such as carbon dioxide and methane, or various aerosols, play a critical role in determining the average temperature.

What, according to the impulse-response models of the earth ensemble, happens when 100 gigatonnes CO_2 enter the atmosphere? As the authors of the initial version of the more recent FAIR model put it:

> Following a CO2 pulse emission of 100 GtC in present-day climate conditions, ESMs [earth system models] (and Earth system models of intermediate complexity – EMICs) display a rapid drawdown of CO2 with the concentration anomaly reduced by approximately 40% from peak after 20 years and by 60% after 100 years, followed by a much slower decay of concentrations which leaves approximately 25 % of peak concentration anomaly remaining after 1000 years (Joos et al., 2013). The speed and shape of this decay is dependent on both the background climate state and the size of the pulse, but a substantial fraction of the emission is simulated to remain in the atmosphere after 1000 years in all cases. (Millar et al 2017, 721)

Like the Lorenz attractor, FAIR focuses on thermal responses. Like **daisyworld**, it couples living and non-living processes. If the Lorenz attractor and **daisyworld** highlight the sensitivity of temperatures to air movements and the growth of living things, the impulse-response models acknowledge the sensitivity of temperatures to technical ensembles in their complexities. In preparing an earlier IPCC assessment report (AR5), scientists had proposed impulse response models as a means of approximating the prediction of the full earth system models. Millar and co-authors extend the impulse-response model to span significantly different social-economic pathways:

> We therefore propose a simple extension of the standard IPCC AR5 impulse-response model, coupling the carbon cycle to the thermal response and to cumulative carbon uptake by terrestrial and marine sinks in order to reproduce the behaviour of the ESMs [earth systems models] under a variety of idealised experiments and future emission scenarios. (Millar et al 2017, 7214)

What the FAIR authors call 'emission scenarios' covers much of the ensemble complexities. They acknowledge this heterogeneous and potentially very lively reactivity in the model itself:

> FAIR is useful for creating large ensembles of future temperature change based on input uncertainties in the carbon cycle parameters and effective radiative forcing strengths. This can be used for instance to assess the impacts of emissions commitment scenarios or committed warming ... or if a certain category of emissions such as aerosols are increased or decreased in the future. FAIR can be used with integrated assessment models to calculate the social cost of carbon in the presence of non-CO2 forcing agents. (Smith et al 2018, 2293)

'Large ensembles of future temperature change' points to this heterogeneity and its complex distribution in experiences of places. FAIR anticipates times lags and feedback loops that impede simple changes in direction: 'commitment scenarios or committed warming'. Like Terrapolis, FAIR envisages the presence of many forms of agencies or sub-ensembles in the forms of 'non-CO2 forcing agents'.

Large ensembles of future change

Like the Lorenz attractor and `daisyworld`, FAIR is sensitive to both initial conditions and the computational approximation to their development. Like them, it has various physical and geophysical measurements scattered through it: ocean heat capacity, the mass of the earth's atmosphere, and so on. Unlike them, it is configured around scenarios chosen by the IPCC to represent a range of near-future developments. The many lines in the plots (see Figures 7.4 and 7.5) show possible global average temperature changes given different scenarios.

The scenarios – SSPs or Shared Socioeconomic Pathways – present in FAIR, and widely in IPCC AR6, are stories about the earth. The SSP database at the International Institute for Applied Systems Analysis explicitly

Figure 7.4: FAIR 2.0 projections of temperature under scenario SSP119

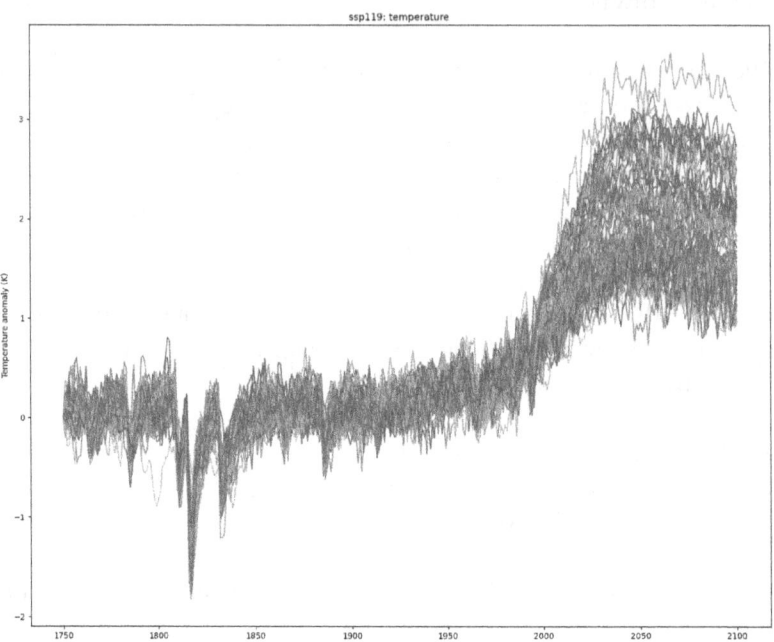

describes them as stories: 'The narratives describe the main characteristics of the SSP future development pathways. They served as the starting point for the identification of internally consistent assumptions for the quantification of SSP elements' (IIASA 2018). These narratives have been extensively described and analysed in scientific literature on environmental change and climate change. The five representative SSPs chosen for the IPCC's CMIP6 range from the 'green road' SSP1 to fossil fuel intensive SSP5 (O'Neill et al 2017), with scenarios in-between mixing sustainability and growing inequality, global fragmentation or regional conflict.

In the light of these narratives, Haraway's speculative fabulation of an integral equation for urbanized earth or Terrapolis is not so far from current best practice. The SSPs, even just the representative ones – SSP119, SSP245, SSP370, SSP460 and SSP585 – chosen for IPC AR6, present a complicated scene, a scene in which many participants ranging from economic institutions (Organisation for Economic Co-operation and Development) through to scientific institutions (US National Ocean and Atmospheric Administration) appear.

We follow the statistically rigorous methodology of Cummins et al (2020) to tune thermal response parameters to 28 CMIP6 models. This

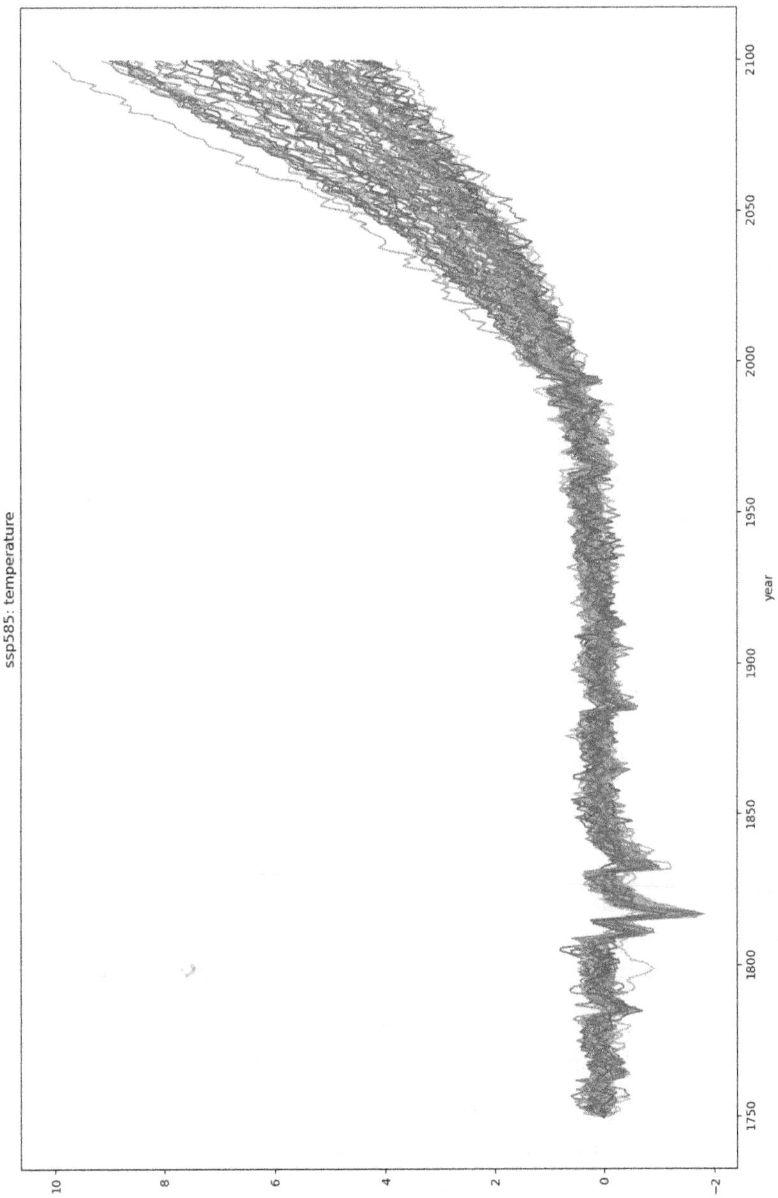

Figure 7.5: FAIR 2.0 projections of temperature under scenario SSP585

involves fitting parameters to the energy balance model outlined in Eq. (9) by recursively computing the likelihood via a Kalman filter; the optimal parameters are those that maximize the computed likelihood. We then transform the optimal energy balance parameters into the impulse response form used in FAIRv2.0.0. (Leach et al 2021, 3016)

The 'optimal parameters' are estimated by fitting the FAIRv2 model to the outputs of several dozen earth system models.

In FAIRv2, the 'energy balance model' is a vertically stacked set of energy boxes representing deep ocean, ocean and atmosphere.

> The ability to tune FaIRv2.0.0 to more complex models ... also allows for estimation of complex model response to a particular scenario or experiment without having to expend computer power to run the model itself, which could allow climate system uncertainties to be introduced more fully into integrated assessment studies by emulating the full CMIP6 ensemble ... with a simpler model. (Leach et al 2021, 3028)

FAIRv2 can be tuned to emulate many other earth system models. The Python notebooks and R scripts that tune FAIRv2 to the various earth system models (Leach and Smith 2021) and the model tuning techniques they rely on (Cummins et al 2020) are central elements in approximating earth ensemble sensitivity to change. This tuning goes beyond that of the Lorenz attractor and `daisyworld` in that it explicitly recognizes the proliferation of models as the problem to be addressed.

Conclusion

The three models – Lorenz attractor, `daisyworld` and FAIR 2.0 – of earth processes each have their own sensitivities to earth processes. They are each experiments in aligning to the ensembles. Each alignment, whether along attractors, through the feedback loops, or through tuning to an ensemble of other models, inclines towards a different way of approaching earth as an ensemble.

In his account of William James' account of stories in things, Didier Debaise insists that for James 'things of the earth' consist of stories:

> What happens when we move from the stories about things, which is essentially the narrative that humans project onto silent things, supposedly unaware of them, to the stories within the things? What narratives do these beings tell that form so many singular perspectives on the world and on other existences? (Debaise and Stengers 2022, 113)

Each of the earth system models considered in this chapter either from the outset or subsequently accrued some world-making sensitivities and potentials, some capacity to dramatize events from a start to a finish. Whatever dynamics, potential or sensitivity they might display have been practically made in numerical solutions, approximation through convergence, or attunement by impulse response.

Their modes of integration of the nonhuman and human are increasingly non-periodic, plural and contingent. The temporalities of the Terrapolis/earth ensemble are increasingly turbulent, ranging from the sensitivity to initial conditions of the Lorenz attractor through the contingent living hysteresis of `daisyworld` through to the avalanching climate changes in FAIR 2.0 reverberating like a hand-clap in a concert hall. I have suggested that three facets of alignment – lack of integration; sense of agreement; alignment as approximation/getting closer – run through the models.

The early 1960s model of atmospheric convection decades later becomes a resonant, popular figure of complexity science and re-surfaces in STS attractor theory because its non-periodic solution offers ways of pluralizing times and generating indetermination amidst situations that seem driven by political, economic or technical forcings. Daisyworld exists as a 'parable', or a moral story animating Gaia theory. FAIR 2.0 gets its name in part from the problem of equity in access to the nation-state supercomputers that run the earth system models of CMIP6.

Alignment might be understood as a practice in experimental ontology. Approaching ensembles in terms of alignments is perhaps a way of doing experimental ontology under non-convergent conditions. Experimental ontology fixes on the difficulty of moving from the analysis of ontological variability, or the many ways in which things make worlds differently, to analysis of how politics and democracy themselves are constituted through and with things in their variability. In order to do that, it re-positions ontology itself as a practice involving all actors, human and nonhuman.

8

Implications

This book anticipates re-grounded worlds in which platforms have become less consolidated as speaking positions, less encroaching along their edges and more seamful in their composition. In their gathering and alignments of devices, numberings, sensings, and closures or captures, platforms pre-figure what they are but cannot affirm: ensembles and their vibratory sensings.

There is something at once deeply theoretically and empirically disconcerting about re-working platforms as ensembles.

On the one hand, the ensemble concept developed in this book can draw on some fairly strong philosophical support. A high-level support comes from Gilles Deleuze's account of Ideas in *Difference and Repetition* (Deleuze 2001). Ideas are ensembles. Ensembles gather 'differential relations and singular points', they 'begin with the inessential', and their 'essences' are constructed 'in the form of centres of envelopment around singularities' (Deleuze 2001, 264). Ideas in this sense gather presentiments of divergences, approximations, and movements of ground and earth found in ensembles. Some instances of singularities or inessential points found in the platform world are terminals, chips, hashing, instruction sets, plugs, and floating point arithmetic. As starting points, they promise little, but much unfolds from them.

On the other hand, anticipating something by doing experimental ontology, and experimenting with such inessential and localized points of departure, seems to avoid central problems and controversies that affect all of us, and that many people suffer from greatly. Many of these difficulties concern the problem of belonging to collectives assembled in collecting.

Under ensemble conditions and bearing in mind the trouble that platforms bring, what is conducive to experimental ontology?

1. Choose places or locate yourself so as to take part in vibrations or movements somewhere along the edge of an ensemble. Vibrational attachments have a particular affective directness. Heading from edge to centre, from lower to higher, vibrational attachments carry their connections with them.

2. Devise methods that have something slightly unstable or a minor transcendence in them. This minor transcendence might be in the form of levels of technicality, detail, performance or scale. Whatever form, methods should in some way stage words, numbers, code, sounds or images together. Ensembles are plays with actors and audiences.
3. Affirm ambivalent attachments to knowledge and power instead of judging truth or falsehood.

Ensembles as vibrational forms

The banded-iron Brockman Formation boulder, the coastal rock platform, a stage platform, the diving platform, the Venetian funerary monument, or a Euclidean proof: how do these rather scattered figures stack up in a post-platform world? In each case and along different lines, inert, stable, flattened, re-configurable support surfaces stand above surrounding ground or water. But in each case, vibrational movements and flows run just beneath the surface, or along the edges, or through the variations and striated levels. Their stories, fragmented, marginal and problematic as they may be, can be points of attachment.

Attachments are not just fastenings or files packaged with emails. They ground psycho-social formations. While 'it is very difficult', notes Deleuze, 'to say why one becomes attached to a particular problem' (Deleuze and Guattari 1994, 12), my forms of attachment to things or situations are explicitly technical. Technical attachments loom large, even in the ensemble of vibrational attachments.

I have, as a result, made efforts to start from technical ensembles, and particularly Gilbert Simondon's account of technical ensembles as an experimental starting point. I imagine Simondon's mid-20th-century audiometry laboratory somewhere in France, equipped with consoles of resonating oscillators and amplifiers, sounding like an early Karlheinz Stockhausen composition such as *Kurzwellen*. It is a striking scene partly because of the biopolitical resonances of psychoacoustic research and partly because the careful isolation, tuning and measuring of oscillations and signals precedes the many recent platform-oriented transformations of sound devices.

Devices and their devisings are less ambivalent figures than platforms. Platforms are nothing but device-specific ensembles. The preceding chapters are filled with them: laboratory balances, low-temperature experiments, single crystals, single chip computers, graphics processing units (GPUs), keyboards, planks, hash functions, ocean buoys, cash registers, antennae, terminals, plugs, tables, boards, libraries in several senses of that term, buildings, and the list goes on.

There is some merit in paying close attention to the way in which developers and software engineers talk about the device-ensembles as an antidote to grand-unifying theories of platform or algorithm. What they say is often much more grounded than the highly polished perorations of platform CEOs on the next disruption or emergence. In the eyes of their CEOs, platforms appear as grand canonical ensembles. In the habits and dispositions of developers, the ensembles have a less homogeneous composition. Their dynamics include embeddings and closures running through devices. The ensemble changes through exchanges, borrowings, and overflows.

The GPU devices, for instance, have varied in ways that attaches sciences, infrastructures, media and money to the shader as a program element. The spread of GPUs depends on habits of coding and terminal work, not to mention the vast architectures of the chip fabs in Taipei and Seoul, or the intricate board assembly work needed to connect advanced microelectronic devices to each other. The intricate configuration work, the many exchanges and borrowings back and forth, the many alignments and closures needed to stabilize an ensemble sometimes surface in collective life. The great GPU shortage of the early COVID-19 years was one such occasion. While the intricacy of configuration work largely goes to ground in contemporary collectives, devices in their embeddings and alignments make platforms possible.

Devices and indeterminacies

Devices are better to think with than platforms because they are more nuanced, proximate and grounded. The verb 'devising' conveys some of this indeterminacy. The analogous verb 'platforming' (the term used in petrochemical refining) does not. In devising, devices more readily slip into ensemble setups. Like musical instruments, they sound very different depending on how they are played and placed. Devices move along integral paths laid out by earth and sky potentials.

MOSFETs (metallic oxide semiconductor field effect transistors), the most common device humans have ever made (around 10^{22} in 2018), fuse silicon, silicon dioxide, metallic oxide layers together through epitaxial crystallization on highly doped polycrystalline silicon to build the crucial junction zones where currents flow differently. Is the MOSFET operation, its zones, its statistical concentrations of donors and depletions, its thresholds and levels, already an ensemble? Their configuration to store charge as a sign of state, to sense or emit light or other electromagnetic radiation, to amplify, filter or switch signals lie much closer to the vibrational attachments to place than the platform formations. It is almost as if the banded-energy materiality of a solid-state is better protection against generalization/platformization than the social organization of the platforms.

What does experimental ontology with devices in view of platform pluralities entail? Devices, as science and technology studies (STS) work has long argued, freeze or slow down transformations. Their 'slight transcendencies', as Latour (2013, 216) termed them, stem from the zigzags and detours they bring. Despite the many shortcuts and accelerations to which they habituate us, devices also slow down or entangle movement in labyrinthine dependencies and repetitions.

For better or worse, all experimental ontology is devised/deviced and the problem is really how to practically sensitize to the chronic dependencies. Tuning to the oscillations, modulating, filtering and combining in practice entails thinking with devices. It is a performance that requires staging, configuration, rehearsal and a panoply of habits, good and bad.

Experimental ontology with devices in ensembles?

The platformate imaginary emerging over the last two decades is beginning to exhaust itself. AI convolutes the platformate imaginary, and precipitates renewed investment in capturing social relationality but seemingly without the liveliness of the 'social graph'. What, if anything, would an STS sensibility want to pick up from this scene?

The core difficulty in the post-platform scene centres on ensembles and their forms of inclusion. Do they engender collective life? Start from the proposition that imaginaries are publicly performed, collectively held, institutionally stabilized visions of social order, sustained by scientific and technical practices (Jasanoff 2015, 4): is there, for instance, a post-platform sociotechnical imaginary?

Many of the platform practices under discussion shape near futures by literally collecting things and arranging them in ways that can be 'collectively held'. The practices of collecting are writ large in proliferating cloud datastores and devices that record. Collecting things collectively is an interaction mode built into platform architectures. Public performances of collecting are myriad.

Yet this collective holding de-couples almost completely from institution stabilization. For instance, the political arithmetic of the hashing function is very different to the tabulations and matrices of statistical, administrative and scientific data forms centred on the State form or even control society operations. The hash code can be a point of connection, a diagrammatic connector running through the crypto, the data storage, the versioning, the cryptocurrencies, the blockchain, the new classes of assets, and then the invention of Web 3.0 with all their community forms, assets and new modes of personalization. In many of these settings, the new political arithmetic devises approximations that re-frame distributions of some-any. Modes of inclusion and belonging provisionally stabilize and then dissolve. More generally, sensings and devices attuned to habits, beliefs, dispositions and indeterminacies of faith also play out in arithmetics of generative content production that at the very least trouble the genres of commodity production in media and entertainment industries.

Institutional stabilization has been right at the heart of platforms too. So many conventions and standards, ranging from the formatting of numbers through to the layout of elements on an app interface, from the file standards for climate science datasets or genomic data through to the user-platforms agreements and their implementation of European Union or other State data governance legislation, not to mention the many emergent forms of contract, token and organization streaming through blockchain and Web 3.0.

Ensembles and subjectivations

The new political arithmetic also runs some new path integrals of subjectivation that cross-multiply living and non-living processes. Ganaele Langlois and Greg Elmer situate the emergent path in terms of attachments and impersonal subjectivation:

> Rather, along the lines of the concept of transindividuation articulated by Simondon (2007) and Stiegler (2010), the individual and the collective are co-constituted through the relationships that emerge between them, and these relationships are in turn technologically and economically mediated, especially through the new infrastructure of impersonal subjectivation. In that regard, alternative models could further benefit from relational psychotherapy (Benjamin, 2004; Winnicott, 2005) in understanding how one's sense of individuality, including the very capacity to think, feel, be attentive to and care for, are not innate but rather given by other human and non-human agents. (Langlois and Elmer 2019, 246)

Their take on data-intensive platformization traces the constitution of the very capacity to attach to something as an ensemble achievement. The transindividuation concept they invoke here is Simondon's philosophical rendering of the potentials of technical things, and technical ensembles in particular, to support and symbolize something that overflows or falls outside the parameters of subjectivity, identity and experience constructed by existing institutions and organized processes of production. What Simondon at times calls the 'pure information' (Simondon 1989, 247) carried in an ensemble can inform a collective in transformative ways.

The formulation appeals to me, especially in its appeal to attachment and its styles of care. That gives something to work with. I'm less persuaded by the transindividual dimension as found in Simondon's version because it is harder to see what experimental practice will be and how that practice has potential to get around the implicit normativities of integrating technology into culture, a culture that Simondon explicitly conceptualizes as an ecumenical 'totality' or 'universality' pre-figured in cybernetics:

> [T]he thought of technical ensembles needs to be inspired by that of elements, and that of the coming-into-being of the human world by the function of totality, in order for these two forms of thought, which must meet analogically but which must not be confused with each other, to preserve their autonomy and not enslave one another. (Simondon 1989, 252)

This vision of transindividual integration of ensembles and totalities is less conducive to experimental ontology than the play of elements. Integration and totality sound like mis-articulated notes. Many elements of the description of the grounded singularities of ensembles remain useful, as does impersonal subjectivation as a term for a reconstructed sense of capacities to think, to care, to attend to or to respond.

Ensembles and self-minimizing platforms

Flickering across edging, closure, embedding, shading, hashing and alignments, the co-constitution of individuals and collectives in ensembles plays out across various levels rather than by the function of totality.

> If and when we collectively decide to dismantle our attachment to Facebook, for example, it will be a messy operation. It is, after all, the minimal integrity of the self, the very space in which each of us has the possibility of existing as a self, that must be restored to integrity now that it has been damaged. (Couldry and Mejias 2019, 204)

Dismantling attachments poses many psycho-technical challenges. Forms of feeling and agency layered up in technical practices and ensemble dynamics reach deep into the base elements of 'the very space' of a possible self. Dismantling sounds very different to the transindividual integration, but can it construct the 'minimal integrity' Couldry and Mejias hope for?

Take, for instance, writing as a way of working with attachments. In writing this book, the number 1000 designates a multiplication of attachments beyond Google/Facebook/X/Instagram/LinkedIn/YouTube/TikTok/Amazon. The 1000 platforms include devices, standardized software arrangements, architecture, conventions, public spaces, infrastructures, geologies and metabolisms, including living bodies and collectives. In synthesizing a 1000 platform ensemble in writing, many attachments are in play. They even overflow 'our attachment to Facebook'.

Attachments develop in different times and places, and are not always consistent with each other. That means that writing, drawing, talking, coding and various other forms of making (wiring up, soldering, and so on) constantly find themselves drawn in different directions. If writing or related practices makes space, it would be space as in an improvising ensemble, where under the right conditions things recombine, elements become more sensitive to activation through encounters and resonance with neighbouring elements. For STS researchers, science perhaps offers an important zone of attachment. The point of the ensemble concept drawn from statistical mechanics is to deal with the enduring uncertainty about how microstates and macrostates connect. The point of the ensemble notion along with its various mathematical and statistical formations is to move between these different levels of experience, one connected very closely to things and the other to changing relations between things. The ensemble figures susceptibility to resonances across scales.

Experimental ontology with ensembles

As far-from-average events become much more normal in life, what is at stake in doing experimental ontology? The most outstanding feature of the attribution of extreme events is their localized differences coupled with their interactive generation.

William James uses the figure of a line of dots on a page and ruler to figure experience and its knowing elements. In James' figure (see Figure 8.1), an instrument – the ruler – stands for sensing, and elements of conceptual abstraction appear as dots:

> Let a row of equidistant dots on a sheet of paper symbolize the concepts by which we intellectualize the world. Let a ruler long enough to cover at least three dots stand for our sensible experience. Then the conceived changes of the sensible experience can be symbolized by sliding the ruler along the line of dots. One concept after another will apply to it, one after another drop away, but it will always cover at least two of them, and no dots less than three will ever adequately cover *it*. You falsify it if you treat it conceptually, or by the law of dots. What is true here of successive states must also be true of simultaneous characters. They also overlap each other with their being. (James 1996, 77, emphasis in original)

Note that in experimental ontology done under platform conditions, the ruler is adorned with many scales, marks and other devices, and the dots as conceptual abstractions are densely wrought in functions, algorithms, models and approximations of many different kinds. In James' idea of the

Figure 8.1: James' ruler and dots; sensing and analysing

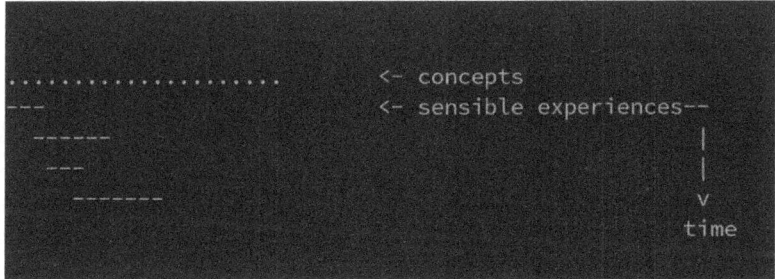

ruler moving along the line of dots, both succession and simultaneity of experience are covered. The ruler moves through changes, sometimes covering layers of dot-concepts simultaneously and always in succession.

It's a strangely obverse figure because here the ruler, with its rigidities, its marks and its sequence of numbers, is experience, and what it aligns are conceptual elements concentrated in dots. The ruler, as a measuring and drawing device, brings so much of the Euclidean constructions of figures, edges and containers with it. This reversal is important to experimental ontology. The many devices and elements taken from platforms in the pages above are like that obverse ruler. They, in effect, offer more intricate, complicated versions of the sensing-attachments of the ruler in Jame's account.

The straight edge of ruler, with its propensity to align things, is the basis of becoming sensitive to the earth and its processes, for instance. Experimental ontology in ensembles is a process of finding and aligning hyperdimensional rulers to the succession, simultaneity and intensities in platforms.

References

Acland, Charles R. 2015. 'Consumer Electronics and the Building of an Entertainment Infrastructure'. In *Signal Traffic: Critical Studies of Media Infrastructures*, edited by Lisa Parks, Jonathan Sterne and Nicole Starosielski, 246–77. Champaign: University of Illinois Press.

Akrich, Madeleine. 1992. 'The De-Scription of Technical Objects'. In *Shaping Technology/Building Society*, edited by Wiebe E. Bijker and John Law, 205–24. Cambridge, MA: MIT Press.

alex. 2015. 'What Is a Practical Use for a Closure in JavaScript?'. Forum Post. *Stack Overflow*.

Amazon. 2018. 'AWS Management Console'. https://eu-central-1.console.aws.amazon.com/console/home?region=eu-central-1#

Amrute, Sareeta. 2020. 'Bored Techies Being Casually Racist: Race as Algorithm'. *Science, Technology, & Human Values* 45(5): 903–33.

Anderson, Don L. 2007. *New Theory of the Earth*. Cambridge: Cambridge University Press.

ARM-Developer. 2023. 'Cortex-M3'. https://developer.arm.com/Processors/Cortex-M3#Technical-Specifications

Atencio, Carlos Pereira. 2023. 'Awesome Micro:Bit'. GitHub, https://github.com/carlosperate/awesome-microbit.

Badiou, Alain. 2008. *Number and Numbers*. Cambridge: Polity Press.

Barad, Karen. 2007. *Meeting the Universe Halfway: Quantum Physics and the Entanglement of Matter and Meaning*. Durham, NC: Duke University Press.

Barney, Darin, Gabriella Coleman, Christine Ross, Jonathan Sterne, Tamar Tembeck, N. Katherine Hayles, et al, eds. 2016. *The Participatory Condition in the Digital Age*. Minneapolis: University of Minnesota Press. http://www.jstor.org/stable/10.5749/j.ctt1ggjkfg

bbcmicrobit. 2023. 'Micropython/Docs/Index.rst at V2-Docs · Bbcmicrobit/Micropython'. *GitHub*. https://github.com/bbcmicrobit/micropython/blob/v2-docs/docs/index.rst

Benjamin, Ruha. 2016. 'Innovating Inequity: If Race Is a Technology, Postracialism Is the Genius Bar'. *Ethnic and Racial Studies* 39(13): 2227–34.

Bergson, Henri. nd. *Matter and Memory*. Princeton: Princeton University Press.

Bergson, Henri. 2021. *Matter and Memory*. Princeton: Princeton University Press.

Bourdieu, Pierre. 2000. *Pascalian Meditations*. Stanford: Stanford University Press.

Bratton, Benjamin H. 2016. *The Stack: On Software and Sovereignty*. Cambridge, MA: MIT Press.

Brooke, Sian. 2021. 'Trouble in Programmer's Paradise: Gender-Biases in Sharing and Recognising Technical Knowledge on Stack Overflow'. *Information, Communication & Society* 24(14): 2091–112.

Butler, Judith. 1997. *Excitable Speech: A Politics of the Performative*. London: Routledge.

Çalışkan, Koray, and Michel Callon. 2010. 'Economization, Part 2: A Research Programme for the Study of Markets'. *Economy and Society* 39(1): 1–32.

Callon, Michel. 1998. 'An Essay on Framing and Overflowing: Economic Externalities Revisited by Sociology'. *The Sociological Review* 46(1_suppl): 244–69.

Callon, Michel. 2016. 'Revisiting Marketization: From Interface-Markets to Market-Agencements'. *Consumption Markets & Culture* 19(1): 17–37.

Callon, Michel, and John Law. 2005. 'On Qualculation, Agency, and Otherness'. *Environment and Planning D* 23(5): 717–33.

Cambrosio, Alberto, Peter Keating and Andrei Mogoutov. 2004. 'Mapping Collaborative Work and Innovation in Biomedicine: A Computer-Assisted Analysis of Antibody Reagent Workshops'. *Social Studies of Science* 34(3): 325–64.

Carter, R.N., and S.D. Prince. 1981. 'Epidemic Models Used to Explain Biogeographical Distribution Limits'. *Nature* 293(5834): 644–5.

Çelik, Ayhan Fuat. 2023. 'The Fall of Stack Overflow / Ayhan Fuat Çelik'. *Observable*. https://observablehq.com/@ayhanfuat/the-fall-of-stack-overflow

Chacon, Scott, and Ben Straub. 2023. 'Git – Git Objects'. https://git-scm.com/book/en/v2/Git-Internals-Git-Objects

Chun, Wendy Hui Kyong. 2016. *Updating to Remain the Same: Habitual New Media*. Cambridge, MA: MIT Press.

Clear, James. 2018. *Atomic Habits: An Easy & Proven Way to Build Good Habits & Break Bad Ones*. Harmondsworth: Penguin Publishing Group.

Couldry, Nick, and Andreas Hepp. 2018. *The Mediated Construction of Reality*. London & New York: John Wiley & Sons.

Couldry, Nick, and Ulises A. Mejias. 2019. *The Costs of Connection: How Data Is Colonizing Human Life and Appropriating It for Capitalism*. Redwood City: Stanford University Press.

Crawford, Kate, and Trevor Paglen. 2019. 'Excavating AI'. https://www.excavating.ai

Cummins, Donald P., David B. Stephenson, and Peter A. Stott. 2020. 'Optimal Estimation of Stochastic Energy Balance Model Parameters'. *Journal of Climate* 33(18): 7909–26.

Dakin, William J., Isobel Benneti, and Elizabeth Pope. 1948. 'A Study of Certain Aspects of the Ecology of the Inter-Tidal Zone of the New South Wales Coast'. *Australian Journal of Biological Sciences* 1(2): 176–230.

Debaise, Didier, and Isabelle Stengers. 2022. 'Stories of Earthly Things: For a Pragmatist Approach of Geostories'. *Subjectivity* 15(3): 109–18.

Deezer. 2023. 'Deezer/Spleeter'. GitHub, https://github.com/deezer/spleeter

Deleuze, Gilles. 1996. *Cinema 1: The Movement-Image: 001*. Minneapolis: University of Minnesota Press.

Deleuze, Gilles. 2001. *Difference and Repetition*. Translated by Paul Patton. London: Continuum.

Deleuze, Gilles, and Félix Guattari. 1981. *One Thousand Plateaus. Capitalism and Antischizophrenia*. Translated by Brian Massumi. Minneapolis: University of Minnesota Press.

Deleuze, Gilles, and Félix Guattari. 1994. *What Is Philosophy?* Translated by Hugh Tomlinson and Graham Burchell. New York: Columbia University Press.

Dewey, John. 1958. *Experience and Nature*. New York: Dover Publications.

Docker. 2022. 'Docker: Accelerated Container Application Development'. https://www.docker.com/.

Donati, F., S. Rusponi, S. Stepanow, C. Wäckerlin, A. Singha, L. Persichetti, et al. 2016. 'Magnetic Remanence in Single Atoms'. *Science* 352(6283): 318–21.

dotnet. 2023. 'NET Platform'. https://github.com/orgs/dotnet/repositories?page=2&type=all

Dummett, Ben. 2021. 'WSJ News Exclusive Stack Overflow Sold to Tech Giant Prosus for $1.8 Billion'. *Wall Street Journal*, June.

Earth System Documentation. 2022. 'ES-DOC Model'. https://explore.es-doc.org/

Edwards, Paul N. 2010. *A Vast Machine: Computer Models, Climate Data, and the Politics of Global Warming*. Cambridge, MA: MIT Press.

Ethereum. 2021. 'Ethereum Virtual Machine Opcodes'. *Ethereum Virtual Machine Opcodes*. https://ethervm.io/

Euclid. 2012. *The Thirteen Books of the Elements*, vol 1, 2nd edn. New York: Dover Publications.

Eyring, Veronika, Sandrine Bony, Gerald A. Meehl, Catherine A. Senior, Bjorn Stevens, Ronald J. Stouffer, et al. 2016. 'Overview of the Coupled Model Intercomparison Project Phase 6 (CMIP6) Experimental Design and Organization'. *Geoscientific Model Development* 9(5): 1937–58.

REFERENCES

Facebook. 2012. 'Registration Statement on Form S-1'. https://www.sec.gov/Archives/edgar/data/1326801/000119312512034517/d287954ds1.htm#toc287954_10

Gabrys, Jennifer. 2019. *How to Do Things with Sensors*. Minneapolis/London: University of Minnesota Press.

Gad, Christopher, and Casper Bruun Jensen. 2010. 'On the Consequences of Post-ANT'. *Science, Technology, & Human Values* 35(1): 55–80.

Gao, Xiang. 2022. 'The Mathematics of the Ensemble Theory'. *Results in Physics* 34(March): 105230.

George, Damian. 2023. 'MicroPython: Python for Microcontrollers'. http://micropython.org/

Gibbs, Josiah Willard. 1902. *Elementary Principles in Statistical Mechanics: Developed with Especial Reference to the …* New York: Charles Scribner's Sons.

Gillespie, Tarleton. 2010. 'The Politics of "Platforms"'. *New Media & Society* 12(3): 347–64.

Gillespie, Tarleton. 2018. *Custodians of the Internet: Platforms, Content Moderation, and the Hidden Decisions That Shape Social Media*. New Haven: Yale University Press.

Goffman, Erving. 1983. 'The Interaction Order: American Sociological Association, 1982 Presidential Address'. *American Sociological Review* 48(1): 1–17.

Google. 2018. 'Cloud Speech-to-Text: Speech Recognition'. *Google Cloud*. https://cloud.google.com/speech-to-text/

Google. 2023. 'Stack Overflow – Marketplace – Ensembles – Google Cloud Console'. https://console.cloud.google.com/marketplace/product/stack-exchange/stack-overflow?pli=1

Google. 2024. 'Containers at Google'. *Google Cloud*. https://cloud.google.com/containers

Granovetter, Mark. 1985. 'Economic Action and Social Structure: The Problem of Embeddedness'. *American Journal of Sociology* 91(3): 481–510.

Gray, George T., and Ron Q. Smith. 2001. 'Sperry Rand's Third-Generation Computers 1964–1980'. *IEEE Annals of the History of Computing* 23(1): 3–16.

Gupta, Abinav. 2019. 'Ascent to the Cloud: How Six Key APAC Economies Can Lift-off'. *BCG Global*. https://www.bcg.com/publications/2019/economic-impact-public-cloud-apac/default

Guyer, Jane I. 2016. *Legacies, Logics, Logistics: Essays in the Anthropology of the Platform Economy*. Chicago: University of Chicago Press.

Hansen, Mark. 2004. *New Philosophy for New Media*. Cambridge, MA: MIT Press.

Hansen, Mark. 2015. 'Prediction in the Wild'. In *The Nonhuman Turn*, edited by Richard A. Grusin. Minneapolis: University of Minnesota Press.

Haraway, Donna J. 2016. *Staying with the Trouble: Making Kin in the Chthulucene*. Durham, NC: Duke University Press.

Hashemi, Mazdak. 2017. 'The Infrastructure Behind Twitter: Scale'. https://blog.twitter.com/engineering/en_us/topics/infrastructure/2017/the-infrastructure-behind-twitter-scale.html

Hookway, Branden. 2014. *Interface*. Cambridge: MIT Press.

Hughes, Thomas Parke. 1993. *Networks of Power: Electrification in Western Society, 1880–1930*. Baltimore/London: JHU Press.

Hutchinson, G. Evelyn. 1959. 'Homage to Santa Rosalia or Why Are There so Many Kinds of Animals?'. *The American Naturalist* 93(870): 145–59.

IBM. 2018. 'IBM Data Science Experience'. https://dataplatform.ibm.com/home?context=analytics

IBM. 2023. 'International Business Machines'. https://github.com/IBM

IIASA. 2018. 'SSP Database'. https://tntcat.iiasa.ac.at/SspDb/dsd?Action=htmlpage&page=20

Intel Corporation. 1986. *Intel 8080 Datasheet*. http://archive.org/details/8080Datasheet

James, William. 1996. *A Pluralistic Universe*. Lincoln: Nebraska University Press.

Jasanoff, Sheila, ed. 2015. *Dreamscapes of Modernity*. Chicago: University of Chicago Press.

Joos, F., R. Roth, J.S. Fuglestvedt, G.P. Peters, I.G. Enting, W. von Bloh, et al. 2013. 'Carbon Dioxide and Climate Impulse Response Functions for the Computation of Greenhouse Gas Metrics: A Multi-Model Analysis'. *Atmospheric Chemistry and Physics* 13(5): 2793–825.

Kauffman, Stuart A. 1993. *The Origins of Order: Self Organization and Selection in Evolution*. New York: Oxford University Press.

Keating, Peter, and Alberto Cambrosio. 2003. *Biomedical Platforms: Realigning the Normal and the Pathological in Late-Twentieth-Century Medicine*. Cambridge, MA: MIT Press.

Kelty, Christopher. 2019. *The Participant*. Chicago: University of Chicago Press.

Kemet. 2023. 'Ceramic Capacitor CBR04C308B5GAC'. https://www.kemet.com/en/us/search.html

Khronos. 2018. 'OpenGL Wiki'. https://www.khronos.org/opengl/wiki/Main_Page

Kindness, David. 2023. 'How Amazon Makes Money'. *Investopedia*. https://www.investopedia.com/how-amazon-makes-money-4587523

Kleene, Stephen Cole. 1956. 'Representation of Events in Nerve Nets and Finite Automata'. *Automata Studies: Annals of Mathematics Studies* 34: 3.

Kopp, Michael, Adrian Mackenzie, Donald H. Chaplin, and G.V.H. Wilson. 1984. 'The Initial AC Susceptibility of a Holmium Single Crystal'. In *A.I.S – Eighth Annual Condensed Matter Physics Meeting*. Pakatoa Island, New Zealand.

Kump, Lee R., James F. Kasting, and Robert G. Crane. 2010. *The Earth System*, 3rd edn. San Francisco: Prentice Hall.

Lancaster, Don. 1974. *TTL Cookbook*. Carmel: SAMS Publishing.

Lancaster University. 2021. 'Low Temperature Physics'. https://www.lancaster.ac.uk/physics/research/experimental-condensed-matter/low-temperature-physics/

Lancaster University. 2023. 'CODAL'. https://lancaster-university.github.io/codal/

Langlois, Ganaele, and Greg Elmer. 2019. 'Impersonal Subjectivation from Platforms to Infrastructures'. *Media, Culture & Society* 41(2): 236–51.

Latour, Bruno. 1987. *Science in Action: How to Follow Scientists and Engineers Through Society*. Cambridge, MA: Harvard University Press.

Latour, Bruno. 1992. 'Where Are the Missing Masses? The Sociology of a Few Mundane Artifacts'. In *Shaping Technology/Building Society: Studies in Sociotechnical Change*, edited by Wiebe E. Bijker and John Law, 225–58. Cambridge and Malden, MA: MIT Press.

Latour, Bruno. 1993. *We Have Never Been Modern*. New York: Harvester Wheatsheaf.

Latour, Bruno. 1996. *Aramis, or the Love of Technology*. Translated by Catherine Porter. Cambridge, MA: Harvard University Press.

Latour, Bruno. 2013. *An Inquiry into Modes of Existence*. Cambridge, MA: Harvard University Press.

Latour, Bruno. 2018. *Down to Earth: Politics in the New Climatic Regime*. Newark: Polity Press.

Latour, Bruno. 2021. *After Lockdown: A Metamorphosis*. John Wiley & Sons.

Latour, Bruno, and Timothy M. Lenton. 2019. 'Extending the Domain of Freedom, or Why Gaia Is so Hard to Understand'. *Critical Inquiry* 45(3): 659–80.

Law, John. 2017. 'STS as Method'. In *The Handbook of Science and Technology Studies*, edited by Ulrike Felt, Clark A. Miller, Laurel Smith-Doerr, and Rayvon Fouché, 4th edn, 31–57. Cambridge, MA: MIT Press.

Leach, Nicholas, and Chris Smith. 2021. 'FaIRv2.0.0 Notebooks', April.

Leach, Nicholas, Stuart Jenkins, Zebedee Nicholls, Christopher J. Smith, John Lynch, Michelle Cain, et al. 2021. 'FaIRv2.0.0: A Generalized Impulse Response Model for Climate Uncertainty and Future Scenario Exploration'. *Geoscientific Model Development* 14(5): 3007–36.

Lee, Ashlin, Adrian Mackenzie, and Gavin Smith. 2020. 'Apps, Repositories and Platforms: Recognising the Dimensions of Urban Platforms'. *Urban Planning*. https://doi.org/DOI: 10.17645/up.vXiX.2545

Le Guin, Ursula K., and Donna Jeanne Haraway. 2019. *The Carrier Bag Theory of Fiction*. London: Ignota Books.

Lenton, Timothy M., and James E. Lovelock. 2001. 'Daisyworld Revisited: Quantifying Biological Effects on Planetary Self-Regulation'. *Tellus Series B Chemical and Physical Meteorology B* 53(January): 288–305.

Lenton, Timothy, and Andrew Watson. 2011. *Revolutions That Made the Earth*. Oxford: Oxford University Press.

Lenton, Timothy M., and Bruno Latour. 2018. 'Gaia 2.0'. *Science* 361(6407): 1066–8.

Leszczynski, Agnieszka. 2019. 'Platform Affects of Geolocation'. *Geoforum* 107(December): 207–15.

Lorang, Noah. 2016. 'Data Scientists Mostly Just Do Arithmetic and That's a Good Thing'. *Signal V. Noise*. https://m.signalvnoise.com/data-scienti sts-mostly-just-do-arithmetic-and-that-s-a-good-thing-c6371885f7f6

Lorenz, Edward N. 1963. 'Deterministic Nonperiodic Flow'. *Journal of the Atmospheric Sciences* 20(2): 130–41.

Lovelock, James E. 1979. *Gaia: A New Look at Life on Earth*. Oxford: Oxford University Press.

Lovelock, James E., and Andrew J. Watson. 1982. 'The Regulation of Carbon Dioxide and Climate: Gaia or Geochemistry'. *Planetary and Space Science* 30(8): 795–802.

Lovink, Geert. 2019. *Sad by Design: On Platform Nihilism*. Pluto Press.

Mackenzie, Adrian. 2002. *Transductions: Bodies and Machines at Speed*. Continuum International Publishing Group.

Mackenzie, Adrian. 2004. 'Has the Cyborg Been Domesticated? (Or, Is Lolo a Disappointing Cyborg?)'. *Metascience* 13(2): 153–63.

Mackenzie, Adrian. 2010. *Wirelessness: Radical Network Empiricism*. Cambridge, MA: MIT Press.

Mackenzie, Adrian. 2012. 'Technical Objects in the Biological Century'. *Zeitschrift Für Medien-Und Kulturforschung* 2012(1): 151–68.

Mackenzie, Adrian. 2017. *Machine Learners: Archaeology of a Data Practice*. Cambridge, MA: MIT Press.

Mackenzie, Adrian. 2018. '48 Million Configurations and Counting: Platform Numbers and Their Capitalization'. *Journal of Cultural Economy* 11(1): 36–53.

Mackenzie, Adrian. 2023. '"This Is a House": Large Image Collections and Their Platform Embeddings'. *Convergence* 29(1): 13548565211052041.

Mackenzie, Adrian, and Anna Munster. 2022. 'Oscilloscopes, Slide Rules and Nematodes: Towards Heterogenetic Perception in/of AI'. In *Distributed Perception: Resonances and Axiologies*, edited by Natasha Lushetich and Iain Campbell, 64–81. London: Routledge.

Marres, Noortje. 2013. 'Why Political Ontology Must Be Experimentalized: On Eco-Show Homes as Devices of Participation'. *Social Studies of Science* 43(3): 417–43.

Marres, Noortje. 2017. *Digital Sociology: The Reinvention of Social Research*, 1st edn. Malden, MA: Polity.

Masson-Delmotte, Valérie, Panmao Zhai, Anna Pirani, Sarah L. Connors, C. Péan, Sophie Berger, et al, eds. 2021. *Climate Change 2021: The Physical Science Basis. Contribution of Working Group I to the Sixth Assessment Report of the Intergovernmental Panel on Climate Change*. Cambridge: Cambridge University Press.

Matplotlib. 2023. 'Matplotlib – Visualization with Python'. https://matplotlib.org/

May, John. 2019. *Signal. Image. Architecture.: (Everything Is Already an Image)*. New York: Columbia Books on Architecture and the City.

McNeil, Maureen, Joan Haran, Adrian Mackenzie, and Richard Tutton. 2016. 'The Concept of Imaginaries in Science and Technology Studies'. In *Handbook of Science and Technology Studies*, edited by Ulrike Felt, 3rd edn. London: SAGE.

Meliorence. 2022. 'React-Native-Snap-Carousel'. Meliorence.

Merleau-Ponty, Maurice. 1964. *The Primacy of Perception: And Other Essays on Phenomenological Psychology, the Philosophy of Art, History, and Politics*. Northwestern University Press.

Meta. 2023. 'React'. https://react.dev/

Micro:bit Educational Foundation. 2023a. 'Hardware'. https://tech.microbit.org/hardware/

Micro:bit Educational Foundation. 2023b. 'Make It: Code It Projects'. https://microbit.org/projects/make-it-code-it/

Micropython. 2023. 'The MicroPython Project'. MicroPython. GitHub, https://github.com/micropython/micropython

Microsoft. 2018. 'Project Brainwave'. Microsoft Research. www.microsoft.com/en-us/research/project/project-brainwave/

Microsoft Corporation. 2023a. 'Azure Functions – Serverless Functions in Computing Microsoft Azure'. https://azure.microsoft.com/en-au/products/functions

Microsoft Corporation. 2023b. 'NET Build. Test. Deploy'. Microsoft. https://dotnet.microsoft.com/en-us/

Mikolov, Tomas, Kai Chen, Greg Corrado, and Jeffrey Dean. 2013. 'Efficient Estimation of Word Representations in Vector Space'. *arXiv:1301.3781 [Cs]*, September. http://arxiv.org/abs/1301.3781

Millar, Richard J., Zebedee R. Nicholls, Pierre Friedlingstein, and Myles R. Allen. 2017. 'A Modified Impulse-Response Representation of the Global Near-Surface Air Temperature and Atmospheric Concentration Response to Carbon Dioxide Emissions'. *Atmospheric Chemistry and Physics* 17(11): 7213–28.

Mittelbach, Gary G. 2012. *Community Ecology*, 1st edn. Sunderland, MA: Sinauer Associates is an imprint of Oxford University Press.

Mody, Cyrus C.M. and Michael Lynch. 2010. 'Test Objects and Other Epistemic Things: A History of a Nanoscale Object'. *The British Journal for the History of Science* 43(3): 423–58.

Morris, R.C. 1983. 'The Origin of the Iron-Formation-Rich Hamersley Group of Western Australia: Deposition on a Platform.' *Precambrian Research* 21(3–4): 273–97.

Nafus, Dawn. 2012. ' "Patches Don't Have Gender": What Is Not Open in Open Source Software'. *New Media & Society* 14(4): 669–83.

Natterer, Fabian D., Kai Yang, William Paul, Philip Willke, Taeyoung Choi, Thomas Greber, et al. 2017. 'Reading and Writing Single-Atom Magnets'. *Nature* 543(7644): 226–8.

NIST. 2015. 'Secure Hash Standard (SHS)'. Federal Information Processing Standard (FIPS) 180-4. U.S. Department of Commerce. doi:10.6028/NIST.FIPS.180-4

NIST, Information Technology Laboratory. 2017. 'NIST Policy on Hash Functions: Hash Functions CSRC CSRC'. *CSRC NIST*. https://csrc.nist.gov/projects/hash-functions/nist-policy-on-hash-functions

NIST, Secure Hash. 1995. 'FIPS Pub 180-1'. *National Institute of Standards and Technology* 17: 15.

Nordic Semiconductor. 2023. 'nRF52833 – Nordic Semiconductor'. https://www.nordicsemi.com/Products/nRF52833

Numpy. 2023. 'NumPy'. https://numpy.org/

Nvidia. 2016. 'NVIDIA Tesla V100'. *NVIDIA*. https://www.nvidia.co.uk/data-center/tesla-v100/

Nvidia. 2018a. 'NVIDIA DGX-2: Enterprise AI Research System'. *NVIDIA*. https://www.nvidia.com/en-au/data-center/dgx-2/

Nvidia. 2018b. 'Programming Guide: CUDA Toolkit Documentation'. https://docs.nvidia.com/cuda/cuda-c-programming-guide/index.html#features-and-technical-specifications

Nvidia. 2018c. 'GTC 2018 Keynote with NVIDIA CEO Jensen Huang'. YouTube. https://www.youtube.com/watch?v=95nphvtVf34

Nvidia. 2018d. 'NVIDIA CLARA Platform'. *NVIDIA Developer*. https://developer.nvidia.com/clara

NXP. 2023. 'MKL27Z256VFM4 Product InformationNXP'. https://www.nxp.com/part/MKL27Z256VFM4#/

O'Neill, Brian C., Elmar Kriegler, Kristie L. Ebi, Eric Kemp-Benedict, Keywan Riahi, Dale S. Rothman, et al. 2017. 'The Roads Ahead: Narratives for Shared Socioeconomic Pathways Describing World Futures in the 21st Century'. *Global Environmental Change* 42(January): 169–80.

OpenAI. 2021. 'GPT-3: Language Models Are Few-Shot Learners'. OpenAI.

OpenAI. 2023. 'ChatGPT'. https://chat.openai.com

Oxford English Dictionary. 2023. 'Git – Quick Search Results Oxford English Dictionary'. https://www.oed.com/search/dictionary/?scope=Entries&q=git

Park, Kun Hee. 2021. 'Daisyworld Resources'. Special Programme in Science. GitHub, https://github.com/nus-sps/earth-daisyworld-article

REFERENCES

Pinch, Trevor J., Wiebe E Bijker, and Thomas Hughes. 1987. 'The Social Construction of Facts and Artefacts'. In *The Social Construction of Technological Systems: New Directions in the Sociology and History of Technology*, 17–49. Cambridge, MA: MIT Press.

Plantin, Jean-Christophe, and Aswin Punathambekar. 2018. 'Digital Media Infrastructures: Pipes, Platforms, and Politics'. *Media, Culture & Society*. https://doi.org/10.1177/0163443718818376

Plantin, Jean-Christophe, Carl Lagoze, Paul N. Edwards, and Christian Sandvig. 2016. 'Infrastructure Studies Meet Platform Studies in the Age of Google and Facebook'. *New Media & Society*. https://doi.org/10.1177/1461444816661553

Porter, Theodore M. 2015. 'The Flight of the Indicator'. In *The World of Indicators: The Making of Governmental Knowledge Through Quantification*, edited by R. Rottenburg et al, 34–55. Cambridge: Cambridge University Press.

Povinelli, Elizabeth A. 2016. 'The Three Figures of Geontology'. In *Geontologies: A Requiem to Late Liberalism*, 1–29. Durham, NC: Duke University Press.

Preciado, Paul. 2013. *Testo Junkie: Sex, Drugs, and Biopolitics in the Pharmacopornographic Era*. New York: The Feminist Press at CUNY.

Python Software Foundation. 2023. 'Welcome to Python.Org'. *Python.org*. https://www.python.org/

Rheinberger, Hans-Jörg. 1997. *Toward a History of Epistemic Things: Synthesizing Proteins in the Test Tube*. Stanford: Stanford University Press.

Rose, Nicholas, and Des Fitzgeral. nd. *The Urban Brain*. Princeton: Princeton University Press.

Ruskin, John. 2009. *The he Stones of Venice*, vol 3, Gutenberg Books. https://www.gutenberg.org/files/30754/30754-h/30756-h.htm

Schneider, Nathan. 2019. 'Decentralization: An Incomplete Ambition'. *Journal of Cultural Economy* 12(4): 265–85.

Scholz, Trebor, and Nathan Schneider. 2017. *Ours to Hack and to Own: The Rise of Platform Cooperativism, a New Vision for the Future of Work and a Fairer Internet*. New York: OR Books.

Schüll, Natasha Dow. 2012. *Addiction by Design: Machine Gambling in Las Vegas*. Princeton: Princeton University Press.

Simondon, Gilbert. 1989. *Du Mode d'existence Des Objets Techniques*. Paris: Aubier.

Simondon, Gilbert. 2017. *On the Mode of Existence of Technical Objects*. Translated by Cecile Malaspina and John Rogove, 1st edn. Minneapolis: University of Minnesota Press.

Skeggs, Beverley, and Simon Yuill. 2016. 'The Methodology of a Multi-Model Project Examining How Facebook Infrastructures Social Relations'. *Information, Communication & Society* 19(10): 1356–72.

Smith, Christopher J., Piers M. Forster, Myles Allen, Nicholas Leach, Richard J. Millar, Giovanni A. Passerello, et al. 2018. 'FAIR V1.3: A Simple Emissions-Based Impulse Response and Carbon Cycle Model'. *Geoscientific Model Development* 11(6): 2273–97.

Smith, Jack. 2015. 'Meet the Man Behind "Solarized", the Most Important Color Scheme in Computer History'. *Observer*, 27 February. https://observer.com/2015/02/meet-the-man-behind-solarized-the-most-important-color-scheme-in-computer-history/

Sperry-Univac. 1973. 'Uniscope 100 Display Terminal'. https://archive.org/details/bitsavers_univacterm701r2Uniscope100DisplayTerminalGeneralDe

Srnicek, Nick. 2016. *Platform Capitalism*. Cambridge: Polity Press.

Stack Exchange. 2023a. 'Stack Overflow Insights: Developer Hiring, Marketing, and User Research'. https://insights.stackoverflow.com/survey

Stack Exchange. 2023b. 'Stack Overflow: Where Developers Learn, Share, & Build Careers'. *Stack Overflow*. https://stackoverflow.com/

Star, Susan Leigh, and Karen Ruhleder. 1996. 'Steps Toward an Ecology of Infrastructure: Design and Access for Large Information Spaces'. *Information Systems Research* 7: 111–34.

Stengers, Isabelle. 2011. *Cosmopolitics II*. Translated by Robert Bononno. Minneapolis: University of Minnesota Press.

Sterne, Jonathan. 2015. 'A Compression History of Media'. In *Signal Traffic: Critical Studies of Media Infrastructures*, edited by Lisa Parks and Nicole Starosielski, 31–52. Urbana: University of Illinois Press.

Stengers, Isabelle. 2004. 'Resister a Simondon'. *Multitudes* 4(18): 55–62.

Stevens, Marc. 2017. 'SHAttered'. https://shattered.io/

Suchman, Lucy. 2012. 'Configuration'. In *Inventive Methods: The Happening of the Social*, edited by Celia Lury and Nina Wakeford, 41–58. New York: Routledge.

Tsing, Anna Lowenhaupt. 2005. *Friction: An Ethnography of Global Connection*. Princeton: Princeton University Press.

U.S. Surgeon-General. 2023. 'Social Media and Youth Mental Health: Current Priorities of the U.S. Surgeon General'. https://www.hhs.gov/surgeongeneral/priorities/youth-mental-health/social-media/index.html

Uprichard, Emma, Roger Burrows, and David Byrne. 2008. 'SPSS as an "Inscription Device": From Causality to Description?'. *The Sociological Review* 56(4): 606–22.

Utzon, Jørn. 1962. 'Platforms and Plateaus: Ideas of a Danish Architect '. *Zodiac* 10: 114–17.

Van Dijck, José, Thomas Poell, and Martijn de Waal. 2018. *The Platform Society: Public Values in a Connective World*. Oxford: Oxford University Press.

Verran, Helen. 2012. 'The Changing Lives of Measures and Values: From Centre Stage in the Fading "Disciplinary" Society to Pervasive Background Instrument in the Emergent "Control" Society'. *The Sociological Review* 59: 60–72.

Vertesi, Janet. 2015. *Seeing Like a Rover: How Robots, Teams, and Images Craft Knowledge of Mars*. Chicago: University of Chicago Press.

Vertesi, Janet, David Ribes, Laura Forlano, Alexandre Camus, Dominique Vinck, Nerea Calvillo, et al. 2019. *digitalSTS: A Field Guide for Science & Technology Studies*. Princeton: Princeton University Press.

von Bloh, Werner. 2006. 'Daisyworld: A Tutorial Approach to Geophysiological Modelling'. Potsdam Institute for Climate Impact Research. http://www.pik-potsdam.de/~bloh/

Voronova, Arya. 2022. 'All About USB-C: Introduction for Hackers'. *Hackaday*.

Wajcman, Judy. 2010. 'Feminist Theories of Technology'. *Cambridge Journal of Economics* 34(1): 143–52.

Wajcman, Judy. 2015. *Pressed for Time: The Acceleration of Life in Digital Capitalism*. Chicago: University of Chicago Press.

Watson, Andrew J. and James E. Lovelock. 1983. 'Biological Homeostasis of the Global Environment: The Parable of Daisyworld'. *Tellus B: Chemical and Physical Meteorology* 35(4): 284–9.

Whitehead, Alfred North. 1925. *Science and the Modern World: Lowell Lectures, 1925*. New York: New American Library.

Wikipedia. 2019. 'Closure'. *Wikipedia*, December.

Wikipedia. 2023. 'Closure (Mathematics)'. *Wikipedia*, July.

Wilensky, Uri. 2006. 'NetLogo Models Library: Daisyworld'. https://ccl.northwestern.edu/netlogo/models/Daisyworld

Yegge, Stevey. 2010. 'Stevey's Google Platforms Rant'. *Gist*. https://gist.github.com/chitchcock/1281611

Index

References to figures appear in *italic* type; those in **bold** type refer to tables.

A

alignments 14–15, 139–40, 157
  approximations as 140–1
Amazon platform 22–3
app interfaces 4, 49
approximations as alignments 140–1
artificial intelligence (AI) 161
'Asus Strix' GPU card 46–7
atomic vibrations 73
attachment-figures 9–10, 17
  alignments 14–15
  closures 13–14
  edging 10–11
  embedding 12–13
  numbering 11–12
  shading 11
attachment listing 8–9
attachments 159, 163–4

B

Badiou, A. 78
banded iron formations 89–91
Barad, K. 76
BBC 92, 94–5, 96
Bergson, H. 48–9, 50, 53, 66
Bezos, J. 22–3
blockchain technologies 86–7
bodies as images 48–51
body-image 45
Brooke, S. 120
Butler, J. 65–6

C

calculation 129–30
Calışkan, K. 129
callbacks 118
Callon, M. 116, 129, 130, 132
Canberra Mini-trains 111, *112*
casinos 106
ChatGPT 126
circuit boards 100–2, 107

Clara Clara 64–5
climate science 14–15
  Finite Amplitude Pulse Response model (FAIR) 141, 150–6
  see also earth systems models
climate sensitivity 150
closures 13–14, 114–33
  and callbacks 117–18
  and data 124–5
  differentiated 121–3
  expansive 123–4
  formatting participation 130–2
  heterodynamic 119–21
  Kleene closure 125–7
  platforms 128–30
  and stagings 116–17
coastal rock platforms 10, 18–19
CODAL platform 95–6
coding practices *see* closures
collecting 161
component habits 105–6
containers 12, 68–70, 71, 72, 74, 75, 86, 87
Couldry, N. and Mejias, U.A. 163
Crawford, K. 72
cryptocurrency 86
CUDA 57–9

D

daisyworld 141, 145–50
DALL.E 50–1
data 124–5
data science 13–14, 92–3, 116–17, 124–33
data storage 73, 84
De Rerum Natura (Lucretius) 48–9
Debaise, D. 156
Deleuze, G. 5, 78, 105, 106, 158, 159
'density-in-phase' 76
developers 26, 119–20
device-ensembles 159–60, 161–2

INDEX

devices 160–1
Dewey, J. 106
Difference and Repetition (Deleuze) 105, 158
differentiated closures 121–3
digital infrastructure 42
diving platforms 134–6
Doge Pesaro door 39–41
dots 164–5
Down to Earth (Latour) 143
Dryhurst, M. 50

E

Earth System Grid Federation 151
earth systems models 137, 139–57
 daisyworld 141, 145–50
 Finite Amplitude Pulse Response model (FAIR) 141, 150–6
 Lorenz attractor 140, 141–5, *146*
ecological theory 19
edging/edges 10–11, 18–19, 20–38
 edge-hardening 22–3, 24, 33
 edge-making 23–5, 33
 gcloud 26–9
 Intel 8080 microprocessor 32–6
 people along edges 25
 terminals 29–32, 36–7
Edwards, P. 139
Elements (Euclid) 68, 69
embedded economy 102–3
embedding 12–13
 as abstraction 108–9
 micro:bit 92–7, 100–6, 107–8, 109–10
 small devices 97–100
embodying 97, 103–5, 107, 110
enclosure 116
ensemble-people 25
ensembles 15–17, 28–9, 48, 108–9, 127
 device-ensembles 159–60, 161–2
 experimental ontology with 158–9, 164–5
 and self-minimizing platforms 163–4
 statistical 75–7, 87–8
 and subjectivations 162–3
Euclidean geometry 11–12, 52, 68–70, 144
expansive closures 123–4
Experience and Nature (Dewey) 106
experimental habits 106–8
experimental ontology 16, 66, 158–9, 160–2, 164–5
'Extending the Domain of Freedom' (Latour and Lenton) 149

F

Facebook 4, 21, 44, 72
 attachment to 163
 hacker culture 23, 26
figures 68, 69–70

Finite Amplitude Pulse Response model (FAIR) 141, 150–6
formatting participation 130–2
fragment shaders 53
Frari basilica 39–41

G

Gaia 149
Gaia hypothesis 141
gcloud 26–9
gendering 120–1, 122
geological formations 89–91
geometry *see* Euclidean geometry
Geontologies (Povinelli) 139
Gibbs, J.W. 75–6
git 83–6
GitHub 85, 87–8, 120, 121, 124, 128–9, 147, 151
Goffman, E. 2, 111
Google 20, 26–8, 63–4, 79, 86, 131
Graphic Technology Computing (GTC) conference 60–1
graphics processing units (GPUs) 160
 shaders 11, 45–8, 51–65
Guyer, J. 78

H

habits
 component habits 105–6
 experimental habits 106–8
hacker culture 23, 26
Hammersley iron 89–91
Hansen, M. 50
Haraway, D. 98, 137–8
Hashemi, M. 81
hashing 12, 77–83, 161
 blockchain technologies 86–7
 containers 86
 git 83–6
heterodynamic closures 119–21
high-diving platforms 134–6
holmium atoms 73
Huang, J. 60–1, 64–5
Hughes, T. 59
human bodies 107
Hutchinson, G.E. 19
hyperscalers 71

I

IBM 73, 116, 128–9, 131–3
images 42, 43–4, 65–7
 #platform 44–5
 bodies as 48–51
 shaders 11, 45–8, 51–65
'Infinite Images and the Latent Camera' (Dryhurst) 50
Instagram 49, 65, 76
 #platform 44–5
institutional stabilization 162

179

Intel 8080 microprocessor 32–6
Intergovernmental Panel on Climate Change (IPCC) 141, 150
IsoLab 74, 75

J

James, W. 6–7, 156, 164–5
JavaScript 114, 115, 117
Joos, F. 152

K

Keating, P. and Cambrosio, A. 80
Kelty, C. 21, 127, 129, 130
Kleene closure 125–6

L

Langlois, G. and Elmer, G. 162
latent camera 50
latent space 50–1
Latour, B. 8, 9, 42, 51, 85, 97–8, 99–100, 143, 149, 161
Law, J. 72
Leach, N. 156
Lenton, T. 149
Lorenz attractor 140, 141–5, *146*
Lovelock, J. 141, 147

M

Margulis, L. 141
Marres, N. 16, 21
Matter and Memory (Bergson) 48
May, J. 49, 51
Merleau-Ponty, M. 107
metal edges 24
micro:bit 92–7, 100–6, 107–8, 109–10
MicroPython 94–5
Millar, R.J. 152–3
MOSFET 160

N

Nafus, D. 120, 124
.NET 123
New South Wales 18
niches 19, 39
numbering 12, 71–2, 87–8
  coldest numbers 74
  hashing 12, 77–83, 161
    blockchain technologies 86–7
    containers 86
    git 83–6
  smallest numbers 73
  statistical ensembles 75–7, 87–8
numericity problem 71, 87
numpy 123
Nvidia 60–1, 64–5

O

One Thousand Plateaus (Deleuze and Guattari) 5, 16

open source software 120, 124
OpenAI DALL.E 50–1
oscillators 108

P

Pandas 123
participation, formatting of 130–2
performance platforms 111–13
Pesaro, G. 39
plateauization 5
#platform 44–5
platform attachment-figures *see* attachment-figures
platform edges *see* edging/edges
platform format 2
platform list 7–8
platform-number problem 71
platform numbers *see* numbering
platform technology 74
platforms / APIs
  edges *see* edging/edges
  as ensembles 15–17 (*see also* ensembles)
  interfaces 23, 29, 37
  as plateaus 5
  programmable 22
  self-minimizing 163–4
  thinning and thickening 5–7
  verticality and flatness 2–5
  see also coastal rock platforms; devices; diving platforms; performance platforms; scientific platforms
platformatization 59, 73, 121, 161
Pluralistic Universe, A (James) 6–7, 164–5
Porter, T. 78
Povinelli, E. 139
Preciado, P. 1
programming interfaces 22
Python code 43, 56, 83, 117, 126
  see also MicroPython

Q

quantum mechanics 74, 76

R

Raworth, K. 102
regulation 80
  see also institutional stabilization
relation 139
Rivest, R. 80
rock formations 89–91
rulers 164–5

S

scale 32
Schüll, N. 106
science and technology studies (STS) 1
  and climate politics 143
  closures 116
  containers 72

devices 160–1
and earth science 137–40
embedding 97–100
embodiment 97
feminist 121
images 51–9, 66
markets 129
numbering 78, 85
scientific images 56–7
scientific platforms 14–15
see also earth systems models
SCOT (Social Construction of Technology) 98
self-minimizing platforms 163–4
service interfaces 22
set theory closure 125
SHA-1 hash 77–8, 79, 80, 84–5
shaders/shading 11, 43, 44, 45–8, 51–65, 67
Shattered attack 79
Signal. Image. Architecture (May) 49
Simondon, G. 16–17, 24, 80, 86, 108–9, 137, 159, 162–3
Skeggs, B. and Yuill, S. 72
smartphone apps 4, 49
Smith, C.J. 153
social media 3
see also Facebook; Instagram; Twitter
software developers 119–20
Stack Overflow 115, 116, 119–21, 122, 123–4, 126, **128**
stacks 35
stagings 111–13, 116–17
statistical ensembles 75–7, 87–8
Stengers, I. 17, 88, 142
Stones of Venice, The (Ruskin) 39
subjectivation 162–3

T

technological closure 116
terminals 29–32, 36–7
Terrapolis equation 137–8, 140
Tesla V100 GPU 60
Tsing, A. 32
TTL Cookbook (Lancaster) 33
Twitter 81–3, 83, 99

U

Ultra Low Temperature Physics Laboratory 74
'Uniscope 100 Display Terminal' (Sperry-Univac.) 29–31
univocity of code 123–4
US National Institute of Standards (NIST) 77, 79
USB plugs 98–9
Utzon, J. 111
performance platform *112*

V

vectorizing loads 60–5
Verran, H. 78
Vertesi, J. 21, 56
vertex chaders 53
video games 52

W

Wajcman, J. 121, 139
Watson, A. 147
Watson Cognitive Computing 131, 133
'Watson Data Science Experience' 116–17

Z

'zones of suspension' 106
Zuckerberg, M. 23